VALUATION

What Assets Are Really Worth

VALUATION

What Assets Are Really Worth

Alfred M. King

JOHN WILEY & SONS, INC.

New York • Chichester • Weinheim • Brisbane • Singapore • Toronto

Library of Congress Cataloging-in-Publication Data:
King, Alfred M.
    Valuation : what assets are really worth / Alfred King.
      p. cm.
    Includes index.
    ISBN 0-471-34983-6 (cloth : alk. paper)
     1. Valuation—United States. I. Title.

  HG4028.V3 K535 2001
  658.15—dc21

                    2001045359

To Mary Jane,
with thanks for your patience

Preface

American business annually spends upward of $1 billion with appraisers, in order to determine, independently and objectively, the value of all types of assets. Whether to secure a loan, insure a building, or sell a business unit, managers need to know the real value of their assets. Financial statements, prepared by accountants, appear to provide information about asset values. But as anyone who has tried to use financial statements for decision making will find out, the rules used by accountants (commonly referred to as generally accepted accounting principles [GAAP]) do not provide realistic value information.

Further, and this is not generally recognized, there is no single number that truly represents *the* value of any asset. Put bluntly, any asset can have two or even three separate values at the same time. Most observers tend at first to question this statement, because it is not intuitively obvious that one asset can have two or even three different values.

A simple example will suffice. Take your own home. Your insurance company needs to know the value of the structure, but not the land, since land is never insured. Your bank needs to know what the house could be sold for in a liquidation or worst case scenario. If you want to sell the house, your realtor will suggest an opening asking price, which you may subsequently have to lower to close a sale with the proverbial willing buyer.

Which of these values is the *real* value? The fact is that every one of them, differ as they might, is correct, but only for the purpose for which the information will be used. You could not sell the house for its insurable value, which represents a cost of reproduction. You would not accept a price from a buyer at the loan value offered by the bank. If you got in a fight with the local tax assessor and wanted to lower your property tax, you would point out to her all the bad points of your structure. These would probably not be items you would necessarily disclose to the prospective buyer.

If there is one key point that readers of this book should understand it is that values are dependent on the purpose for which the information will be used. Change the purpose, and you change the value answer.

This book is *not* a do-it-yourself handbook on how to perform an appraisal. Many other books purport to teach one how to do an appraisal. It is interesting that there are very few college or graduate courses in valuation. In practice, most professional appraisers have learned on the job. The author has more than 32 years of professional experience.

The author once had a colleague who after 20 years in the profession made a flat statement that anyone would have to have a minimum of 15 years in order to be fully qualified. Five years later, when he himself had 25 years' experience, his judgment had changed. Now it took a minimum of 20 years to be fully qualified. And yes, when he was near retirement, with 30 years experience he let everyone know that without 25 years' experience the individual's answers as to value might be questionable.

Things are not quite that extreme. An individual with five to ten years of business experience can learn the fundamentals of valuation, and become a proficient practitioner, in perhaps five years. A newly minted MBA, with only two or three years' experience, will probably require seven to ten additional years to be able to determine values on a supportable basis.

The truth is that actual appraisal experience is far more valuable than theories, equations, formulas, or rules of thumb. When I see an ad in the back of a financial magazine for a $195 software program that will allow the purchaser to value a business, I just laugh. If it were that simple, why would sophisticated senior financial executives, in the very largest companies, hire outside appraisers? After all, they could invest the $195 and tell one of their hotshot MBAs to get the job done. Somehow, in practice, things do not work out very well if that is the course of action that is chosen.

The basic principles of valuation are indeed simple. Application of those principles to a specific situation is far from simple. The best analysis we have heard, in describing the real world of valuation, is that "Valuation can be done by any three year old, as long has he has 30 years' experience."

I do not mean to dwell too long on the role of experience, but one other point has to be made here. Individuals who go into the appraisal profession rarely leave. The work is interesting, challenging, and always changing. No two valuation assignments are ever the same. You deal with dozens, if not hundreds, of different industries. Intellectual curiosity is perhaps the one requirement we look for in hiring prospective appraisers. Interest in business, and studying new business problems, is a key part of the learning process for any appraiser.

What does all this have to do with readers of this book? As mentioned above, this is not written to turn you into an appraiser, nor is it designed to intrigue you into exploring valuation as a career.

What we do want is for you to understand how appraisers go about their work in developing values for virtually any purpose. Why do you need this insight? Most valuations are performed because of some prospective transaction or potential conflict. For example:

- A seller wants to obtain the highest price, yet make sure the asset is priced correctly.
- A buyer wants to pay the minimum he can. One wants a high price, one wants a low price. An independent third-party appraiser can provide an answer that is fair to both. But just how can either party be sure that the appraiser is not favoring the other side? This book will show you.

Another example:

- The owner of a closely held company wants to give a 10 percent interest in his company to his children, and pay the minimum gift tax.
- The Internal Revenue Service (IRS) wants to maximize the taxes it collects, so it often challenges the values placed on closely held stock. How can the business owner obtain the greatest tax benefits and minimize the risk of attack from the IRS? A well-documented valuation report should withstand challenge, but how much documentation, and what type of assumptions, is reasonable? This book will show you.

A final example:

- In a business combination (a merger or purchase) the buyer wants to maximize future reported earnings. How the total purchase price is allocated over the assets acquired, that is, property, plant and equipment, intangible assets such as patents and brand names, and goodwill, will affect future reported earnings.
- The Securities and Exchange Commission (SEC) often challenges such allocations, on the grounds that the buyer is trying to enhance earnings, at the expense of conservative accounting. How can the buyer convince the SEC that the allocation is not biased, and in effect has been prepared in accordance with GAAP? A well-prepared valuation report is often required. How can the financial executive determine the quality of the appraisal? Readers of this book will be able to make this determination.

In short, the purpose of this book is to make you, the reader, a well-informed buyer of appraisal services. Conversely, if an adverse party hands you an appraisal report, you will be able to determine its quality and whether or not it should be utilized by you in negotiations.

Virtually every business transaction revolves around value. The parties ultimately must agree as to the value of the asset in question in order for the transaction to take place. Many buyers and sellers are thoroughly knowledgeable about values of assets in their own field, for example, a women's clothing store owner knows design and quality of dresses. When it comes to an infrequent transaction, for example, selling the store itself, the prospective seller usually has little or no experience. The only solution is to obtain expert assistance, often an appraisal.

There are well-designed dresses and poor-quality dresses, and it takes an expert to tell them apart at a glance. While most appraisal reports are reliable, unfortunately there are far too many poorly designed and even inadequate appraisals out there. Any appraiser can judge the quality of another valuation report very quickly. But how can you, the prospective user of a single report, tell whether you should or should not rely on it?

Most financial managers may see only one or two valuation reports in a lifetime. Yet, when faced with one, there may be many dollars at stake. This book, written by an insider, reveals what you, the client, should know about appraisals in order to make you an informed buyer or user.

Although the primary focus of this book is corporate financial transactions and how appraisers determine value, it should be noted that a significant number of valuation reports are basically prepared for tax planning and to preclude future litigation. Thus, tax practitioners and corporate attorneys will find this book helpful as they deal with appraisers and appraisal reports.

A typical appraisal report may cost in excess of $15,000 to $25,000. Before investing that amount of money, the buyer should become as informed as possible. This book has been written to make you, the reader, such an informed buyer.

Alfred M. King
Spotsylvania, VA
Fall 2001

Acknowledgments

With more than 30 years' experience in the field of appraisals and valuation, it would be foolhardy to try and name everyone who has helped me. If I started to list the names, it is certain that someone would inadvertently be left off the list and I would be in deep trouble. All I can say is that all of my colleagues at Valuation Research Corporation have been generous with both their time and their knowledge.

Each of my colleagues has had unique experiences. It is this willingness of the Valuation Research staff to share our knowledge that, in the final analysis, has contributed both to the success of the firm and to this book.

There is, however, one individual who must be named. Ettore Barbatelli first got me into the appraisal business in 1969. He founded Valuation Research Corporation several years later, and I joined him shortly afterward. He has been an inspiration all these years, and I have told anyone who will listen that Barb, as he is known, is the most knowledgeable person who has ever worked in the profession. Much of what I have learned, I owe to him.

The views expressed are solely those of the author. They do not represent the position of Valuation Research Corporation. Any reader who disagrees with what is written should contact the author directly.

Contents

CHAPTER 1

Cost, Value, and Price

- Company A stock closes today at a price of $35.00, down $5.00 from yesterday's close.

- At a Sotheby's art auction two bidders are tied at $40 million for a Van Gogh painting, one raises the price to $41 million, and the other drops out. The winner now has bought the painting for $41 million.

- Your brother-in-law just paid $21,000 to a new-car dealer for a Toyota Camry.

- A local bidder offers to put up a newly constructed house on a lot you own at a cost of $300,000.

- Privately held Internet Company B sells shares to a Venture Capital firm at $7.00 per share and offers options to employees the next day at $5.00 per share. Six months later the company has an initial public offering (IPO) at $18.00.

- A business buys a used milling machine at a "bargain price" of $50,000 and insures it for $65,000; the bank will lend only $35,000 to the company with the milling machine as collateral.

- Company C is currently selling on the New York Stock Exchange at $55.00 per share, and an unfriendly tender offer is made at $75.00 per share.

- A 40 percent short-term spike in lumber prices causes homes built in October 20xx to cost 7 percent more than the identical house next door built just one month earlier, as well as one built on the other side two months later. A *current* buyer today couldn't care less about lumber prices five years ago, so the market value of the three homes is identical. Yet homeowner's insurance premiums are based on original cost, multiplied by a current cost index. The October home is now paying $70 a year more for insurance than its two neighbors, although the three homes are physically identical.

• The trustee for your uncle's estate, in order to close the estate, sells his residence for $200,000, even though it is assessed at $240,000, and you thought nearby houses were selling for about $265,000.

• A jewelry firm advertises a contest on the Internet, the winner to receive a pair of diamond stud earrings "valued at $1,000."

• Construction equipment is a highly competitive industry. During the annual budget preparation a worksheet showing the "standard cost" for both the current and following year of a high-volume tractor was left out on the desktop overnight. One of the analysts was extremely concerned the next morning that a competitor could possibly have gained access to this highly confidential material. Fears were expressed that the company could be hurt badly. The analyst, however, was unable to explain the exact nature of the adverse impact.

Each of these mini-cases has a common element. In one form or another they demonstrate how in our capitalist form of society the *market* determines cost, value, and price. Unfortunately, while cost, value, and price are three separate and distinct concepts, many business managers, as well as consumers who are buyers, get these concepts confused. Cost and (selling) price differ. Selling price and value differ. And, finally, cost does not equal value. Yet in common parlance the three terms are all too often used interchangeably, albeit incorrectly.

The primary reason that people hire an appraiser is to determine *value*. To accomplish that, appraisers use cost and selling price as aids in determining value. However, cost does not equal value, and neither does selling price.

Value, to simplify things, represents the amount at which "willing buyers and willing sellers" would transact a purchase/sale, as long as both parties had full knowledge and were under no pressure to buy or sell.

There are many reasons people want to know the value of something, and it is usually related, in one form or another, to a prospective transaction. Rarely do people want knowledge of values just for the sake of knowledge. But when a transaction is imminent and it is important that the deal be fair to all parties, people call on appraisers.

An appraisal is nothing more or less than an opinion of value, usually expressed by someone with knowledge, training, and experience in the area under consideration. To the extent that the appraiser is neutral and unbiased, and to the extent that sufficient research has been performed, the answer provided as to value can:

- Be relied upon by both parties; and
- Is probably accurate to within 10 percent, plus or minus.

Unfortunately, because of the confusion among cost, value, and price, parties to a transaction often have difficulty in truly communicating with each other. Let us look at each of these mini-cases in precise terms and then derive some general principles.

- **Company A stock closes today at a price of $35.00, down $5.00 from yesterday's close.**

One of the basic concepts taught in every business school is that we have an "Efficient Market," particularly as it refers to the stock market, where at least in theory all relevant knowledge is impounded in the current price of a stock. Many studies have demonstrated that, in one form or another, the Efficient Market exists. Some analysts have found that for small firms, not followed by many analysts, it may take some time for the market to comprehend the latest information. Nonetheless, study after study demonstrates conclusively that the market is indeed efficient.

But if the market is so efficient, how do we explain the large and sudden swings we see listed every day in the *Wall Street Journal?* Every day at least 20 companies have swings—up or down—of more than 15 percent. Does it really make sense that a company that misses its quarterly earnings forecast by one cent per share is really worth *15 percent less* the next day? The same security analysts who put out the earnings forecast now punish the company for missing their projections by issuing an immediate "sell" signal.

In this instance, is the company selling less product to customers? Have costs of doing business suddenly risen. Have strong new competitors come on the scene? Has management changed? In every case the answer is probably NO. The sales are the same today as yesterday. The costs of doing business are the same today as yesterday. The management is the same today as yesterday.

In fact, *nothing* basic to the company has changed, other than the market price of a few shares at the margin, those that traded yesterday. The fact that a few shares were traded between buyer and seller at a lower price than the day before does not mean the *value* of the company has diminished.

The *value* of the company is unchanged, if you define value in terms of the present value of future cash flows. Revenues are the same. Costs and expenses are the same. Investor perceptions may have changed, but perhaps those investor perceptions are themselves incorrect. Not only is the public often wrong, but the public also often changes its mind!

Many of the same companies, whose stocks drop precipitously one day, come back over the next month or so to the old level. What then is the real value of the business? Is it based on the number of shares outstanding multiplied by today's market price (assuming no outstanding debt), or is the value *independent* of the current day's price? In this instance, market price and real long-term value are not the same.

- **At a Sotheby's art auction two bidders are tied at $40 million for a Van Gogh painting. One raises the price to $41 million, and the other drops out. The winner now has bought the painting for $41 million.**

The price at which the painting sold is clear, that is, $41 million. But is that the *value?* The standard definition of *fair market value* states:

Fair market value is defined as the price for which property would exchange between a willing buyer and a willing seller, each having reasonable knowledge of all relevant facts, neither under compulsion to buy or sell, and with equity to both.

This implies both a buyer and a seller. Two aspects must be kept in mind with regard to the day after the Van Gogh buyer paid his $41 million. Since there is only a single copy of the painting, the present owner from the previous day probably does not want to sell, so he is not the willing seller of the definition. Even more important, the most logical buyer would be the so-called underbidder. But we saw that he had dropped out at $40 million and had been unwilling to go up even one more bid. Presumably, that individual (or institution) would still be willing to pay $40 million, but that means an immediate diminution in value to the auction winner. What is the *value* of the painting?

An interesting example of this phenomenon was reported in the *New York Times* (May 11, 2000). A Cezanne painting was up for sale with an estimate of $5 to $7 million. "The circa 1898 landscape had bad luck tonight. It sold for $4.5 million but was reoffered late in the sale due to a misunderstanding with the winning bidder. The second time, it died at $4.3 million." What this particular Cezanne painting was worth in May 2000 is far from clear.

There is a second factor that might indicate the painting's *value* differs from its *cost* to the buyer. "Auction fever" is a well-known phenomenon, whereby two bidders go far above what either of them anticipated, just to make sure the other bidder does not walk off with the prize. In practice, auctioneers attempt to stimulate this type of rabid bidding, knowing that the highest possible price will be realized. Inasmuch as the auction house receives a percentage of the final selling price, the higher the final bid the more the auction house collects.

But once the auction is over and Auction Fever has been eliminated, it is likely that the winning buyer now suffers from another phenomenon called *buyer's remorse*. Were he to put the same object back up for auction a few months later, he might only receive 75 to 80 percent of what he himself had paid.

In short, reported auction *prices*, which represent a true willing buyer and willing seller *at the moment of the transaction*, may not represent *value* as we usually think of it. Put a different way, one man's *cost* may not be another man's *value*. This does not mean that auction prices realized should be discounted. After all, money did change hands at that moment.

Just as auction fever can raise the current price *above* true value, so can an auction result in *lower* prices. If there has not been sufficient publicity about an auction there may be too few willing buyers to arrive at so-called market prices. That is the reason many auctions have reserve prices. If the bidding does not reach some predetermined minimum, the item is not sold. But an item can meet the minimum reserve price and be sold, and yet represent a true bargain purchase.

The moral is clear. Auction *prices,* the *cost* to the buyer, may well not reflect long-term *value*.

- **Your brother-in-law just paid $21,000 to a new-car dealer for a Toyota Camry.**

Assume for the time being that the dealer really sold the car at his cost, as so many dealers advertise. In order to stay in business a dealer has to make a profit, so most people are somewhat skeptical of a car dealer's claim he is selling for cost. But it can happen; to simplify the example, perhaps it was the last day of the month and this one sales transaction meant the salesperson or the dealer reached quota, thus generating some additional bonus.

At this point the *cost* to the dealer was $21,000. The *price* paid by the buyer was $21,000; thus, the *cost* to the buyer was $21,000. With all of this, what is the *value* of the car?

Answers to this type of valuation question keep appraisers and valuation professionals in business, albeit not for single automobiles. If value were simply a matter of determining the cost or looking up the most recent price, life would be a lot simpler, but perhaps less remunerative for appraisers.

In this situation the answer to the question of the car's *value* is a function of the *purpose* for which the value information is needed. For example, the State Farm insurance agent wants to value the car on the basis of *replacement cost*. In this situation the replacement cost might be $22,000, inasmuch as the dealer sold the car at his cost, and presumably cannot do this all the time. A $1,000 gross profit appears reasonable, so State Farm would value the car at $22,000.

The local assessor, looking at the appropriate property tax assessment, might go to an automobile Blue Book and look up the retail price of a current year's used car. This could well be $19,000. At this point we have a car for which the buyer paid $21,000, insured it for $22,000, and is paying tax on $19,000 of valuation—One car, three values.

Suppose the buyer sees a Ferrari for which he has had a lifelong desire. The Ferrari dealer offers him a $25,000 trade-in on the new sport car. How can the dealer do that? Easily, because it is no more nor less than a sales discount on the high-priced Ferrari, in the form of an over-allowance on the trade-in.

Finally, suppose the prospective buyer of the Ferrari decides he wants a straight cash discount and offers to sell his original car to his neighbor at the current market price. They go to the newspaper and see that similar cars are being advertised at between $17,500 and $19,500. To save time and enmity between friends they decide mutually to split the difference and the neighbor buys the virtually new car for $18,500.

Now we have one car and five different values. All of them, while different, are correct—for the specific purpose and transaction. This is the reason that the very first question any appraiser asks before taking on an assignment is, "What is the value information to be used for?"

- **A local bidder offers to put up a newly constructed house on a lot you own at a cost of $300,000.**

This is pretty straightforward. When a builder, contractor, or other professional says "that will *cost* . . ." what he is really saying is that $300,000 is his *selling* price. You, as the buyer, do not know the seller's *cost* to perform the work.

Only the U.S. government tries to have a seller reveal his costs. What may not be well known is that many government contractors have to expose their books to government auditors, and the final sales price they receive is a function of the approved costs. Unapproved costs are not paid for by the government and come out of profits. Needless to say, this approach to contracting and procurement leads to numerous differences of opinion as to just what cost really is or should be.

- **Privately held Internet Company B sells shares to a Venture Capital firm at $7.00 per share and offers options to employees the next day at $5.00 per share. Six months later the company has an IPO at $18.00.**

This example represents a true-life situation. Companies want to reward employees and managers with low-price options prior to an IPO, essentially compensating the individuals for the sacrifices they made during the early start-up days. But to avoid compensation expense, options have to be granted at their Fair Market Value.

The Securities and Exchange Commission (SEC) is very sensitive to this issue, because of its emphasis on protecting investors in the IPO. The question they ask is, "How can the same company double in value just a few months before the public is being asked to invest?" Implicit in this question is the question, "What is the value of a privately held firm planning a future IPO, a transaction that may or may not occur?"

The sale to an investor at $7.00 and the granting of options at $5.00 at the same time appears, on the surface, to be a conflict. Examined more closely, it may not be.

An appraiser might value the company as a whole and conclude that the $5.00 per share option grant was truly at fair market value. The appraiser would be willing to defend that price with the IRS and SEC.

Then how can the $7.00 price be justified to the Venture Capital firm? The large investor may have a lot of money to put to work, like the subject company, and need a substantial position to make the investment worthwhile. He is willing to pay a premium to acquire a large block, which may well encompass a seat on the board of directors. The $2.00 premium truly reflects the law of supply and demand; looked at a different way, to the Venture Capital firm, they are willing to pay a premium to "get in on the ground floor" if they believe that a future IPO not only is likely, but will take place.

Meanwhile, the employees granted the options are probably working at compensation levels below the normal market, anticipating their reward as and when the company goes public.

In this situation all sides are satisfied, and the differing price truly represents value, given their individual circumstances.

The SEC, however, is uncomfortable about this situation. If the IPO is closely tied to the previous bargain prices, they raise a question about favoritism and inside dealing. It is beyond the scope of this chapter to explain the SEC's rationalization. Suffice it to say here that it is possible to rebut the SEC's presumption about value's increasing sharply just because of an IPO. What is not so easy is to determine whether this difference is of the order of magnitude of 50 percent or 150 percent. (This topic is covered further in Chapter 16.)

- **A business buys a used milling machine at a "bargain price" of $50,000 and insures it for $65,000; the bank will lend only $35,000 to the company with the milling machine as collateral because that is its liquidation value in the case of a forced sale.**

The insurance company insists on valuing the machine at $65,000, because in case of loss that is the amount it will take to replace the machine. Similar to the example above, where insurable values are often more than cost, here is a situation where cost on the one hand and *liquidation value* on the other are far apart. In this instance, the issue has to be looked at from the perspective of the lender.

No bank or finance company wants to pay off its loan through sale of the borrower's collateral. It is far better for the borrower to repay the loan from current cash flow. But if the business fails and there is only negative cash flow, the only hope for the bank lies in sale either of the business as a whole or of the individual assets on a piecemeal approach.

Hence, financial institutions value assets put up for collateral on a worst case basis. They assume that the asset may be in poor physical condition because of lack of maintenance while the borrower was suffering financially. They assume a forced liquidation, wherein prospective buyers realize the bank is not the proverbial willing seller.

The bank or finance company cannot utilize the milling machine in its own activities. Further, some cash is better than none. It costs the bank money to hold assets for sale, and requires management time and effort during the sale process. The quicker the sale, the better, from the lender's perspective. Thus, to a lender the value of the milling machine is not what it sold for, the recent cost to the borrower. Rather, the value is what the machine could realize in a forced sale "under the hammer," in an undetermined, but probably poor, condition.

- **Company C's stock is currently selling on the New York Stock Exchange at $55.00 per share and an unfriendly tender offer is made this evening at $75.00 per share.**

The fact is that the $55.00 share price and the $75.00 price are both correct. The reason is that based on current facts and investor perceptions, the $55.00 is the fair market value (FMV) for shares that have *no control* over the firm's activities. This is sometimes referred to as a *minority* price.

Now if someone wants to acquire control of the company, by owning over 50 percent of the voting shares, it is necessary to pay a *premium* to induce existing shareholders to sell their stock. If nothing else, individual shareholders will now be responsible for paying a capital gains tax, not to mention the need to identify some other investment with the cash they received from tendering their stock to the raider.

What we have here is a two-price system. Shares that control the company are worth more than shares that can receive only what management decides to give them.

- **A 40 percent short-term spike in lumber prices caused homes built in October 20xx to cost 7 percent more than the identical house next** door built just one month earlier, as well as one built on the other side two months later. A *current* buyer today couldn't care less about lumber prices five years ago, so the market value of the three homes is identical. Yet homeowner's insurance premiums are based on original cost, multiplied by a current cost index. The October home is now paying $70 a year more for insurance than its two neighbors, although the three homes are physically identical.

Insurable values are based on the cost of reproduction, what it would cost today to rebuild the structure in case of loss. Obviously, the cost of reproduction today is totally unaffected by lumber prices from five years ago.

However, the most cost-effective way to determine the cost of reproduction today is to apply a *cost index* to the original cost. Cost indexes are relatively blunt instruments that are not sophisticated enough to distinguish short-term fluctuations in original cost from five years ago. In short, determining the cost or value today, based on application of an index, can be no more accurate than the underlying information.

- **The trustee for your uncle's estate, in order to close the estate, sells the uncle's residence for $200,000, even though it is assessed at $240,000, and you thought nearby houses were selling for about $265,000.**

The basic definition of FMV assumes a theoretical willing buyer and an equally theoretical willing seller. Ordinarily, when individuals are selling their own home, they will attempt to obtain the maximum price, even if this means waiting for the right buyer to appear. Waiting an extra month or two may well result in selling the home at its true market value.

In the case of an estate, however, the trustee is under pressure to close things out and settle with the heirs. Thus, the trustee is likely to accept the first reasonable offer received, irrespective of the possibility of obtaining slightly more by waiting.

If you or an appraiser are now researching actual reported transactions to try and determine comparable prices for your own home, it is imperative that you understand the full nature of reported and recorded sales. That is, all sales reports are not of equal validity. Several years ago, during the Savings and Loan crisis, it was reported in the press that market participants had formed rings and colluded to report a series of ever-higher prices for the same property. Those transactions were then used to justify a very large loan that was never repaid.

- **A jewelry firm advertises a contest on the Internet, the winner to receive a pair of diamond stud earrings "valued at $1,000."**

In the final analysis, value represents what someone is willing to pay for an asset. So it is probably true that a piece of jewelry is valued at a certain amount; the announcer's wife might well pay $1,000, and who can say she is wrong? But that does not mean that *you* would pay that amount. Value is in the eye of the beholder.

- **Construction equipment is a highly competitive industry. During the annual budget preparation a worksheet showing the standard cost for both the current and following year of a high-volume tractor was left out on the desktop overnight. One of the analysts was extremely concerned the next morning that a competitor could possibly have gained access to this highly confidential cost information. Fears were expressed that the company could be hurt badly. The analyst, however, was unable to explain the exact nature of the adverse impact.**

Cost information is usually considered to be one of the most highly confidential types of information within a company, exceeded in sensitivity only by salary and compensation data. But just exactly what can Company A do with knowledge of Company B's cost information?

Suppose Gateway knows to the penny what Dell has to pay to buy a computer made in Korea. Just what can Gateway do with this information? Each firm has its own design, its own distribution system, its own marketing program. You cannot change one element in an integrated system without affecting all parts of the system. If Gateway found that Dell was paying less for a display screen, how would this help Gateway without perhaps requiring a basic engineering redesign of the product?

Or suppose that ExxonMobil finds out that Shell is paying less per hour to its workers at a Texas refinery. What can ExxonMobil do? It cannot move its refinery. It probably cannot renegotiate its contract with the union.

Dozens more examples would only confirm the statement that cost, like value, is in the eye of the beholder. There are many definitions of cost, which will be discussed in Chapter 5. For different business purposes it may help to know one or more of these levels of cost. But, as a generalization, cost is always related to a specific set of circumstances, and can only be used as a basis for decisions when all the parameters are known.

GENERAL PRINCIPLES

The first lesson to be learned is one of semantics. The terms *cost, value,* and *price* are *not* interchangeable. They relate to three separate and distinct concepts. When used improperly, erroneous ideas may be communicated.

Cost accountants may differ on the meaning of the term *cost.* The cost of any manufactured item may range from the prime cost of just material and direct labor, through various levels of full cost including overhead, up to an amount that bears a proportionate share of all sales, general and administrative (SG&A) expenses. From a seller's perspective, cost does not include profit, so a seller's selling price consists of cost plus profit, however measured and for whatever purpose.

From a buyer's perspective, the price he pays to acquire an asset then becomes his cost, at least for purposes of financial accounting and tax accounting. Further, in the absence of compulsion, the *value* to the buyer at the moment of acquisition is the *price* he paid, which was his *cost,* again however cost is measured in terms of cost accounting concepts. But almost immediately after the asset is acquired, the value is likely to change, as we have seen in the mini-cases discussed in this chapter.

There are as many definitions of *value* as there are of *cost.* The cost of a product for transfer pricing will differ from the cost for calculating gross profit upon sale to a third party. If considering outsourcing a production part, then the cost to make the product will *differ* from the cost used to buy the part from an outside vendor.

Similarly as we have seen, *insurable values* are usually based on the *cost of reproduction.* The value for financing of the same asset will be based on *liquidation value.* Liquidation value and cost of reproduction are at opposite ends of the value spectrum. In the middle is the concept of value in use. Appraisers use the term *value in use* to refer to the *replacement cost* of an asset, less depreciation from all causes.

12

In allocating the purchase price in a business combination, the value in use concept is widely utilized. As one can see, this value concept in turn depends on an estimate by the appraiser of replacement cost. Replacement cost, then, is the price that would have to be paid to buy an asset of equivalent utility, not necessarily a one-for-one replica of the subject.

The term *value* has almost as many definitions as the term *cost.* While cost is usually related to an actual or anticipated cash outlay, value relates to an assumed transaction. Appraisers, in determining an estimate of value, may look to cost as one element. But there is an alternative if deriving value, and that is to look at the actual selling price of other comparable transactions. Thus, in valuing the stock of a closely held corporation for which there have been no sales, an appraiser would search out comparable publicly traded companies and see the price(s) at which they sold. Adjustments to reflect size and marketability might be required, but the starting point would always come back to actual reported prices.

CONCLUSION

Professional appraisers deal with the concepts of *cost, value,* and *price* in every aspect of their work. With regard to *cost,* whether in trying to develop a target costing approach to new product development or installing a new enterprise resource planning (ERP) system to reduce inventories and increase quality, decisions have to be made about product and material costs, prices (both selling and purchase) and values of existing assets.

With regard to *price,* it is necessary to understand the actual nature of the transaction. The price at which a Van Gogh painting sold at auction differs from the price of lumber in a competitive market, and both differ from the price at which IBM stock closed yesterday.

With regard to *value,* we must always understand the purpose for which the information will be used and the kind of decision that will be made with the answer. There are as many different values as there are purposes.

Precise and accurate use of the three terms will avoid miscommunication as well as enhance the dialog among the parties at interest. Cost may or may not be the same as price. Price may or may not be the same as value. Value may or may not be based on cost. What has made these terms confusing for many users is that the same reference term has many different uses or definitions, *depending on the purpose.* When defined clearly and used properly, each of the concepts can be highly valuable. When not defined at all, or when used improperly, communication will be lost.

CHAPTER 2

Accounting for Value, Not Cost: Financial Reporting at the Crossroads

Financial reporting is controlled by generally accepted accounting principles (GAAP). For the last 100 years GAAP has meant historical cost. Assets are on the balance sheet at their original cost less depreciation. Any resemblance between book value and fair market value (FMV) is purely coincidental. When businesspeople are going to buy or sell an asset, they want to know what it is worth today, not what it might have sold for x years in the past.

A businessperson was looking for a new accountant, advertised the position, and received resumes from three applicants. Given the current requirements of the Equal Employment Opportunity Commission (EEOC), the only fair way to select the winning candidate was to give each of them the same objective test. The question was, "How much is 2 + 2?"

The first candidate answered "4."

The second candidate answered "let's say, about 4, plus or minus."

The third candidate answered "How much do you need?"

This old story is still appropriate for the subject of this chapter. If the manager doing the hiring were an accountant by background and training,

14

obviously the first candidate would be hired on the spot. He was accurate and understood the question.

However, if the manager doing the hiring were a salesman, not overly concerned about precision, candidate two might well be hired. Being a good personality match and not overly precise is more likely to be accepted by other members of the management team.

If the person doing the hiring were an entrepreneur planning an initial public offering (IPO), guess which candidate would be hired? Number three was the one who knew that it is results that count and was responsive to the real underlying business issues, not necessarily governed by perhaps outmoded conventions and rules.

Why this little parable? Businesspeople make decisions every day on the basis of *value*. Accounting statements may be interesting and provide a clue as to value. Even the most ardent accountant has to admit that financial statements produced in accordance with GAAP do *not* tell the reader the value of the assets shown.

Accountants insist on precision, reliability, and verifiability. They like to be right. They want to be trusted. They are trusted. That is why, in most surveys of Americans, accountants rank up near the top with pharmacists and physicians, and way above lawyers and used-car salesmen. This trust has been earned over the years because accountants are trained to take nothing for granted, to verify the source of all data in a company's books. The only way to do this is to trace every entry back to an invoice, a payroll register, or a sales receipt.

Accountants put assets on the books only when they can "kick the tires," that is, see the asset, and can determine the exact cost of the asset. Since most property, plant and equipment (PP&E) is purchased, it is easy to go back to the original invoice and see how much the asset cost when originally acquired. Accountants have to use judgment in determining the life of the asset, but once this is done they can compute an annual depreciation charge. Then each year that depreciation charge shows up as an expense, the original cost of the asset is reduced by that year's depreciation, and the result is the current *net book value*. Then, once the asset is fully depreciated, the dollars representing both the original cost of the asset and the total accumulated depreciation are removed from the balance sheet.

This is a system that has been in place for over 100 years, and it works except for one thing. The net book value at any point in time bears little relationship to the real value of the asset, if we define *value* as what someone would be willing to pay for the asset. The net book value is actually the original cost of the asset, less the depreciation charge determined by the accountant. It is not tested by reference to the market, either what used assets sell for, or what new assets could be acquired for.

WHAT ARE THE INFORMATION NEEDS OF BUSINESSPEOPLE?

Accountants are sometimes accused of looking backward, in a rearview mirror. The dollar amount on a balance sheet for the cost of PP&E is precisely accurate. We can have a high degree of confidence that, in fact, the firm spent exactly what is shown for the assets. While less precise, the accumulated depreciation on the balance sheet at least has been computed on some sort of rational basis, that is, straight-line or accelerated. The net of the two is, therefore, reliable.

But how *relevant* is this information? How can it be used? In the real world unless information is useful, it is superfluous, if not irrelevant. When assets are going to be bought or sold, or shares of a company bought or sold, virtually everyone is interested in *cash,* not accounting entries.

One accounting convention we have is that land is not depreciated. The underlying theory is sound. Land values more often than not stay the same or go up. Therefore, writing down land from its original cost is probably unrealistic.

This seemingly conservative tradition, that land values are never written down, albeit never written up either, leads to the situation that land worth hundreds or even thousands of dollars an acre is shown on the balance sheet at the original 1915 cost of less than $1.00 an acre. This is true of many companies in the forest products industry.

Over the years several large firms have been subjected to takeovers by outside raiders. These businessmen understood that the potential cash flow from selling the land would be well in excess of the dollar amounts shown on the balance sheet. If the then current stock price were controlled by the balance sheet amounts, there was substantial hidden value waiting to be grabbed. In fact, this type of adversarial takeover has been quite common.

The justification by the raider almost invariably is that he is interested in unlocking shareholder value. Translated, it means he believes he can buy low and sell higher. There is nothing wrong in buying at one price and selling at a different, higher price—unless you are part of the management team and lose your job.

Kern County Land Company was formed to hold land in Kern County, California. The original owners in the 1890s had paid less than $1.00 per acre, and the company owned literally hundreds of thousands of acres used mostly for agriculture. The company essentially was going nowhere until one day oil was discovered on its property.

Soon, Wall Street perceived Kern County Land Company as an oil company, with some agricultural land as a bonus. Because the land value was essentially zero, there was no cost of sales for the oil, and all the revenue flowed to the bottom line, except for the general and administrative expenses involved in running the company.

With tremendous cash flow and no way of reinvesting in more land in California, Kern management began a diversification program. They bought 100 percent of Walker Manufacturing, a company in the automobile muffler business, and a controlling interest in J.I. Case Company, a farm and construction equipment firm. Walker was modestly profitable under Kern management, but the deep-seated problems at Case were beyond their capability of fixing and Case was a drain on Kern's cash flow. However, with substantial oil revenues continuing to pump in cash, the bottom line on the Kern County financial statements continued to look very good.

Company management bragged to its shareholders about the very high return on investment (net income/equity) being realized. The implication was that company management was doing an outstanding job. This was true, if the investment base was the original 1890 cost of the land, combined with the recent purchase of Walker and Case.

A few shareholders, however, had the temerity to ask, "What is the *current value* of the land owned by Kern County Land Company?" The shareholders did not know just how much the land was worth, but the one certain fact was that the current market value was substantially in excess of $1.00 per acre! Perhaps the company's income was not so great, if measured against the real market value today of the thousands of acres of land with oil reserves underneath.

Arguing that their reported return on investment (ROI) was just fine, Kern County management did *not* disclose the current land value to its shareholders, perhaps because they themselves did not want to know. The truth was that the high profits and superb ROI resulting from those profits were in fact mediocre when related to the *current market value* of the land.

In reality, the Kern County management was doing a poor job of managing its assets, not a great job. But by failing to disclose the market value of the land and the oil underneath the land, they could maintain the fiction that they were doing a great job for the shareholders.

Armand Hammer, the entrepreneur behind Occidental Petroleum, knew the oil business and had made a career of identifying good values in oil property. He made a tender offer for Kern County Land Company stock at a price significantly above the then current market.

All of a sudden, Kern County management started bleating to their shareholders that the Occidental offer was *below* the real value of the company and its assets, even though the offer was way above anything at which the stock market had heretofore valued Kern County.

After attempts to get Mr. Hammer and Occidental to go away, Kern County management turned to Tenneco as a white knight. Tenneco bought all of Kern County, including Walker and Case.

Within a few years all the Kern County management team was gone. Tenneco expanded the Walker and Case holdings. Recently, Tenneco spun off Case, by this time a $5 billion firm, and only Walker and one other company were all that was left of Tenneco. The acquisition of Kern County in 1969, an acquisition that itself was due to poor financial reporting, caused the management to lose their jobs.

Let us look at another example of the perils of relying on historical cost information. NationsBank recently acquired BankAmerica. Shortly after the merger, the former chief executive officer (CEO) of BankAmerica, who had been promised the top position in the new firm in several years, was forced to resign because of substantial losses (several hundred million dollars) from an investment made by his bank that had turned bad. Commenting on this situation in the October 27, 1998 *Wall Street Journal,* noted financial writer Martin Mayer, a guest scholar in the economic studies program at the Brookings Institution, wrote:

What are the Information Needs of Businesspeople?

The revelation that BankAmerica lost $372 million in a complicated joint venture with the New York hedge fund operator D. E. Shaw—and in the process acquired a portfolio of bonds with a face value of $20 billion, which could generate further losses—has raised troubling commercial and legal questions about the recent merger of NationsBank into the old BankAmerica.

BankAmerica and David Shaw, a former Columbia University professor, launched their partnership in March 1997. Their plan was to use the bank's money and Mr. Shaw's software to exploit the range of opportunities for arbitrage opened by the expansion of trading in debt instruments and derivatives.

The real results of such trading were not predictable if market volatilities exceeded certain almost impossible parameters. That of course is just what happened. The Asian tigers rolled over, the Japanese banks ran out of let's pretend room on their bad assets, the Russian state imploded—and so did the computer models. Bids for the instruments the computers had modeled simply disappeared. So far as the outside world knew, however, the BankAmerica venture was the Chevy truck of trading—like a rock. Stockholders in Nations-Bank and BankAmerica who voted in September to approve the merger had no notion that one of the partners was bleeding hundreds of millions of dollars.

Asked in October why the bank continued to carry its Shaw investment at cost in August, when the losses in the deal became overwhelmingly apparent, a spokesman said the bank had believed that the values would come back with the passage of time—and, anyway, the Comptroller of the Currency, the bank's federal supervisor, had known all about it. If Shaw as an investment company had tried to value its holding in the joint venture at cost, somebody could have gone to jail. But the bank could do so, because banking regulators have long permitted banks to state their assets at "historic cost," without reference to market value.

About a decade ago, the FASB [Financial Accounting Standards Board] decided that valuations of financial instruments should be standardized across industry lines, and commercial banks—like investment banks, brokers, and mutual funds—should have to carry their securities at market price. Federal Reserve Chairman Greenspan objected strongly, warning that if they had to carry government bonds at market price, banks might not buy such stuff, making it more difficult for the government to fund its deficit; and in 1991 the banks were in such trouble that Richard Breeden, the SEC chairman who had led the charge for reform, was pushed aside.

In 1996, however, the FASB went ahead anyway, proposing a set of rules for valuing all bank investments, including derivatives. Again, Mr. Greenspan and Comptroller Eugene Ludwig objected; valuing the assets, after all, is what their bank examiners do for a living. Mr. Greenspan went so far as to write letters to the chairman of the congressional committees that supervise the SEC opposing such a plan.

But the Shaw–BankAmerica saga makes the FASB case. It demonstrates the need for imposing market-value accounting on banks, especially larger banks, which increasingly rely on the market rather than on deposits for their funding.

It would be interesting to interview the former CEO of BankAmerica about his views today on market value financial reporting, as contrasted with historic cost accounting. He might still have his job.

FAIR MARKET VALUE OF ASSETS

Rigid reliance on historical cost has hurt the usefulness of financial reports. "Driving looking into the rear-view mirror" is how some critics have characterized today's financial reporting model.

Almost 30 years ago a distinguished body of accountants, headed by Robert Trueblood, studied the subject of what information users of financial statements really need. The conclusion was both simple and clear. Users of financial statements, both investors and creditors, wanted a handle on anticipated future cash flows. Since nobody can foretell the future, the best evidence as to what is most likely to happen is based on the recent past and the present.

Future cash flows to a company are going to come from customer revenues, less expenses incurred in deriving that revenue (i.e., salaries, rent, materials and supplies). In addition, cash requirements for new capital investments and working capital needed to support increased sales and inventory levels have to be considered.

In addition to profits to be generated from sales, companies can finance their cash requirements:

- By borrowing (occasionally by selling stock)
- By selling assets

If a company chooses to borrow, say from a bank, the lender wants to know how it is going to be repaid. Loan repayments, including interest, come from operations, as long as the business remains profitable. But lenders are skeptical by nature ("A banker is someone who lends you money only when you don't need it"). Bankers invariably take a worst-case assumption and assume that there will not be profits. If not from profits, then where will loan repayments come from? The answer is clear—from *asset sales.*

This is why bankers always try to obtain a secured position, laying claim to a borrower's assets, so that in case of financial difficulty the bank will be in a preferred position. It will have the legal right to sell the assets and apply the cash received to the loan.

If you were a banker and were going to lend money to a customer with the customer's assets as collateral, what would you want to know about the assets? Would you be interested in what the borrower paid for the assets sometime in the past? Would you prefer to know what the asset(s) could be sold for today, irrespective of original cost?

Merely stating the question this way provides its own answer. Borrowers have to know how much cash could be generated in case of financial stress. Here the key point is that accounting conventions, displaying assets at depreciated historical cost usually is of little probative value to a lender. The lender needs to know the *value,* today, of the assets. For this purpose, *value* is defined in terms of cash receipts if the assets were sold to a third party.

If creditors and shareholders need information about future cash flows, as the Trueblood report indicates, then at least from the perspective of creditors, value information should be disclosed. And it is hard to believe that shareholders are not interested in the value of the assets of the company they own! Why is value information not typically disclosed?

WHAT IF VALUE INFORMATION WERE DISCLOSED

There appear to be four main reasons why companies do not disclose the value of their firm's assets:

1. Fear of competitive reaction.
2. Natural conservatism.
3. Values can—and do—change.
4. Changes in values will overwhelm normal operating results.

Competitive Reaction

For almost 100 years financial managers have complained that disclosure of information by their firm will lead to irretrievable harm. At one point, some 70 years ago, firms were reluctant to disclose their sales level! *"If our competitors know how much we sell, they can focus their energies on our customers—or perhaps they will cut prices to capture market share."* Somehow, nobody was ever able to point out a single concrete example of such harm. Fifty years later, when the accounting rule makers required companies to disclose sales and operating profit by business segment, the lineal descendants of the earlier financial managers complained, *"If our competitors know how much we sell and make in each product line, they can focus their energies on our customers—or perhaps they will cut prices to capture market share—or our customers will demand price cuts if they see how profitable we are."* Again, nobody has been able to point out a concrete example of such harm.

The bottom line is that financial managers are conservative and simply are reluctant to disclose information about their own firm—at the same time they of course like to obtain information about their customers, suppliers, and competitors. Virtually every observer has commented that one of the strengths of our economy and our business system is the free flow of information. By definition this has to be a two-way street, no matter how reluctant any one player is to abide by the rules.

In point of fact the real criticism about our disclosure system today, one made increasingly by financial journalists and financial analysts, not to mention individual shareholders, is that there is *too much information* being disclosed. Pick up the annual report of any major U.S. firm. Try to read the entire financial statements and related footnotes, plus management discussion and analysis (MD&A). Sara Lee is a medium-sized company by many standards ($18 billion in sales). The Operations Review, Financial Review, Management's Report on Financial Information, Report of Independent Public Accountants, plus the financial statements and footnotes add up to over 40 pages of information. For all except the most devoted analyst, this is information overload.

Thus, when management complains about disclosing value information on top of everything else, they have a point. Would readers of the Sara Lee annual report—which, by the way, is an excellent example of financial reporting—have a better grasp of the company with an additional two to five pages of value information? Perhaps not, and that is the real argument in favor of the status quo, not the specious argument about competitive disadvantage.

This begs the question as to whether value information, *instead of* historical cost information, should be supplied, a subject to be discussed in this chapter.

Natural Conservatism

The basic personality trait of financial managers, by and large, is conservative. Change is considered doubtful; risks are to be avoided. What has worked in the past is tried and true and should be maintained until the evidence is overwhelming that something new is needed. This is not meant as criticism, but simply a description of what is. The financial manager of a firm is responsible for the continuing ability of a firm to meet its payroll, pay its suppliers, and finance growth. Risks must be avoided that could jeopardize the existence of the firm. In contrast, the personal characteristics of sales personnel must be different from that of the financial staff. Conservative advertising and marketing may be just as deleterious as aggressive financial management.

The author has known many financial managers and almost without exception they are comfortable following the rules. Most financial executives started their career in accounting and auditing. An auditor's job is to see that the rules are followed and write up those who have not followed the rules. Auditors like rules. Rules provide guidance and obviate the need for initiative and judgment.

Today's accounting rules, developed over the past 100 years, were based on the convention of historic cost. For a long time, in fact, the historic cost of assets, after accounting depreciation had been subtracted, probably did reflect the then current value of the assets.

In a period of relatively stable (or even declining) prices and relatively slow technological change, the current value of an asset could be expected to decline more or less in line with its age. Inflation in the past 30 years, combined with rapid technological improvements, as well as worldwide competition, all mean that the rate of change has greatly sped up.

The old paradigm that accounting book values essentially equaled market value lost its validity. This was accentuated by high tax rates that encouraged:

- Firms to choose short lives for assets that did not necessarily reflect the underlying economics; and
- Mergers and acquisitions.

In a merger the buyer is required to allocate the purchase price, resulting in new book values that differ from the amounts previously shown on the acquired firm's financial statements.

In short, as the pace of change has accelerated, the accounting conventions have slowly had to change. Unfortunately, the economic and social conditions in the world changed faster than the accounting. This has meant that the emphasis on original historic cost has been maintained, even at the expense of relevance and accuracy.

This is what we meant by conservatism. The world appears to have changed, but the rules have remained the same. Who, among accountants, wants to be a trailblazer and propose new rules? Accountants and financial executives, almost by definition, are not trailblazers!

Thus, it has been left to critics in academia and journalism, to point out the flaws in today's accounting. They may be right, but academics and journalists do not make the rules. Accounting rules are set in the private sector by the Financial Accounting Standards Board (FASB), and enforced by public accountants as well as the SEC, which itself is a conservative government regulatory agency.

From the point of view of the critics of today's accounting rules, the deck is stacked. The very people who apply the rules, and are comfortable with those rules, are the same people who write the rules. No wonder change is slow.

Values Change

If using a historical cost convention in accounting, the only entries required are the original cost of the asset, based on the vendor's invoice, and the succeeding years' charges for depreciation, usually calculated on a straight-line basis. The original cost does not change from year to year; only the accumulated depreciation charge increases, and the net book value decreases each year in regular and predictable increments. No judgment is required. In effect the accounting system is on autopilot.

If companies were to go to a system of reporting current value information, there would be several problems, because as is discussed throughout the book, there is no single definition of value.

First, is the determination of the appropriate definition of value, what we sometimes refer to as the *premise of value*. Are we looking for the cost to replace the asset? Or do we want to know what the asset could be sold for to a third party? Are we valuing the asset on a stand-alone basis, or is it more appropriate to consider it as part of a larger grouping, for example, as a single hotel versus one of a group of 15 hotels? In each case the values will be different, so who is to determine which is the most appropriate?

Second, whatever is chosen as the premise of value, it is certain that the values will not be static. Since there is a cost to determine value information, how often should values be determined? Monthly? Quarterly? Annually? Monthly and quarterly appear ridiculous, but even annual revaluations would be costly. Every five years, then? Since accountants and auditors need rules, to avoid complete anarchy, who will set the rule about revaluations and how will the determination be made? It is easier to ask the questions than to answer them. But it is these types of issues that critics of today's accounting conventions have to answer before seriously proposing a change.

That values change quickly, in some cases, was demonstrated in an appraisal prepared for a bank. The borrower was a large contractor in Florida who owned most of his own equipment. The construction equipment was to be the basis of securing the loan. The bank asked the appraisal firm to determine the fair market value of the assets, and the premise of value was what could be realized by a sale to a dealer.

The appraisal firm inspected the assets, reviewed used equipment prices in the relevant blue book, and then, as a final step, checked the validity of the values through personal discussions with major equipment dealers in Florida, dealers who bought and sold the exact type of assets being appraised. The appraisal firm's values were developed, the appraisal report prepared, and the loan approved and disbursed.

Nine months later the bank called the appraisal firm. The loan officer was in a panic. The contractor had defaulted on the loan. Then, when the bank went to try and sell the equipment—the collateral supporting the loan—the dealers offered less than half of what the equipment had been appraised at only a few months earlier. The message to the appraisal firm from the bank was clear, "You are liable for our losses. If your appraisal had been correct, that is, with the 'real' lower values, our bank would not have made the loan and hence we would not be losing money now."

For a brief period of time there was panic at the appraisal firm. "How could we have been so wrong?" After all, the first assumption was that the bank must be correct.

Further investigation, however, revealed the truth. The contractor declared bankruptcy because economic conditions in Florida deteriorated rapidly and there was no new construction going on. Further, the sharp decline in the price paid for used construction equipment was related to the same circumstances: With no construction there was no demand for equipment and if the dealers could not sell what they had in inventory, they had no interest in acquiring any more. In short, the same set of economic conditions affected both the contractor and the used equipment market.

The key point was that the appraisal was correct as of the date it was made. Nine months later, it could no longer be used. Values had changed. The appraisal had not changed.

The purpose of this mini-case study is not to discuss the validity of valuation work by an appraisal firm. Neither is it to try and assess blame or responsibility. The point is that values do change. In less than one year, the value of used construction equipment in Florida dropped by more than half.

For those who support a requirement that firms disclose the current value of their assets, a major difficulty is that the cost of developing this information may exceed the benefits to be derived. The truth is that for most assets used by most companies, asset values do *not* change that rapidly. Obviously, the construction equipment example described above is the exception, not the rule.

Certainly, examples can be easily developed where rapid fluctuations in market values take place. Every day, at least 50 stocks are reported in the *Wall Street Journal* that have risen or fallen by more than 10 percent. And that is a 10 percent change in total value in a single day. Over a six-month period many companies have changes in total value in excess of 50 percent. As a shareholder you are affected accordingly.

Other than mutual funds, few companies own blocks of stock in other publicly traded firms, so stock market fluctuations actually do not affect most industrial firms. The point is that 50+ percent changes in values are common, but would not necessarily affect the reported financial information of other firms.

Real estate is another area in which market values can go up or down rapidly, depending on development in a locality, and also on a global basis by changes in interest rates. Popular financial columnists often opine on the desirability of individuals buying a house if interest rates are going down, because "house values go up when mortgage payments go down." But the history of real estate prices and values suggests that sizable changes are the norm, not the exception.

Operating Results are Affected by Changes in Value

What happens to a company's reported operating results if values of assets change during a period, and if a company then has to reflect these changes in its financial statements? Debits have to equal credits in every balance sheet and income statement. If a company reduces the value of an asset because it is impaired, this is a credit to the value of the asset. There has to be a corresponding debit, which in this case has to be to expense.

If you were the manager of a profit center and being measured on your performance, your main emphasis should be on sales volume, gross profit, expense control, new products, and so forth. In short, you should be focused on operations and operating profit. Operating profit comes from operations.

Now what if someone forced you to take a charge to expense because of a *change in asset values?* Depending on the magnitude of the value change and the dollar amount of the operating income, it is totally conceivable that a full year's profits could be wiped out by a single accounting change (i.e., the change in the fair market value of your assets). To reduce the value of your assets, say, by $1 million requires a $1 million expense charge. If operating profits were $900,000, you would report a net loss, even if the $900,000 operating profit were above budget. You worked all year to generate a profit, and then on December 31 some accountant would come along and say that because real estate values in the neighborhood had gone down, you have to take the $1 million charge. Nothing in the business has changed. You still use the same buildings, in the same condition. But because the market says the buildings are suddenly worth less, you have to show this in your financial statements.

For many—if not most—firms, a 5 percent change in the fair market value of their assets could either double reported profits or completely wipe them out for a year. After all, since values go up as well as down, reported profits could go up. Even a doubling of reported profits in a period may not be all that great. What about one year later when the new year's operations are compared with the previous year's results. At that point, the doubling of profits is going to make the current comparison look bad. Once you start mixing operating results with changes in values, the utility of today's financial statements is in question.

CAN OPERATING RESULTS BE KEPT SEPARATE?

Perhaps the strongest single argument *against* developing and disclosing current market value information is the impact on the usefulness of the income statement, sometimes referred to as the profit and loss (P&L) statement. Management is hired to produce products or services, at a profit. It is provided capital by the owners of the business, and expected to add value to the assets.

The income statement, the report to shareholders, is essentially a report card, measuring performance. Most companies prepare financial statements for internal purposes each month and report quarterly to outside parties (i.e., shareholders and creditors). Publicly traded firms must, by law, report quarterly to the SEC and hence to the public.

It is true that changes in the value of assets are important, and may affect future cash flows of the business. Even more significant, in terms of future cash flows, are the underlying sales and profits of the basic products and services produced by the firm. With the exception of mutual funds and real estate businesses, virtually no other companies are in the business of increasing the value of assets owned by the firm. Companies are in business to produce products and services. IBM makes computers. General Electric makes jet engines. Merck makes pharmaceutical products. Microsoft makes software. Exxon Mobil produces, refines, and distributes petroleum products. AT&T provides telecommunications services.

In the final analysis, shareholders are interested in how well management is doing. Management is measured in absolute terms, in terms of dollars of profit, earnings per share. Comparisons are made with previous years' results for the company, and expectations are generated for the future. In addition, most financial analysts attempt to compare the subject firm with others in its industry, to arrive at a judgment as to relative performance. This, in turn, involves understanding the effect of the external economy, domestic and international, on the market(s) for the firm's products and services. How well did the management of Company A respond to industry conditions and economic conditions? Is it gaining market share? Is it developing new products through research and development, or is it expanding through acquisitions? Investors ask these and a hundred other questions.

The primary source of information to answer these questions is the firm's own financial statements. For single-product firms, the total P&L statement is the basis of analysis. For multiproduct firms, those operating in several different industries, supplemental information about segment

28

performance is provided in footnotes to the financial statements. This book is not a text on financial statement analysis; most readers are knowledgeable on the subject.

What is important is to understand that if changes in the values of assets are included in regular operating results, then the usefulness of the operating results is going to be compromised. In effect, information would be provided about two different functions—results of operations and changes in asset values.

We have seen that small changes in asset values may well overwhelm the dollar amounts of profit generated from sales to customers. So, which is more important, operating results or asset values? Virtually every observer would agree that to understand long-term results, asset value changes are at best of secondary interest. Continuing profits have to come from sales to customers.

Asset value changes, either up or down, are limited in how far they can go. Vacant land, for example, can become worthless or it can increase in value by thousands of dollars an acre. But the amount of land held by a company for future growth is limited, unless it is in the real estate business. Excess land can be sold only once. There could be a one-time impact on cash flows, and such a potential gain might be important to shareholders and creditors. But once the land is sold, at either a profit or at a loss, the future course of the firm is going to revert back to its basic business.

There is a potential solution to this problem of mixing apples and oranges, combining operating results with changes in the value of assets. The solution would be to separate the two types of income in the same statement. A company could disclose operating profit, and then show changes in asset values as a separate line with a separate caption.

The sum of these two would be net income, either before or after tax. But the detail making up the net income figure would be available. Is this the best of both worlds? Yes, but only if one has the detailed financial statements in hand.

Perhaps more often than we realize only summarized information is used. Take the daily stock market listings in the *Wall Street Journal.* They show a price/earnings (P/E) ratio for each stock. The P/E ratio is composed, obviously, of two factors: the current price of the stock per share and the current earnings per share (EPS) of the stock. If changes in asset values are going to be included in the financial statements, and in net income, should that final bottom line be the basis for calculating earnings per share? If you exclude changes in asset values and rely solely on income from operations, you have defeated the purpose of measuring and reporting changes in asset values. However, if the single earnings per share figure *includes* changes in asset values, it is highly likely that some very unusual results will be reported, results that do not reflect the underlying economics of the business.

Readers may say that the single earnings per share number used to calculate the daily P/E ratios is an exception or an anomaly. It is a price worth paying, or it can be overlooked because of the greater benefit of having the new additional information.

But the daily P/E ratio in the *Wall Street Journal* is not the only place that the new information would have an impact. Go to any financial publication, *Forbes, Fortune,* or *Business Week,* or to any stockmarket newsletter. Comparisons are continually being made among companies. Past results, present results, and anticipated future results are all the subject of journalistic inquiry.

Now what is going to be the impact on these multicompany comparisons if the basic financial statements are a combination of operating results and unrealized changes in asset values? It is not hard to foresee that mass confusion will result. Sooner rather than later, some analyst is going to plead, "Will the *real* earnings please stand up?" But what is the *real* earnings? Is it the amount *with* the asset value changes, or is it the amount *without* the asset value changes? Frankly, neither answer is going to be correct all the time. Some analysts, for some purposes, are going to want one figure; other analysts for other purposes are going to want the other.

There are some problems for which there are no good answers, and this is one of them. At times, readers of financial statements would be helped by having information about changes in the value of assets held by the company. At other times it would be confusing, if not positively harmful, to mix operating results with changes in value.

Presenting both sets of information, and letting financial statement users choose their own data sounds good at first. But what if you read in publication A that EPS for your firm was $2.55 and then in publication B that EPS was only $1.69. One figure was operating results only, and the other included changes in value of assets. Will the *real* earnings figure please stand up?

REAL-WORLD EXPERIENCE

If changing the accounting system to reflect current values has problems, is there a compromise possible? Could value information be developed and disclosed to readers of financial statements without changing the basic accounting conventions we are all used to? The answer is affirmative.

Two approaches are possible. One would be to retain today's historical cost accounting model, and then on a supplemental basis provide a second set of financial statements based on current values. Readers would have today's numbers as the real financials, and the additional data would be considered as informational, but not definitive. The *Wall Street Journal* would pick up as earnings and EPS the same data they do today. For those interested in the supplemental value information, the only source would be the firm's printed financial reports available to shareholders, creditors, and others.

A second approach would be to provide even less than a full set of financial statements prepared on a value basis. Here, a firm would provide, but only in a footnote, current value information on fixed assets, at least for those assets whose value today differs from historical cost. If there were other assets on the balance sheet, like goodwill, the value of which differed from cost, that presumably would be disclosed also. Finally, some observers have suggested that companies fully disclose the value of intellectual property, which is usually thought to consist of such intangible assets as patents, trademarks, brand names, and research and development. At least today there is virtually nothing shown on the balance sheet for intellectual property. Many observers say that for high-tech firms the major asset is intellectual property and showing nothing on the balance sheet for these assets implies that they have no value. In practice, of course, the most valuable asset of many high-tech firms is the idea and how it is being implemented, even if there are no reported assets as defined by accountants.

Many readers may not be aware that over 20 years ago the accounting profession was faced with a requirement to do just what was stated above. The SEC required companies to disclose the replacement cost of their assets and the impact on reported profits if depreciation were taken on the theoretical replacement cost of those assets. The effect of the SEC proposal was to suggest that historical-cost financial statements greatly overstated real income.

A second and different approach was mandated by the FASB. Rather than develop what it would cost today to replace the assets, the FASB required that companies apply price indexes to the original cost of the assets.

Both the SEC and FASB requirements were a response to the high rates of inflation being experienced in the late 1970s. Take Brazil as an example. With inflation of 50 percent to 100+ percent per year, the historical cost of assets becomes useless information on a financial statement in less than two years. Business still has to be carried on in a high-inflation economy. Management has to manage. Shareholders need some measure of performance.

Consequently, there are well-established techniques for adjusting historical-cost financial statements to reflect the impact of inflation. Essentially, an index such as the consumer price index or the gross national product deflator is chosen (some inflation-adjustment methods allow for several indexes simultaneously). The index is applied across the board. The effect of such indexing is to reduce reported profit drastically.

Let us look briefly at the application of the SEC and FASB methods and how they worked out in practice. If we don't learn from this past experience, some have suggested we will be condemned to repeat it. As one who lived through the experiments and criticized them at the time, the author has no wish for either technique to be required again. We can learn from the past.

At this point, let us go back to fundamentals. What is value? There is a definition that is generally accepted by appraisers, the courts, and the Internal Revenue Service.

Fair market value is defined as the price for which property would exchange between a willing buyer and a willing seller, each having reasonable knowledge of all relevant facts, neither under compulsion to buy or sell, and with equity to both.

This definition assumes an exchange, a purchase by one party and sale by the other party of an asset. Implicit is the assumption that if the deal is consummated, then cash will change hands. The definition of value, therefore, is the estimate of the price at which both parties would be happy to undertake the transaction.

Both the SEC and FASB inflation reporting requirements, one based on replacement cost and the other on price indexes, suffered the same impediment. Both requirements were theoretical. They asked the question: If the assets were replaced, or were bought at today's prices, what would they cost?

To those at the FASB and SEC who mandated these requirements it seemed perfectly obvious. Wouldn't it be nice if we knew what the assets would cost today? We then would know the impact on depreciation expense (which obviously would be much higher in a period of high inflation). Finally, we as managers, creditors, and shareholders, could see that reported income on the historical cost model was plainly overstated. The unstated assumption on the part of the FASB and SEC was that those who prepared financial statements and those who used them had to be saved from themselves. By mandating additional information, "better decisions" could be made. There was a high degree of arrogance that a select group of accountants in Washington (SEC) and Connecticut (FASB) knew what statement preparers and users really needed.

It only took a few years for the SEC and FASB requirements to be withdrawn. The face-saving argument at the point of withdrawal was that the rate of inflation had declined dramatically, and the inflation-adjusted information no longer was needed.

The truth was that even at the point of greatest inflation the so-called value information developed to meet the requirements of replacement cost (SEC) and indexed historical cost (FASB) was of *no use* to management or to readers of financial statements. Study after study was unable to find any examples of better decisions as a result of all the supplemental information disclosed during the period the experiments were under way.

Why did the replacement cost and indexed historical cost experiments fail? The answer is found in the Trueblood Committee report, mentioned above. The primary objective of financial statements is to allow users to estimate future cash flows. In turn, an understanding of real cash flows will help readers arrive at their own estimates of value. The fundamental premise of valuation and financial investing is that the value today of an asset is the *present value of future cash flows*. Know what the future cash flows are going to be and you can derive the value.

The simplest example proving this theorem is the valuation of U.S. government bonds. There is zero risk of default, because the government can always print more money. The value of future dollars, in terms of purchasing power, may be less, because of inflation, but there is 100 % certainty that if you buy a $1,000 bond due in 2010, then in the year 2010 you will receive $1,000 from the U.S. Treasury. No other body, foreign country, or AAA-rated corporation can make that promise. Every other issuer of bonds has some risk that the bonds will not be paid at maturity.

Thus, for valuing U.S. government bonds the only issue is the rate at which the known future cash flows should be discounted. Changes in the discount rate affect today's value of a U.S. Treasury security, but at any one point the discount rate and hence the price of the security is known.

The value of any security other than a Treasury bond has to incorporate risk that the anticipated future cash flows may not be met. The point is that despite the risk element, the value of any security, including the common stock of publicly traded firms, is affected by investors' perceptions as to the timing and uncertainty of future cash flows.

For a bond, the future cash flows are carefully laid out in terms of semi-annual interest payments plus the face value of the bond at maturity. For common stock, the future cash flows are far less certain, both in timing and amount. Nonetheless, in the final analysis, stocks are bought and sold on investors' overall expectations for future profits and cash flows.

Usually implicit in the valuation process is the assumption that what has happened in the past is likely to continue in the future. If a company's sales have been growing 5 percent per year on average for the past three or four years, it is reasonable to assume continuation of this trend. If a company has been making capital expenditures approximately equal to its annual depreciation charge for the past three or four years, it is reasonable to assume continuation of this trend. If a company has been paying out 40 to 45 percent of its reported income as dividends, it is reasonable to assume continuation of this trend.

The SEC proponents of replacement cost accounting, and the FASB proponents of index-adjusted historical cost both assumed that inflation was distorting the financial statements relative to corporate business policies. As prices rose, the current cost today to buy the inventories and fixed assets was a lot higher than the historical-cost amounts shown on the financial statements. A milling machine that was bought five years ago for $55,000 (and had a 10-year life for financial reporting purposes) might cost $75,000 today. The $5,500 annual depreciation charge on the books therefore *understated* what the depreciation charge would have been ($7,500) if the milling machine were to have been bought this year.

The FASB's indexing requirement was said to apply a machine tool index to the balance sheet value of the asset, and to the income statement amount of depreciation expense. The effect was to show higher depreciation expense and lower profits than the unadjusted historical-cost financial statements. The reason is that the older the asset, and the greater the cumulative impact of inflation, the larger will be the new depreciation expense. Inflation is cumulative each year, so the index for current year's sales and cost of sales is low, but the index for depreciation expense, based on assets purchase several years earlier, was high.

For capital-intensive firms, with low operating profit margins and high depreciation expense, the FASB's indexing resulted in firms showing losses instead of profits! The FASB response to corporate officers who complained about the result was "Well, that's economic reality," followed by, "That's why we require you to show the lower income."

The problem with the FASB approach, which in their minds provided better information to statement users, was that companies were *not* replacing five-year-old milling machines with new. The indexed depreciation expense was just that, a mechanical application of an index that had nothing to do with future cash flows.

The FASB assumed that when it did come time to replace existing assets with new, higher-priced assets (higher priced because of inflation), depreciation expense would increase at that time. By showing the impact today of potential replacements in the future, the FASB methodology provided only "what if" information, not information on actual or potential cash flows.

The fatal flaw in the FASB indexing of historical cost was that virtually no capital expenditures—for any firm—are one-for-one like-kind replacements. The truth is that most capital equipment does not wear out. Good maintenance will keep most assets going for far longer than the arbitrary life used to calculate accounting depreciation. Two examples prove this point. Buildings are never depreciated over more than a 40-year life. How many buildings constructed before 1963 are still being used? In fact, one appraiser pointed out that French cathedrals constructed in 1350 are still being used today for their original purpose, and are just as functional today as they were 650 years ago. How much depreciation expense should have been charged over that period? Would indexing it for inflation have made the number more useful?

A second example is jet aircraft. Few airlines use more than 12 years as the life of a jet, for purposes of calculating depreciation for tax and book purposes. Yet, as critics have pointed out, there are many jets still flying today that are more than 25 years old. Continuous maintenance allows the airlines to utilize the aircraft. The process of parts replacement is ongoing, so after 25 years there may be virtually no original parts, yet it is the same plane. A new jet may cost more than double, in today's dollars, what the specific aircraft cost 25 years ago. But since the maintenance expense is being reported at current levels, and the plane continues to fly, does it make sense to double up on the depreciation expense?

The reason the FASB experiment failed was that they forgot their own requirement that financial statements should help readers anticipate future cash flows. Indexing historical-cost depreciation, and in effect doubling the dollar amount, tells you nothing about real-life plans for future capital expenditures. Companies typically spend their capital dollars for new product projects on the one hand and cost reduction projects on the other. They spend only an insignificant portion of capital expenditures replacing assets that have literally worn out.

While computers are a poor example in talking about the impact of inflation, they are an excellent example for a discussion of asset valuation. It would be a safe assumption that over the past 20 years virtually no computer has ever worn out. Maybe a hard disk drive crashes and it is not worthwhile to fix it. But a 10-year-old Pentium computer will still perform today the functions for which it was acquired 10 years ago. The problem is that today's software is far more powerful and requires a newer and more powerful computer to run on. But if all you are doing is straightforward word processing and you do not need to access the Internet, for example, then your Pentium should last a long time, far longer than whatever five-year life, plus or minus, had been chosen for financial reporting purposes.

In the final analysis the FASB indexing approach failed for two reasons:

1. The rate of inflation dropped to levels which no longer required adjustments
2. The methodology did not reflect actual cash flows.

Indexing is a statistical technique, and the results are no better than the index. Developing indexes for all the types of assets utilized in American industry was a daunting task, one that ultimately collapsed of its own work. Utilizing a single index, say the gross national product (GNP) deflator, did not capture diverse price trends, such as electronics prices going down, versus the cost of medical care that increased far faster than overall prices. A one-size index cannot fit all circumstances, but the development and maintenance of numerous different indexes was costly. Even worse, different companies in the same industry used different indexes, thus destroying comparability among companies.

The SEC, in its replacement cost proposal, took a different approach, even though its objective was the same, that is, to reflect the impact of inflation. The SEC said, "Let's look at what companies would spend today to replace their productive capacity, allowing for technological changes." This way the financial information would not be distorted by indexing historical costs for assets, without reflecting the fact that new assets are more efficient than old assets.

Given the fact that technological improvements are commonplace, indexing what was bought in the past does appear incorrect. Further, if companies replaced assets today, with the latest technology, operating costs would decline. Taking the jet airplane example above, a brand new jet may cost significantly more than the 15-year-old model it replaces, but operating costs (fewer staff, lower fuel consumption) would drop, sometimes dramatically.

The SEC told registrants to determine the cost today to replace its existing productive capacity and show the depreciation expense on the current replacement cost, but then offset this expense with the savings (if any) from utilization of the new complement of assets.

Just trying to describe this approach in words is difficult. Imagine the difficulty in applying it. For large, complex, and diverse conglomerates, operating in many industries, the difficulty in trying, for practical purposes, to reengineer and redesign a total company was literally mind-boggling. Because of the latitude provided in deciding how assets might be replaced and what operating economies might be realized, the exercise ended up being totally subjective.

Replacement cost accounting, as promulgated by the SEC and implemented by U.S. industry, turned out to be worthless and was soon withdrawn as a requirement. The SEC methodology failed to pass the test of its own objectives. It did not reflect the impact of inflation.

Why did replacement cost accounting fail? Three reasons seem to account for this failure. First, it was subjective. The SEC asked companies to determine, in effect, how they would reconfigure and reconstruct their business as though they were starting over again. This is patently unrealistic and has zero relevance to actual cash flows.

Second, while the new depreciation figure showed what the impact of inflation was, *if* all the assets were replaced at today's cost, the SEC also allowed firms to take credit for the *savings* the new assets would have generated. How do you calculate these savings? Most firms did not want to show that they were much worse off in the then current inflationary environment than they were in more "normal" times. So if depreciation expense went up (and earnings went down) under the new accounting, there was tremendous pressure to assume the best regarding operating efficiencies. Nobody could prove you wrong, since there was never a real-world test of anyone's actually replacing all their assets at once and measuring the performance improvements. Neither outside auditors nor security analysts could get a handle on the resulting numbers.

Finally, replacement cost accounting failed because it did not give readers of financial statements either a grasp of current management performance or of future earnings and cash flow. The SEC requirements were theoretical, while investors want practical help in deciding whether a particular stock is or is not going to go up or down in the future. The replacement cost information provided no help in making this analysis because it was not grounded in economic reality.

WILL VALUE INFORMATION BE DISCLOSED IN THE FUTURE?

The fact that two experiments failed did not stop accounting rule makers from continuing their quest to provide better information to readers of financial statements. The real problem with the experiments was that they made the assumption that the rule makers knew better than the statement users what information would be useful. Mandating a new accounting system unrelated to actual transactions in the market simply did not help management, much less outsiders, understand the impact of inflation.

But as we saw earlier in this chapter, values do change. Cash flows can be affected by changes in values—if the company decides to sell assets whose values differ from the amounts shown on the financial statements.

The key is the ability or intent to convert the asset(s) into cash. At that point disclosing the fair market value has relevance. Disclosing the value—no matter how defined—of assets that cannot or will not be converted into cash is an exercise of little practical value to anyone.

As discussed in Chapter 1, the very first question an appraiser asks a potential client is: "What are you going to do with the information?" How information will be used affects both what an appraiser does and in what form he discloses the answer.

In 1996–1998, the SEC and FASB issued requirements calling for the disclosure of current values (or fair value, since accountants seem to use the terms interchangeably) of financial instruments. By definition, financial instruments include securities that are usually marketable, and so-called derivatives that are used to control risk and hedge future circumstances. The effort on the part of accounting rule makers has been to get companies to mark to market the price of securities and financial instruments they hold.

The principle is that rather than showing on the balance sheet the original cost of a bond, the balance sheet should show the current price of that bond, since the company could literally pick up the telephone and sell the bond in less than one minute. There was great opposition to recording marketable securities and financial instruments at current market prices. Why?

Just as we discussed above, management teams have felt, and probably correctly, that if the current market values were displayed and *changes* in values flowed through, the income statement operating results would be distorted. A real-life example occurred recently when the stock market dropped by 15 percent in a matter of weeks. Harvard University's endowment, aggressively invested, went down by at least that percentage, which amounted, in real terms, to a loss of value of over $1 billion. This made

38

fund raising very difficult for Harvard as alumni asked the question, "Why should I give money to Harvard to offset their stock market losses?" The answer, of course, was that the losses were temporary. The losses were not permanent. The market came back and so did the endowment. Over the long pull, Harvard's investment policy had compound gains at or above industry levels. But showing short-term fluctuations on a quarterly basis distorts long-term results.

Another example of a distortion from showing changes in values of marketable securities as part of current income came in an appraisal of a hospital.

The 300+-bed hospital, with revenues of $100 million a year, was embroiled in a dispute between the county's hospital district, which owned the hospital, and the board of directors, which ran the hospital. The county hospital district trustees asked for an appraisal of the hospital, implicitly threatening the independence of the board of directors because the appraisal might be used as the basis of selling the hospital to a third party, at which point the board of directors would lose its power.

The hospital had been very conservatively managed and over the years had accumulated liquid assets in excess of $100 million, that is, more than one year's revenue. Most hospitals that size might have had only a third as much cash and investments.

The appraisal was as of September 30, and the stock market had collapsed in the previous 60 days. Between June 30 and September 30 the market value of the hospital's investments dropped by $12 million, which showed up as a *loss* on the income statement. Yet for income from operations, based on serving patients, the hospital was still slightly in the black.

Did the hospital make money that year or did it lose money? Obviously, the answer affects the value of the hospital. The hospital made money from operations and lost money from investments. The net of the two was a loss. But should the two be netted? Was the loss a real loss? Could the market be expected to come back at some point in the future and offset the loss? These are all questions that had to be answered in the appraisal.

The answer we took as an appraiser was to value the hospital based solely on operations and operating results. We then added the current market value (down some $12 million from previous levels) of the investments to the value of the hospital as a hospital. As and when the market would come back and restore the previous loss, the value of the entity would increase.

What we did not do is to incorporate the current year's drop in market value of the investments as part of the ongoing operating results, and then apply some sort of price/earnings multiple to overall net income, or net loss in this case.

So here is a practical example of how even appraisers approach the current value of assets with care and discretion. The changes in value of Harvard's endowment and the hospital's investment portfolio were both real. The market values were down from previous levels, with no guarantees that they would recover in the future. But in evaluating the overall position of the institutions the changes in market value of financial instruments and marketable securities have to be put in perspective.

What is the impact on alumni gifts to Harvard if individuals are being asked to contribute $1 billion, simply to push the endowment's market value back to where it was? Patients and health care organizations wonder why they should be asked to pay, through their health-insurance premiums, for a drop in the market value of securities at the hospital. In both cases was management incompetent for allowing the drop in value of the securities? If not, who is responsible?

The truth is that there is risk in holding any investment. Increases and decreases in value will happen over time, and such changes are to be expected and anticipated. They are inevitable, in fact. What is wrong is to measure short-term management performance with temporary fluctuations in the value of an investment portfolio.

PROPOSED SOLUTION

Investors and creditors need to know the underlying values of assets held by an organization, primarily to understand the actual or potential impact on future cash flows. Having the information, however, does not require that changes in the value from one period to the next must necessarily be considered part of operations for the period. Running the changes in value through the income statement is an artificial construct of accountants, not some immutable law of nature.

Further, any proposal to go to a value-based system of accounting must face the fact that there are not enough appraisers in the world to value all the assets of every organization every year, much less every quarter. We make a flat prediction that, absent some fundamental change in the way business is carried on, the United States will never go to a value-based accounting system.

What can and should happen is that the management of an organization should be held responsible for determining the current value of assets that conceivably could be sold for cash. This would *not* relate to sale of the total company. Investors cannot and should not expect management to value its own business as a whole.

Owners of a business, as well as creditors, should understand what cash flow potential is available if nonoperating and even noncritical assets were sold. Knowledge that either a potential gain or a potential loss would be reflected in the financial statements if a particular action were taken is important.

Our suggestion, therefore, is that management be required to disclose current values of those *assets that could be disposed of.* The information on values would be disclosed in a footnote, not in the body of the financial statements, and changes in value would not be included in income for the period.

Under this proposal, the burden of proof would be on management to determine what might be sold, without materially changing the character of the organization. For example, if a conglomerate owned five different and disparate companies in five different industries, any one of them could be sold at any time without affecting the value of the others. In such a situation the company would have to determine the approximate FMV of each unit.

For a single-product firm, integrated among manufacturing and distribution functions, sale of any part of the business would affect the rest, and the firm's financial reports probably would not disclose any value information, unless there were nonoperating assets such as vacant land or a securities portfolio.

Independent accountants would have to review the organization's operations and determine whether management complied with the value disclosure requirements. The auditors would not be responsible for providing an opinion on the values themselves.

The factor that would put teeth into the requirement would be some sort of penalty, enforced by the SEC for publicly traded firms, which would come into effect if material assets were disposed of—at a gain or at a loss—and the firm had not previously disclosed potential value information on those assets. However, the company would not be held liable, within say a 20 to 30 percent band, for the specific *accuracy* of the previously disclosed value information. Values do change, as will be discussed in subsequent chapters. The ability to realize value is often a function of negotiating skill and specific circumstances. Thus, it would be unrealistic to require that footnote disclosure of values have pinpoint accuracy.

This proposal, for supplemental disclosure of value information on assets that could be disposed of, appears to resolve many of the issues that have caused difficulty in the past. Energy would not be expended on determining the values of assets that were not going to be sold or replaced. Calculations as to the "what if" impact on operations of replacing assets that won't be replaced will be precluded. Inflation, or deflation for that matter, does not affect asset values if the assets are going to be continued in use for the purpose for which they were acquired, so disclosing theoretical information that has no future cash flow impact will not be required.

Our proposal would give shareholders and creditors information that can affect cash flow. If a plant or division with a book value of $10 million has a fair market value of $30 million, then the current returns on that investment must be related to the $30 million cash potential. Management cannot hide behind high ROI, when the "I"—investment—was made many years ago.

It is likely that management will oppose this proposal, just as they have all previous proposals for more information. In this case, the burden will be on them to show why shareholders (who own the firm!) are not entitled to know the real value of what they own. Useful information will be disclosed. Useless information will not be disclosed. That sounds like a pretty good solution.

CHAPTER 3

Investing for Value:
Buying and Selling Assets

The "premise of value" sounds like an arcane phrase, but really gets to the heart of the valuation process. What is *the* value of a new automobile? The answer is, "It depends." The answer depends on *who* is using the information, and for what *purpose.*

For the sake of discussion, assume the following is true for a 2002 Ford.

Manufacturing cost (labor, material, and overhead)	$15,500
Total cost on Ford's books (including SG&A)	$18,000
Selling price to dealer	$19,500
Manufacturer's suggested retail selling price	$22,000
Typical actual customer purchase	$21,000
"Used" price—1,500 miles	$20,000

Which of these is the value of the car? The fact is that all of the above amounts represent value at some point in the production and sales cycle. For different purposes, each of these is correct and should be used for making appropriate decisions.

"Are you buying or are you selling?" In our capitalistic, free-enterprise society there is nothing wrong with making a profit. Further, there are costs involved in buying, holding, and selling any type of asset. These costs all have to be recovered by the seller, even before any profit is generated. Consequently, the value of any asset, at each stage of production and distribution, changes. Obviously, the value of an automobile at the end of the assembly line ($15,500 above), with 2,000 units a day being produced, differs from the value ($19,500 above) to the dealer at his showroom. To a consumer, the value of the car the day he buys it ($21,000 above) will not be the same a week later inasmuch as used cars typically sell at a lower price ($20,000 above), often irrespective of mileage.

While we will not go through the exercise, most readers will realize that any of the dollar amounts between $15,500 and $22,000 could be considered *the* value of the 2002 Ford, depending on who was using the information and for what purpose. The value for insuring the car while it is in transit from the factory to the dealer will undoubtedly differ from the insurable value once the customer has bought it from a dealer. The value for property tax purposes will differ among the manufacturer, the dealer, and the consumer. If the car is to be used as collateral by a lending institution, say Citibank, then the bank would lend one amount to Ford, a different amount to the dealer, and a third amount to the consumer. In each case the maximum loan amount is a function of the value, but only at that time and to that owner.

"TO WHOM AND FOR WHAT PURPOSE?"

The very first questions an appraiser asks when obtaining with a new appraisal assignment deal with:

- The purpose of the valuation;
- How it will be used; and
- The exact date of the valuation.

In Chapter 2 we related the story of how the used construction equipment market can change so rapidly that values as of one point in time were totally out of date only six months later.

The same issue, as to the necessity of being totally explicit as to the purpose of a valuation, can be seen in the following.

An appraisal company was asked by a reputable business to prepare an appraisal for insurance purposes. This requires the appraiser to determine the *cost of reproduction* of the assets as of the appraisal date. The reason is obvious. In case of loss, the insured looks to the insurance company to replace the lost assets. In turn, this would require going out and acquiring the assets from suppliers, manufacturers, or contractors. Thus, the insurance company wants to know how much they would have to spend to make the insured whole.

An insurance appraisal, with the *premise of value* being cost of reproduction, will typically have values that are in excess of the current *fair market value,* usually defined to mean what the assets could be *sold* for to a proverbial willing buyer. *Selling* the assets on the open market will usually bring less than would *buying* the identical assets from the producers. Besides the differences between new and used assets, there is also the cost of transportation, setup, run-in, and debugging. Finally, there is an obvious difference between the two amounts related to the inventory carrying costs and profit margins of the market participants.

In this case the appraisal firm performed its assignment and delivered the report to the client, on time and within the agreed upon fee.

About a year later the appraisal firm was somewhat surprised to receive a call from a bank asking why the values were so high. It seemed that the bank's customer, the appraisal firm's former client, had borrowed a large amount of money and now could not repay it. When the bank went to sell the assets, used as collateral for the loan, the assets brought very much less than the amounts shown in the appraisal report. In fact, the bank complained that the report "was less than a year old."

The appraisal company went to its files, retrieved its file copy, and reviewed the valuation. Of course, it immediately became clear that the borrower had utilized an *insurance appraisal* to support borrowing from the bank.

Usually, it is the lender who requests the appraisal directly from the appraisal firm; the lender usually specifies that the *premise of value* be orderly liquidation, which will be discussed in this chapter. In this case the borrower, perhaps inadvertently, went to the bank and told them, "We already have an appraisal," and the bank accepted the document.

The bank went to the page of the report that showed the *total* insurable value, read that as *the* value, and based its loan on that amount. What they did *not* do is *read the report.* The report clearly stated that the purpose of the report was insurance, and the premise of value, in this case, was cost of reproduction. The bank officer made a very costly mistake; he assumed that all appraisals are the same and that only the total dollar amount was critical.

PREMISE OF VALUE

One of the most difficult concepts to accept, particularly for financial managers and certified public accountants (CPAs), is the idea that different values are possible at one and the same time for the same asset. The author once was testifying at a hearing of the Financial Accounting Standards Board (FASB), dealing with impairment of assets, and made that statement. One of the board members literally pooh-poohed the idea.

This is because many people think of value in terms of the price of a share of stock. For them, the only way to determine the value of such an asset is to look up the quotation in the *Wall Street Journal.* Barring unusual circumstances, the value of a 1,000-share block of IBM or Microsoft can be obtained in 10 seconds—and the answer is accurate as well as supportable.

Even this, however, is not so clear-cut. One paper may use 4:00 P.M. closing prices and another a 6:00 P.M. A second difference can arise if one analyst uses closing price to value the stock, as compared to another that chooses to use the average of the day's high and low. Finally, at least for lightly traded stocks, what happens if we are valuing a block of stock that represents five days' volume of trading. Putting that block on the market will itself affect the price realized.

Consequently, as can be seen, even something as simple as pricing a block of publicly traded stock may have certain difficulties. Securities that are not frequently traded provide a more difficult situation, as was the case with a mutual fund holding somewhat illiquid municipal securities that were considered high risk by many investors. One day the mutual fund shareholders found the net asset value of their fund was marked down by 50 percent, and the explanation was that the previous approach to pricing the securities every day turned out to be flawed. Many observers would agree that a 50 percent drop in one day did represent a flawed model.

That, however, is the exception. Most of the time, utilizing yesterday's closing price for New York Stock Exchange (NYSE) and National Association of Securities Dealers Automated Quotation System (NASDAQ) securities will provide reasonably accurate answers. But it should be remembered that in most corporate business situations, listed securities represent a very small percentage of a company's assets. Far more common are joint venture investments, potential product line divestitures, employee stock options, and so forth. These types of assets, and many others, must often be valued, and there is no published source one can go to. This is the reason why there are professional appraisers. Businessmen, attorneys, and accountants need to know current values, and the information is *not* in the *Wall Street Journal.*

ALTERNATIVE INVESTMENT OPPORTUNITIES

Appraisers use three different ways to estimate value. These are commonly referred to as the income approach, the cost approach, and the market comparable approach to value. These are discussed in Chapters 5, 6, and 7. What is important here is the concept that the value of any asset has to be determined in relation to all other assets.

The underlying premise of the income approach to value is that there are numerous independent investors who have funds to invest and an entire range of investment opportunities. How realistic is this assumption?

Let's look for a moment at the residential real estate market. There is a saying among realtors, "For every house there is a buyer out there somewhere." What this is, in addition to a consolation to a seller whose house has been on the market already for 10 months, is a recognition that at the right price anything and everything will sell.

Similarly, in the business investment market, there are always prospective buyers, usually looking for a bargain, but nonetheless with funds available for purchase of a business. Talk to any business broker and the answer is the same: "We have far more prospective buyers than good sellers." Regardless of the economic conditions, the U.S. economy is so large and diverse that there will always be buyers and sellers. In fact, it is probably a rare business that is not periodically approached by a broker or investment banker to find out if the business is for sale.

The real issue is the usually unrealistic expectations each side has. Buyers want to pay less than full value, and sellers expect to receive a premium, usually because it is "their baby." The trick is to price a business, or any asset for that matter, at fair market value. Placing it on the market at the right price, and with an aggressive marketing campaign, any business will sell. There are literally thousands of individuals who have always wanted to own their own business, and have the resources to finance a purchase. That there will be hard negotiations, and that the seller may have to accept installment payments, are facts of life; a good valuation report will have considered these factors.

The standard definition of *fair market value* defines it as the price at which the property would exchange between a willing buyer and a willing seller. There will always be a willing buyer for a business, assuming the price is right. The real question is whether there is such a thing as a true "willing seller." A very experienced appraiser told the writer, shortly after he had started in the valuation business, "There is no such thing as a 'willing seller.'"

For larger businesses, outside the scope of an individual entrepreneur, or a retired business executive, many corporations are looking for expansion

opportunities through acquisition. This is exactly why the national and regional investment banking firms exist and continue to prosper. The fees
charged to either the buyer or seller or both reflect the fact that transactions
do not happen in a vacuum. Buyers and sellers must know about each other
and then meet. Nonetheless, even the larger investment banking firms are
looking for businesses for sale. So while there is no shortage of willing
buyers, there is a dearth of willing sellers.

Let's look for a moment at why people sell their business. For smaller
family businesses, the reasons include:

- Death or retirement
- Financial and operating difficulties, including competition from larger
  firms
- Need for expansion capital that is not available
- Family disputes, including divorce

For larger businesses sales are usually triggered by:

- Focusing on core business, which suggests voluntary divestiture of
  noncore units
- Operating and financial problems of the business as a whole, in turn
  caused by any one or more of innumerable management failures
- Underperformance from the stock market's perspective, leading to a
  takeover
- The need to raise capital for other parts of the business

In almost every one of these circumstances, sellers are motivated to sell
because of a condition outside their control. There are one or more factors,
in effect, forcing them to sell. So, whereas prospective buyers have many
alternate opportunities to use their investment dollars, the seller has only a
single decision: sell or not sell. If not sell is unrealistic, then the seller may
not be willing, in the sense of having true freedom of choice.

What is the implication of an unwilling seller? Basically, it means that
the final transaction price might be below true fair market value (FMV).
Take, as an example, the executor of an estate of an individual who had
built up a successful small business. The executor in effect must sell the
business because of the need to raise money to pay the estate taxes that are
due. Further, without the principal who founded the business, it is entirely
possible that the firm will slowly lose value without the founder's guidance. It is to the executor's benefit to sell as soon as possible.

Now what are the implications of this situation for a prospective buyer? Presumably, any interested party is going to perform due diligence. This will uncover the fact that it is an executor who is selling and that the founder of the business is no longer there to provide leadership and guidance. The time pressure on the one hand and the potential diminution in value over time on the other not only will be known to buyers, they will take advantage of this situation. They will offer less than the fair market value of the business, expecting that the executor will want to close the deal just to get it done. The executor may not feel he has the luxury of waiting and obtaining the true FMV of the business.

There is no good answer to this conundrum of most sellers not being truly willing. When appraisers look to comparable transactions in the market for guidance as to value, were those very transactions affected by a strongly motivated seller? If so, how much lower than FMV was that deal consummated at?

This discussion began in the context of the income approach to value. It was stated that one of the premises of the income approach was that prospective buyers had alternate investment opportunities. This led into the discussion that sellers might not have the same range of alternatives.

Many years ago the author heard a presentation in business school by an individual who was in the corporate liquidation business. He bought sick and failing companies and decided whether to hire new managers or to sell off the pieces and liquidate. He referred to one very successful acquisition he had made as a case study.

Penn Central, at that time a major railroad, was being reorganized. New management was divesting businesses not directly connected with rail transportation. One entity was a small barge operation that was losing money.

The entrepreneur studied the company and discovered that the railroad required some 200 people to run the barge company, essentially because they had applied railroad requirements and corporate overhead standardized requirements to what was essentially a very simple business. The businessman determined he could literally run the company with no more than 25 people and that it would be profitable. He offered Penn Central a real "lowball" offer, which was accepted because management believed the company was losing so much that the quicker it was sold the better.

He immediately fired 175 people and almost instantly had a profitable business, albeit without all the record keeping and staff. He then turned around and sold the business for a very handsome profit.

The business school students, suitably impressed, then asked the $64 question, "How could you do this—couldn't Penn Central management see this and do the same?"

His answer was instructive. "Two things. First of all, railroad management knew only one way to do things and they had no flexibility of thought. Second, I was able to negotiate a very low purchase price because I have bought 200 companies, and usually the seller has never sold a business before. I have a tremendous advantage in negotiation because I know how to do it [buy a business] and they don't [sell a business]."

There are two lessons to be learned from this example. First, before selling a business, one should obtain an independent valuation before starting the negotiation process. Second, before selling, ask if "out-of-the-box" changes to the way the business is being run are feasible and should be considered.

Most corporate liquidators, who generally have a bad name, nonetheless are successful because they can see how and then implement changes in the way to run the business. This is not to say that whenever a business gets into trouble one should go out and fire every second employee. It does mean that one should look realistically at alternatives. This is what an appraiser does, although the appraiser does not expect to actually implement the potential changes himself.

ASSUMPTIONS ARE THE KEY

If the premise of value is key to determining the appropriate value for a specific decision or specific purpose, then understanding the role of assumptions in an appraisal is equally important. When appraisers differ among themselves, and this is all too common in litigation, the explanation can usually be found in the underlying assumptions.

It is common in a divorce, with a closely held business, for each side to engage an expert appraiser who presents his opinion of value to the court. Often, these valuations are far apart.

The judge is faced with two seemingly valid opinions of value, but one can show a high value and the other a very low value. Typically, a judge will throw up her hands and draw the conclusion that appraisers cannot be trusted to be objective.

However, the difference between two opinions of value regarding a closely held business can usually be traced back to differing assumptions regarding the outlook for the business. It is not uncommon for the husband, who is probably running the company, to favor a low value. The wife, who may expect to receive half of the value of the company in cash, will probably be looking for an optimistic outlook.

One appraiser will assess the future growth prospects for the company as being in excess of 10 percent compound growth annually, leading to a high value. The other appraiser, in the interests of conservatism, will assert that the basis for valuing the company should start with an assumed growth rate of only 2 percent per year.

Which is correct, 2 percent or 10 percent? When dealing with the future there is no certainty, and either could turn out after the fact to have been more accurate. But it is necessary to come up with an answer now, not five years from now. In such situations a judge will probably choose between the two appraisals on the basis of which side has the most convincing arguments supporting the growth assumption.

Undoubtedly, if you change the assumptions, you change the answer.

WHEN THE LAWYERS GET INVOLVED

The legal system is not necessarily the best way to determine values, but in our society the courts often provide the ultimate answers. The reason is that when values become a matter of contention, say the value for purposes of estate tax or property tax, the only arbiter is the judicial system.

The difficulty is that lawyers are advocates for their clients, quite properly, and are not necessarily interested in arriving at the "right" answer. Thus, when a closely held business is being valued for estate tax purposes, the IRS's lawyers will argue for the largest amount they think they can support, while the estate takes a position that the business is on the verge of Chapter 11 bankruptcy. Neither side, at least initially, is interested in determining the true FMV. Then, at some point, the two sides compromise or they end up in court.

The legal system is not set up to determine real values, but it does come up with definitive answers. "Splitting the difference" between two extreme positions probably does *not* arrive at the real value that a totally impartial appraiser would find.

Value can ultimately be determined or validated only by a transaction. Most valuation disputes cannot be settled that way. Litigation, therefore, is the final refuge when a lot of money is at stake.

SPECIAL-PURPOSE ASSETS

One of the most difficult valuation issues arises when special-purpose assets are involved. A commercial bakery is designed and built to accomplish a specific purpose and cannot be used to manufacture semiconductors. Similarly, a semiconductor facility with a very expensive "clean room" would be considered overbuilt with respect to a warehouse. A bowling alley would require a lot of upgrading and lots of improvements if it were to be used as a restaurant. Yet, in the case of condemnation for a public housing project, each of these assets would have to be paid for in terms of their present use.

Special-purpose assets can be valued in terms of their original cost only if they are to continue in use for the purpose for which they were designed and built. Appraisers are often called on to place a value on assets that will *not* be utilized for their "highest and best use." In such situations, the value of the components related to their original purpose is lost, and a cost penalty is involved to allow for the cost of putting the building in shape for its next intended use.

In such situations, the original owner (the prospective seller) often feels that the initial indication of value is too favorable for the prospective buyer. From the buyer's perspective, however, the only reason to acquire an asset originally designed for some other purpose would be if the *net* cost were attractive.

Once again, the FMV of an asset is directly related to its prospective use and the cost of alternative assets. Essentially, appraisers are correct in assuming that buyers and sellers are rational and that they act in their own best interest. Further, appraisers correctly assume that there are always alternatives available to both buyers and sellers.

Only in the case of truly unique assets in the antiques and fine arts area (e.g., there is only one of any Vermeer painting), can we approach it differently. If a collector has his heart set on buying only a painting by Vermeer, and not a Picasso or a Rembrandt, we can value it only in terms of relative bargaining strength. This is why the papers are full of stories of startling price realizations in the fine arts area, whereas one never sees such stories in the commercial and industrial areas. Buyers and sellers have many choices in commercial and industrial properties. Buyers have very few choices in fine arts, and if two buyers start competing for a unique work of art, there is only one solution. The price keeps going higher until one or the other gives up.

This is why appraisers have a lot more confidence in the answers they provide clients when dealing with real and personal property for commercial and industrial uses. Yes, one location may be better than another for a regional warehouse, but a second-best site will still work, although there may be a small cost penalty associated with the slightly higher transportation costs. One asset can be substituted for another in most commercial and industrial situations. They cannot in the antiques and fine arts arena.

CONCLUSION

Investing means taking risks, in effect buying into the unknown future. Appraisals and the valuation process can help both buyers and sellers, borrowers and lenders, taxpayers and the IRS.

Because there are many different values that can possibly be associated with the same asset at the same time, it is important for the parties to understand the premise of value. If that can be established, then the next step is to agree on the relevant assumptions for valuing that asset, that is, the purpose for which the appraisal is being performed.

Finally, a good appraisal report will clearly lay out the steps that were followed in arriving at the valuation conclusions, with indications of the extent to which the answer would change if certain sensitive assumptions were changed.

If all these steps have been followed and there are reasonable parties on both sides, a common answer will be found and be acceptable to both. This may seem like a scenario from an ideal world of make-believe, but with goodwill on both sides, and a competent appraiser, this should be the expected solution.

CHAPTER 4

Adversarial Nature of Valuations: "Why Can't I Get a Higher (Lower) Answer?"

Appraisers are virtually never asked to determine the value of a particular asset unless some sort of transaction is going to take place. Sometimes people ask themselves, "Wouldn't it be nice to know what ____ is worth?" Let's say the asset in question is your car. Why would you really want to know what your three-year-old Lexus is worth, unless you were going to trade it in or it is coming off lease and you have an option to buy?

Perhaps you have to fill out a financial statement to obtain a mortgage and one of the blanks where you list your assets is for the value of your automobile. No bank is going to care whether you put down $20,000 or $30,000 for the three-year-old Lexus, because the difference is truly immaterial to your net worth, and particularly to your ability to make the monthly payments on the proposed mortgage. Without a transaction involving the car itself, its value is purely theoretical.

But if you are going to buy a new car and use the Lexus as a trade-in, then the value of the car is important. The more it is worth, the less will be the cost of the new car. In turn, this translates into either a lower cash outlay or lower monthly payments, depending on whether or not you finance the new car or pay for it outright.

As the owner of the Lexus you want to receive the highest possible price. But, at the same time, the dealer wants to minimize the amount he allows you on your old car. His profit margin on reselling the three-year-old Lexus is going to be directly proportional to his ability to obtain the car at a low price. In short, there is an adversarial relationship relative to your car. One party wants a high price. The other party wants a low price.

Put this way, it seems both obvious and commonsense. These valuation issues are usually settled on the basis of negotiation and compromise between the parties. And for something as common as an automobile, wherein there are thousands of transactions, the range between the buyer and seller is going to be fairly narrow.

Now, however, look at something more complex than an automobile. Houses are usually the most expensive possession anyone owns. Let's say you have a home that you think is worth $300,000, and you want to sell it. How do you determine the price at which you should put it on the market? Most people will call a real estate broker, whereas a few will obtain an independent appraisal.

Many people who have sold their homes have found that the recommended listing price the broker put on the house initially has to be lowered a few months later. Why? Did the broker misunderstand the market? The answer is probably not.

People who have a house to sell typically call in three or four brokers, and more often than not the "winner" is the broker who recommends setting the initial offer at the highest price. Since brokers are compensated not only for selling houses, but listing them, there is great competition to obtain the listing. How better to obtain the listing than by suggesting a higher value? If it does not sell at that price, she can always come back later, suggest lowering the asking price, and probably retain the listing.

In short, there is a conflict between the broker and the home owner. The broker wants the listing, even at an unrealistic price. The home owner wants to receive the maximum price the house is really worth. The home owner would be better off selling the house in four weeks at $310,000 than hoping to get $340,000 (the listing price) and then three months later have to start lowering the price before the house becomes stale on the market.

The solution, of course, from the perspective of this book at least, is for the home owner to obtain an independent and unbiased appraisal. Then the sales price can be set correctly, the house will be sold quickly, and all parties to the transaction will walk away happy.

In this situation the appraiser is truly independent. The fee for the appraisal, perhaps $300 to $400, is totally unrelated to the final answer, and is not dependent on a sale's taking place. It is all right for a broker to be paid a percentage of the transaction. The ethical standards for appraisers absolutely preclude fees that are some percentage of the value. This is the difference between a broker and an appraiser.

Whenever an asset is going to be bought or sold, there will be a conflict between the buyer and seller. As we saw earlier, for an automobile obtaining the right answer is easy. A quick perusal of the ads in the Sunday newspaper or going to the Internet will get a good approximation. There are lots of transactions, and the product is fairly standard.

For homes, the market is not so well established. The range of values is more a function of the unique characteristics of the specific house and how much a prospective buyer will value such feature(s). Professional appraisals, an informed judgment by the home owner, and even a recommendation by a broker are all going to be reasonably close.

There are a number of situations in which the market is limited, the determination of the fair market value (FMV) is not so easy or clear-cut. In the remainder of this chapter we look at a number of situations in which the prospective parties to a transaction have real differences, where a lot of money is potentially at stake, and some means must be found to resolve the issues.

SETTING UP JOINT VENTURES

This form of business organization is becoming increasingly popular. Most companies are recognizing that they cannot be all things to all people; rather, they should concentrate on their core competencies. This means that if Company A develops a new product, but perhaps does not have experience selling into that market, it will find a partner with marketing experience. Rather than just sell the right to the product on an outright basis or license its use for a period of years, the idea of setting up a joint venture (JV) has great appeal. If there are going to be significant profits from making and selling the new product, the "JV" probably has to be considered the best organizational structure.

By definition, a JV involves contributions from both parties. A new company is organized, with ownership split between the two companies. (In theory, there can be three or even more parties, but the concepts regarding valuation are the same.) The question is, "How much is my contribution worth, relative to yours?"

If the ownership of the JV is going to be split 50/50 or 49/51 (so that one party runs the operation), each side wants to make sure the other is putting in sufficient assets. Each side, in other words, wants its contribution valued at the highest possible amount. How can this potential conflict be resolved? Clearly, the answer is by an independent appraisal.

It is imperative that the *same* professional perform both valuations. Otherwise, the result will be two separate valuations, each perhaps very high and with neither being accepted by the other side. There is always that germ of suspicion that the appraisal was "*M*ade *a*s *I*nstructed"; the initials MAI also stand for the professional designation of real estate appraisers who have earned the professional MAI designation, *M*ember of the *A*ppraisal *I*nstitute.

What is the procedure for valuing the relative contributions to a JV? The best way is to start with a business enterprise value (BEV) of the new company. One would start with the best possible financial projections, showing projected sales and cost of sales, as well as sales, general and administrative (SG&A) expenses. This, in turn, would allow reasonable estimates of operating profit, or EBITDA (earnings before interest, taxes, depreciation, and amortization). One would also project capital expenditure requirements as well as working capital needs from which would be derived future cash flows.

Utilizing EBITDA multiples found in the market for publicly traded firms that are comparable, one would be able to estimate an (FMV) utilizing the market comparable approach. Then, utilizing the cash flow projections, an estimate of FMV utilizing the income approach would be developed.

These two approaches to value would have to be correlated by the appraiser, utilizing his best professional judgment. At this point it is critical that *both* parties to the projected JV "buy in" to the estimate of FMV for the new joint venture. The key variables, of course, are the sales and profit projections. Unless both sides agree as to the reasonableness of the sales and profit projections, they will certainly not agree on the FMV estimate of the JV itself.

Assuming at this point that the parties do agree on the projections, and hence on the BEV of the joint venture, the next step in evaluating the relative contributions of the two parties is to look at what each is contributing. At least in theory the sum of the two contributions should total the BEV of the new company. As shown above, if one company is providing the new product, and the other marketing expertise, it is obviously necessary that both be joined together. Either one without the other cannot support the BEV of the new enterprise.

Company A has invented a new drug that has been approved by the Food and Drug Administration (FDA), but A has virtually no marketing experience. The contribution of Company B is the marketing experience and distribution channels developed over the years. Assume we are talking about

57

a pharmaceutical company that has a large staff of detail representatives. How did Company B get to the point at which they have such resources?

It is probably easier to value the marketing channel and distribution experience than to place a value on the new drug. Even though there are sales and income projections for the JV, there is a degree of speculation. Will there be competition from somebody else's drug that we don't know about? Will there be unexpected side effects, despite the rigorous testing already performed? There are no certainties in introducing any new product, much less a new prescription drug. Consequently, the sales and profit potential of the drug by itself is necessarily speculative.

However, it is relatively easy to determine the value of the marketing channels and sales staff. The cost approach would be used. In fact, if Company A did not form the JV and wanted to sell the product itself, it would have to develop its own marketing program. Making some assumptions about elapsed time and depth of coverage desired, it would be a matter of adding up the number of people to be hired, including managers. Costs for travel, training, office space, and support are all readily available. The one unknown would be how long it would take a new staff (even if those hired had industry experience) to become fully effective. Even in a worst-case scenario, one should be able to put together a first-class marketing effort in two years.

This cost approach will provide a supportable estimate of the resources required replicating Company B's marketing team already in place. The one thing it does not do is determine whether, in practice, Company A has the financial strength and cash resources to hire and train a new staff of, say, 100 people. There could easily be costs of $20 million, and then it would have taken two years to start generating meaningful sales revenues.

Utilizing Company B's existing marketing resources, therefore, using this valuation approach could easily be worth $25 to $30 million, allowing for the lost profits during the two-year buildup. If the BEV of the new joint venture had been appraised at $75 million, and the marketing contribution of Company B at perhaps $30 million, then the value of Company A's contribution of the new product invention could reasonably be estimated at the residual, say $45 million.

If the JV were to be set up on a 50/50 basis, then Company B would have to put in an additional $15 million to the JV, or pay Company A a one-time payment of $15 million. It is beyond the scope of this book to hypothesize how negotiations would actually take place. The concept, however, is clear.

One firm should do the valuation of the contributions of both parties in forming a joint venture. Agreement has to be reached about the potential benefits, assuming the JV works. The relative contribution of each party has to be evaluated and any balancing payment worked out by the parties.

SPLITTING UP JOINT VENTURES AND PARTNERSHIPS

Conflicts in valuation, which become adversarial in nature, all too often end up in court. That may be a function of our litigious society. It may be a result of poor negotiating skills. It may be a result of poor drafting or execution of the original agreement between the parties. Or, finally, it may be because of true disagreements about the real value of an asset or a business.

The total subject of dispute resolution is obviously outside the scope of this book. Resolving disputes about the valuation of companies and/or assets *can* be done outside the courtroom. But first, let's look at a real-life case study in which the parties did not reach an amicable solution and ended up in court.

The company was an importer from Europe of automobile parts for auto racing cars. The exporter had a very high reputation in auto racing circles, and demand for the parts in the United States appeared to be significant. For a while the European firm just exported directly to end users who were ordering direct from the factory. This was inefficient, and the next step was for the company to set up its own U.S. warehouse. Limited sales efforts were conducted from the parent company utilizing occasional U.S. trips by management or technical staff. Effectively, the business was simply accepting orders.

The next step was to set up a U.S. subsidiary, with the warehouse as base. Then a U.S. employee was hired who had significant experience in auto racing. The individual hired was allowed to buy 10 percent of the U.S. subsidiary stock for a nominal amount. Sales prospered and significant profits were generated.

As a result of personal differences between the U.S. employee and the parent company, the employee was suddenly terminated, almost without warning. The issue then became the value of the 10 percent interest in the U.S. subsidiary.

Negotiations were fruitless, and the parties ended up in court. Each side hired its own appraisal expert. Each party then submitted its appraisal report to the court, with copies to the opposing parties. The judge (no jury) then heard testimony from both sides about the history of the company and the dispute about the individual's managerial and sales performance. Of course, the latter was virtually irrelevant to the real issue regarding value. Each side's appraiser appeared on the witness stand and qualified as an expert.

The trouble was that the two "experts" were themselves far apart. The company's appraiser came in, logically enough, with a very low estimate of value, while the plaintiff's appraiser determined that the real fair market value was almost three times as high as the company's expert had estimated.

Put yourself in the position of the judge. He received two appraisal reports with different methodologies and significantly different assumptions about what the future course of events would have been in the absence of the termination of the one key employee. Two reports, two vastly different answers, both prepared by "experts." How does a judge in that situation make a decision?

In practice, one of two things happens. He may split the difference, arguing that the appraisals are so far apart that there is no way to reconcile them and the only fair thing is to go right down the middle.

Alternatively, he will read the reports, listen to the testimony, and judge the credibility of the two parties. What ends up then is a decision that essentially is a subjective judgment. Personality, demeanor, writing skill in the report, and reasonableness of assumptions probably all weigh into the final decision.

In this case the plaintiff's valuation report estimated what future sales would have been based on past sales trends. Profit projections were also consistent with actual reported results. In projecting the future, and then discounting those projections on a present value basis; it is tempting if one is trying to support a particular position, to assume very rapid growth.

But any such assumption, to be credible, has to be supported by past experience. If sales growth had averaged 20 percent a year, how can one support a 35 percent growth over the next five years? If gross profit margins have been running at 25 percent, why would a reasonable person suddenly expect them to change markedly—either up (plaintiff's benefit) or down (defendant's benefit)?

In this case the defendant's appraisal report essentially argued that, with regard to the manager, past sales trends were irrelevant and that he had had little real impact on results. Then they turned around and argued that future sales would be low without him. This was an internal conflict that probably destroyed the credibility of the valuation report. They were trying to have it both ways, and lost.

In this imported parts case the judge found 100 percent for the plaintiff; essentially, the defendant's valuation report did not appear credible.

Two lessons can be learned from the above. First, litigation is risky, as well as expensive, and should be avoided if at all possible. But if this is not possible and a valuation dispute does end up in court, the best strategy is to have *your* appraiser be as objective as possible. The author has testified frequently, and so far has virtually a 100 percent batting average. In every case we took the approach of using *reasonable assumptions*. Rather than take an extreme position and hope that the judge will split the difference, we have consistently valued the assets in question on the basis of what an outside party would really be prepared to pay.

Does a proposed indication of value pass the smell test? Credibility is perhaps most important in court testimony. Credibility is a combination of:

- Professional experience
- Ability to articulate one's position; and
- Reasonableness of the answer.

Adopting this approach ends up with an indication of value that is lower than the highest amount that could conceivably be supported. The trade-off of a lower value (higher if you are on the other side) for increased credibility is, in this appraiser's opinion, well worthwhile.

DIVORCE

In the typical divorce case the husband and wife own a company that the husband runs. In the divorce the wife typically wants her half of the value of the company paid in cash, while the husband will continue to run the firm. Therefore, it is to the husband's advantage to assert the company (almost always privately held) is not doing well. Conversely, the wife believes that the company is little short of the next Microsoft.

The dispute about the value of the company is always inextricably tied up with many other disputes within the marriage. If a lot of money is at stake, all these other interpersonal issues get played out, in negotiations and in court, as well as in the respective valuation reports. Marital disputes are bitter and take a long time to resolve. Typically, neither party wants to pay for valuations until the case is settled. The first thing we require, if we even take on a case, is 50 percent of our estimated fee up front.

Leaving out the psychology and emotions of a divorce, the basic dispute about the value of the company inevitably revolves around the future of the business. As has been discussed several places in the book, the FMV of any asset, including a closely held business, is ultimately a reflection of how one thinks the business will do in the future.

Usually, the wife's appraiser only has access to historical financial statements and does not have access to real management projections. Even if a budget is presented following discovery, the wife's lawyer will argue that the projection was lowballed to decrease the valuation. So the issue boils down to how to estimate future results, short of putting the business up for sale and letting the market decide.

The husband will testify that the market for the firm's products is weak, customers/clients have been lost, costs are going up, competition is worse than ever, and the future is bleak. In fact, a Chapter 11 filing is "just around the corner!"

The wife's advisers are at a disadvantage because they do not have access to current information, only what shows up in the previous financial statements. With no formal projections from management that can be relied on, any forecast made by the wife's appraiser is going to be suspect and can readily be challenged by the husband's experts.

The wife typically does not have a lot of cash to pay for an in-depth approach that would involve interviewing customers, suppliers, and competitors. The only way to obtain supportable information would be for the wife's appraiser to perform such an in-depth analysis. Even then the husband could argue, "You don't really understand our business, the industry, the products, technology, and competitive conditions."

The divorce situation is 180 degrees away from the more normal situation in which the owners of a business that is being sold go out of their way to try and be helpful to the prospective buyer. Often, there are unfriendly takeover attempts of publicly held companies in which the prospective buyer receives no help from the target. But if the target is publicly held, there is very substantial information already filed with the Securities and Exchange Commission (SEC), information that had to be prepared accurately and audited.

In a divorce situation, with a privately held firm, this information source (10-K) simply is not available. Developing an informed opinion of value of a publicly traded firm, with or without cooperation, is an order of magnitude easier than in the divorce situation.

While there is no perfect solution, our professional advice in a divorce situation would be to try and have the parties agree on the projections for the firm. These projections could be discussed, and while there would undoubtedly end up being a difference of opinion still, any narrowing of the differences is at least some progress.

At worst, whichever side one is on, the most credible valuation in court is going to be the one that is most reasonable, the one that relies most heavily on recently reported financial results. Reasonable people can disagree on the trend of future events, but substantial discontinuities are rare. In the long run, developing "far-out" valuations will usually *not* be supportable. If "half a loaf is better than none," our suggestion makes sense. The trouble with bitter divorce situations is that the parties end up hating each other so much that unreasonable and unsupportable positions are taken. As mentioned, in these circumstances there simply may be no good solution. Maybe the judge will just have to split the difference, and both sides will be equally unhappy!

BUY AND SELL AGREEMENTS

Often, in setting up a new business, either a partnership or a corporation, the principals will anticipate the possibility of one member's leaving the organization. The original agreement will then spell out what has sometimes been referred to as a "buy and sell agreement." In such agreements the document itself specifies the approach, methodology, or formula under which a departing member will be paid out. Assuming that the remaining partners are doing the buying, then the buy and sell agreement becomes a contractual commitment between or among the parties.

Basically, there are two different approaches utilized in the majority of buy and sell agreements. One is based on a more or less arbitrary formula; the other commits the parties to utilizing fair market value, which requires

63

the answer to be developed by an outside independent party, usually an appraiser. If the agreement is that the parties will be bound by the answer of an independent appraiser, then the valuation approaches discussed in this book will be applied.

Some closely held firms have annual appraisals (occasionally every six months) to allow employees a chance of acquiring or disposing of shares internally. Firms with employee stock option plans (ESOPs) must by law have annual appraisals. When firms regularly have periodic appraisals, the answer for a buy and sell agreement is simple: Use the latest appraised value, or alternatively: Use the next appraised value.

As long as the appraiser is truly independent and professional in his approach, all the parties at interest are protected. In performing a periodic valuation assignment of a closely held firm, the appraiser knows that someone will be buying and someone else selling. The appraiser is totally indifferent to the personal financial situations of the individuals involved.

Trouble arises when the buy and sell agreement does *not* utilize a professional valuation, but rather tries to accomplish the same result through application of some predetermined formula. In other words, the parties have actually agreed in advance to what amounts to a do-it-yourself appraisal. Disregard the conflict of interest in which the author, as a professional appraiser, does not want to lose potential client assignments. The fact here is that *no single formula or approach is going to be fair to both sides of any agreement.*

Two common formula approaches to valuation are:

1. "Stock will be purchased at book value, based on the latest audited balance sheet."
2. "Stock will be purchased at five times EBITDA, based on the latest audited financial statement."

In both cases the formula is applied to audited financial statements. This means, at a minimum, that an outside professional accountant has reviewed the statements and that they were prepared "in accordance with generally accepted accounting practice." So far, so good.

When buy/sell formulas are based on book value, the underlying assumption is that the balance sheet in some way reflects the value of the assets and hence the value of the business.

A small jewelry manufacturing firm was owned by the father. The sons had been running the business for several years and they wanted to

buy the business. While there was no formal agreement, the parties tried to utilize book value as a starting point.

The company manufactured pins, rings, and other jewelry with the seal or logo of the customer. The customer had to pay for the engraving of the original die, which the jewelry firm then kept in case of future orders. On receipt of a second order the company would go to its die inventory, retrieve it, and therefore the customer would obtain the second and subsequent orders at a much lower unit price.

The inventory of dies, in this case some 60,000, represented an asset of the business in that customers with repeat orders would almost certainly order from our client, because they would save the cost of engraving a new die. The value to the business of the dies was in future repeat business, because technically the customer could (but never did) ask for "his" die. However, the jewelry company had consistently put the original cost of the dies on its balance sheet on the basis that the dies had future value.

Consequently, the book value of the business included the original cost of 60,000 dies. At an average cost of perhaps $500 each, this meant that there was at least $30 million on the balance sheet representing the dies. There was a corresponding $30 million in the equity section of the balance sheet, from which book value was calculated.

The father believed that the sons should pay him for the book value, including $30 million for the 60,000 dies. He argued, somewhat persuasively, that the dies represented the source of a lot of repeat business, the sales of which were profitable.

The sons were uncomfortable paying for the 60,000 dies, even though they were physically on the shelf and *could* be used in the future. Their argument was that many, if not most, of the dies would *never* result in repeat orders. The customers had changed business, the logos had changed, there was little demand for, say, cuff links and so forth.

In this case, while there was no argument about what the book value was, the sons felt that the book value essentially overstated the value of the business. If 50,000 of the dies were not going to result in future business, the company book value was overstated by $25 million.

One could argue that the accountant should not have gone along with carrying potentially obsolete dies as an asset. In defense of the accounting, it was virtually impossible to predict whether any specific dies would or would not ever be used again. Many times very old dies did result in repeat orders! Further, the accounting for the dies had been handled consistently for the history of the company.

The resolution of this conflict, from a valuation perspective, was relatively simple. An actuarial analysis was performed on a limited sample of 200 of the dies. The objective was to see how many times in the last 5 years repeat orders had been received for any of the 200 dies. If 20 of them had resulted in repeat orders, we then estimated that 10 percent of the dies had economic value. We then calculated the gross profit on each of the 20 orders from which we derived a "value per good die", say, $1,000 each. We then said that 6,000 of the dies had an economic value of $6 million, while the remaining dies had no real economic value.

This did not mean the parties should throw out 54,000 dies. It did mean that we ascribed no economic value to them, and the sons should not pay a replacement cost for dies that would never, in total, be utilized again.

Once the logic of our approach was demonstrated to the parties, a more or less amicable settlement was reached.

We have been discussing why buy/sell formulas based on book value may not provide a fair answer. In an attempt to get away from a static balance sheet approach, many buy/sell agreements are based on some formula of earnings. At least in theory, value is a function of future cash flows; current earnings (cash flows) are probably the best indication of future results. So a formula based on current results looks fair, at least on paper.

A particularly good example of valuing a business on the basis of earnings, using a *predetermined formula,* arose recently with a privately held appraisal company. Imagine the difficulty of coming up with *the* value of an appraisal firm, when every one of the current and potential shareholders is, almost by definition, an expert in valuation. Obviously, there is a conflict inherent in a buy/sell agreement for a professional services firm. The existing shareholders (management) want to maximize their own return when it is time to sell, usually because of retirement. The prospective new shareholders, representing the up-and-coming younger professionals, want the lowest possible price, at least on the day they are buying. And with both sides experts at valuation, the potential for conflict is large. The last thing a professional services firm needs is major conflicts between top management and younger staff.

The appraisal firm being discussed was privately held, but primarily by outside investors, with only a minority of the stock held by current management. The exit strategy of the outside investors was for the company either to be bought out by employees (or another company) or to go public and have an initial public offering (IPO).

The initial valuation formula was based on weighting the most recent year's results at 3x, the previous year's at 2x, and the third year's back at 1x. The weighted average was then multiplied by a fixed factor, say 6, that appeared fair to both buyers and sellers.

This formula worked well while the company was going through good times; each year was equal to or better than the previous year so the 3,2,1 formula appeared to be equitable.

Then the firm ran into a bad year. Expenses increased in anticipation of higher volume, which was not achieved. Of course, the expenses were achieved, and the company had a small loss.

Now the 3,2,1 formula kicked in with a vengeance, weighting the current year's loss as 50 percent of the total value! This had not been anticipated, and it was obvious to the CEO that the formula was wrong. The only solution was to *change the formula.*

Analyzing the situation, it was apparent that making all the results dependent on what *had happened,* not looking to the *future,* was out of line with investors' thought process. The company in question prepared a budget each year that was approved by the board of directors. Sitting on the board were the very outside investors who wanted to protect the nominal value of their investment.

At the urging of the CEO, the board approved a change in the formula that weighted the valuation based on one-fourth for the budget for next year and three-fourths based on the previous 3,2,1 formula of current and past years' results. Effectively, this had the result of diluting the current year's loss, and more accurately reflecting the anticipated (profitable) results. After all the reason for using past results was that it was supposed to be a guide for the future. If the current year's loss was only a statistical blip, then changing the formula made sense. In fact, perhaps the original formula was wrong and the company should all along have been looking to the future.

Guess what. The next year there was a second consecutive loss. Expenses had not been cut, in anticipation of an upturn in sales. Now the formula provided an answer as to the value of the company and the stock. But the answer was not acceptable to the outside investors who still had faith that the company was worth a lot more and did not want to sell their stock to employees at a price that was unfairly low.

Only one solution was possible. Change the formula! The new formula weighted the next year's budget at 50 percent and past results at 50 percent. Again, on the surface this appears fair. The problem from the employees' perspective was that the new even more fair formula was introduced only when it suited the convenience of the prospective sellers, the investors who sat on the board.

The final straw came the next year when operating results were in the black, but nowhere near what had been budgeted. The final change to the formula now weighted the budget at 60 percent and previous three years (losses or nominal profits) at just 40 percent.

Even that formula could be considered fair had it been in place all along. It was the moving yardstick that appeared to be unfair, at least to the prospective buyers of company stock. And it was those prospective buyers who were selling and executing the work, thus generating the cash flows on which the valuation formula(s) depended.

The final straw that broke the proverbial camel's back was not the new 60 percent budget formula—even though that was bad enough. What caused a revolt was approval of a budget for the next year (now weighted at 60 percent) that appeared to many of the staff as totally unrealistic. A budget that showed an essentially unobtainable level of earnings and cash flows would put the current stock price so high that current buyers might never obtain a decent return on their investment.

Of course the sellers running the board and controlling the company were happy with the CEO and the ever-increasing annual valuation of the stock.

The dénouement was that the employees went to the outside board members and said either the CEO was fired or they would all quit. When all the facts were laid on the table, the board understood the situation. Shortly thereafter, the CEO left, and the employees bought the company. The transaction was at a low price, based not on any formula but 100 percent on the current and prospective financial condition of a firm that should never had had outside investors in the first place.

This example of a formula approach to a buy/sell agreement may appear far-fetched, although it is true. What is not so common is the constant tinkering with the formula. What is common is the inability of a formula—*any* formula—to reflect changes in underlying business and economic conditions. In this case the 3,2,1 formula was predicated on increasing volume and earnings. As soon as that paradigm changed, the formula started to produce bad results, at least from the perspective of the sellers.

Based on over 30 years' professional experience, we have *never* seen a buy/sell formula that works under changing business and economic conditions. The truth is that in the real world buyers and sellers of businesses evaluate each situation separately. The past results of a company are important. The outlook for the future is important. What is happening in the industry—to competitors, customers, and suppliers—is important. What is happening in the domestic and world economies is important. How can any formula, developed at a point in time, possibly encompass all these variables? The answer is clear. Formulas are static. Business is dynamic.

Valuing a closely held business cannot be done by formula, whether based on book value or based on some fixed multiple of past, current, or future earnings.

Is there a solution to the problem? Yes. Many partnership and closely held companies have a statement that "The value of the company will be determined [annually, or quarterly] by an independent valuation firm." Sometimes, the firm is named; at other times, management chooses the firm. Ordinarily, however, in such situations the same appraisal firm will do the periodic valuations. There are real economies in having any firm update prior appraisals. At a minimum the appraiser becomes familiar with the company and its industry. Also, it has access to the previous projections and can measure how closely actual results equaled those projections. Finally, valuation is still an art and not a science. While two different appraisers will come close to each other, if they value the same company, there still can be a difference of up to 10 percent between them. No company would want the appraisal in year one to be at the top end of the range, and then the next year a different appraiser coming in 10 percent lower at the bottom of the range. Consistency, in and of itself, is valuable.

LOANS: BORROWER VERSUS LENDER

Most loans are based on the potential cash flow of the borrower, that is, the lender expects to be repaid out of future profits and cash flows. But just in case the loan cannot be repaid from future profits and cash flows, lenders often ask for the borrower to put up collateral. If the loan subsequently goes into default, the bank then has a claim on the specific assets that had been pledged.

In practice, the maximum loan to a borrower may be some percentage of the value of the assets that are going to be pledged. Many lending institutions will lend perhaps 80 percent of the value of accounts receivable, 65 percent of inventory value, and perhaps 50 percent of the value of property, plant and equipment (PP&E). Finally, a recent trend involves lending against the security of *intangible assets,* such as *brand names* and *patents.*

Put this way, it is easy to see how a conflict may develop between the borrower and the lender. The greater the value of the collateral, the larger the loan. On the assumption that many companies would like to increase the maximum amount of their borrowing, for a borrower the key then is to demonstrate that the value of its collateral to be pledged is as high as possible.

It is fairly hard for a company to increase the valuation of its accounts receivable. The latest balance sheet, if it has been audited, pretty much sets forth the dollar value of the receivables, with only a slight degree of judgment involved in the size of the reserve for bad debts.

Similarly, the ability to increase the valuation of inventory is quite limited. In practice, depending on the type of inventory, the lender will apply an above-average haircut to the book value of inventory on the balance sheet. While finished goods inventory, whether shoes or steel, can always be sold to a jobber, and raw materials can usually be sold either to the producer or a competitor, work-in-process inventory is virtually worthless. If the borrower has trouble producing positive cash flow in other words, (is losing money), how is a bank or other lender going to come in, finish the production process, and sell the resulting product? Since it is unlikely, lenders do not like to use work-in-process as collateral.

One further problem with using inventory as collateral is that most companies have a significant percentage of their finished goods inventory in what charitably is referred to as slow moving. Because such product is quite unlikely to be sold easily, lenders usually insist on a substantial discount from book value. A good inventory control system, one that tracks on-hand inventory and sales history, should enable the prospective borrower to clean out the inventory that does not sell, incidentally saving on property taxes as well as insurance.

Then, with good records, and fast-moving inventory the bank will have more confidence. At that point the bank will be able to increase its loan-to-value percentage, providing the borrower with greater availability of funds.

With regard to PP&E as loan collateral, what usually happens is that the lender (bank or finance company) tells the prospective borrower that they, the lender, will obtain an independent appraisal that the borrower has to pay for. Working for the lender, the appraiser tends to be conservative. Then the borrower sees the draft report and starts screaming that the values are too low.

Solution? The appraiser has to explain the assumptions and methodology to the borrower. If the premise of value is orderly liquidation, the numbers in the report are probably correct and supportable. What the borrower is really objecting to is using liquidation value as the basis, as opposed to a cost of replacement or value in use basis. But, in the final analysis, it is the lender that is calling the shots and liquidation value that is required for the loan decision.

GIFTS AND ESTATE TAX

This chapter deals with conflicts in valuation. Probably the two areas where there is the greatest disagreement about the value of assets is:

1. With the IRS in valuing closely held firms for gift and estate tax returns
2. In messy divorce fights

Divorce valuations have previously been covered in this chapter.

Why there should be disputes between taxpayers and the IRS should be evident. A revenue agent believes that his or her job is to collect the maximum amount of taxes. In theory, they are supposed to be neutral and objective. Talk to any agent, one to one, and you will find that they are reasonable people with a very tough job.

The problem comes about because a lot of taxpayers, employing high-priced tax advisors, develop ever more complex tax avoidance strategies. Given the complexities of tax laws and regulations, and the court interpretations that follow, many legal schemes are developed with the sole purpose of minimizing or eliminating taxes. The creativity of tax professionals in the private sector far exceeds the ability of the IRS and Congress in closing loopholes.

So, from the perspective of a revenue agent, he sees very wealthy people paying minimal taxes, while he and all other salaried employees pay their full fair share. We are supposed to have a progressive tax system, with ability to pay being one of the criteria. Yet wealthy individuals, following the advice of their sophisticated tax advisors, adopt many seemingly egregious tax schemes. Unfortunately, from the revenue agent's perspective, many of these schemes on the surface appear to be legal in the sense that they comply with all the regulations and court decisions. So a relatively low-paid salaried civil servant sees far wealthier individuals paying less than he does. It is no wonder that many revenue agents become somewhat cynical after many years.

This is all by way of introduction to the topic. How do you determine the fair market value of a closely held business, which has never been traded publicly, for which there is no current market, and which was essentially built up by the founder based on his personal skills and resources. That founder has died, the estate must be settled, and inheritance taxes at rates quickly approaching 50 percent of the value of the company are due quite quickly.

Every $100,000 reduction in the value of the company means a cash savings to the estate and beneficiaries of perhaps $50,000. The value of any closely-held company is far from clear, because there is no market quotation; whatever answer is finally arrived at is still theoretical, while the tax payment due based on that value is real.

As one can imagine, disputes about valuation of closely held company securities, for gift and estate taxes, are very common. The IRS will *always* want to maximize the value, while the taxpayer wants to minimize the value. What happens?

The taxpayer will obtain an appraisal from a reputable appraisal firm that, not surprisingly, often shows a very low value for the business. The IRS can then obtain its own valuation, first from its internal staff and occasionally from an outside independent valuation firm. As six-year-old kids are fond of saying, "Guess what?"—the IRS valuation is higher than the taxpayers. In fact, we have *never* seen a case in which the IRS says that the taxpayer has *overvalued* the closely held securities.

The next step is negotiation, followed occasionally by going to court and having a judge decide the case. There have been a tremendous number of cases over the years dealing with valuation issues. It is very hard to draw conclusions as to how the courts will decide in a specific instance.

It appears that significant weight is given, in many decisions, to the reasonableness of the position taken, and the credibility of the *assumptions* inherent in every valuation. Finally, if there is direct oral testimony by the experts, the ability to testify (often gained by previous testimony experience) can tip the scales one way or the other.

In almost every gift and estate tax valuation case there are three points at issue:

1. Business enterprise value (BEV)
2. Discount for lack of marketability
3. Discount for lack of control

Disputes can arise over all three of these value considerations. While discussed in Chapter 15 in more detail, the reason these three factors are subject to dispute is that they most greatly affect the final answer for tax purposes.

If the IRS can successfully argue that the business itself, its BEV, is higher, then the tax payment will go up proportionately. This is common sense. But how does the IRS successfully argue for a higher BEV? As discussed in Chapter 7, the key to any valuation is the fundamental assumptions relating to the future course of the business. The difference in value between a company that is expected to grow 5 percent a year and one that is expected to grow 10 percent a year is substantial. At any point in time, who knows what will happen in the future? I argue for 5 percent growth if I want a lower value. The IRS argues for 10 percent growth for the sake of increasing the value. Which is correct? Only five years from now will we really know for sure. Meanwhile, we need an answer today, not in five years.

The second area of dispute relates to the lack of marketability of closely held stock. There is relatively little dispute with the IRS when dealing with a block of shares in a publicly traded firm. One can call a broker and sell at a price very close to that listed in that day's *Wall Street Journal*. Taxpayers rarely argue about publicly traded securities.

The appropriateness of a marketability discount for private firms is generally recognized by both sides, although disagreements still arise as to the appropriate amount in each case. Once again, a reasonable assumption is going to be accepted by the courts if it gets that far.

The discount for lack of control, the knowledge that a minority share-holder is at a disadvantage, is also generally recognized by both sides. There is probably greater disagreement about the correct discount. Many taxpayers or their advisors split up shares among several family members, each of whom by definition is a minority shareholder, but in total it is still one family business. Resolution of this conflict is ultimately a matter of negotiation, based on the facts and circumstances of the specific situation.

Because so much money is often at stake in tax disputes, and it is a zero-sum game, more tax disputes end up in court than almost any other type of valuation issue.

SUMMARY: CAN ADVERSE PARTIES AGREE ON VALUE?

As Adam Smith said more than 200 years ago, when each individual looks out for his own best interests, society as a whole gains. Standing back, and looking at disputes from 50,000 feet, this concept is essentially correct.

Yet at the time you are participating in such a debate—say you are trying to sell your stock back to the other owners of a closely held business—the contentious issues probably seem insuperable. As mentioned above, most valuation disputes are truly a zero-sum contest (i.e., what you win, I lose and vice versa).

The lessons that can be learned from those who have participated in the battles are as follows:

- There is no exact figure for FMV, only a range of ±10 percent.
- The parties have to agree on the premise of value, cost of reproduction, value in use, or liquidation value.
- The parties have to agree as to the basic outlook for the business or specific asset.
- Rather than pay the expenses of going through the legal system, both parties should hire a competent and truly independent appraiser and agree to abide by his valuation.

CHAPTER 5

Cost Approach to Value

There are three, and only three, ways to determine the value of any asset. This stark statement may, at first reading, seem hard to accept. There are at least 50 "proofs" of the Pythagorean theorem. There are hundreds of translations of the Bible. Many different roads all lead to Rome. But in the history of valuation the world's leading thinkers have never been able to develop more than three ways of measuring value:

1. *Cost approach.* This asks the question, "What would it *cost* today to buy or build the same or a similar asset?" The underlying assumption is that a 'willing buyer' would not pay any more for the asset being valued than he would have to pay for some other comparable asset. If a builder would build a new 3,000 square foot, four-bedroom house for $325,000, you would not likely pay $375,000 for an identical house in the same subdevelopment that was 1 year old. Typically, the cost approach places an upper limit on the value of the asset being appraised.

2. *Income approach.* It asks the question, "Considering the risks involved, what type of return can I obtain from an investment in this asset?" The income approach is used for intangible assets, including business enterprises, as well as for patents, brand names, and other intellectual property.

3. *Market comparable approach.* It asks the question "What are comparable assets being *sold* for in the open market?" It is often surprising, but for many types of assets there is a well-established market, with buyers and sellers. Comparable assets sell for prices within relatively narrow limits. In a virtually perfect market, perhaps for

U.S. Treasury bonds, the difference between the bid and asked prices is substantially less than 1 percent. In other markets, the bid/ask spread can be as high as 25 to 35 percent. Knowledge of the relevant market is essential in utilizing the market comparable approach.

In over 30 years in the appraisal and valuation business, we have seen only a single instance in which professional appraisers were unable to utilize one or more of these approaches to respond to the client's concern or business problem.

A Ripley's Believe It or Not Museum came to an appraisal firm and asked for the value of the contents for the purpose of insuring the property at replacement cost. In case of a fire, flood, or other loss, the insurance company would then be responsible for paying an amount sufficient to replace the lost objects.

Included in the contents were such unique items as an Eiffel Tower made out of toothpicks and a shrunken head from Peru. The appraisers took a look at the project and backed off.

They told the client that they were capable of valuing the business itself, based on revenue generated from ticket sales. This was the income approach. There did not appear to be a viable market for shrunken heads, so the market comparable approach had to be discarded. In terms of the specific contents, there was no feasible way to estimate the cost of producing a shrunken head! So the cost approach could not be used.

In short, the appraisal firm struck out.

In the remainder of this chapter, and the next two, we will discuss the strengths and weaknesses of each approach to valuation. Readers of any valuation report should find reference to the methodology utilized by the appraiser, as well as a discussion of which approaches to value were utilized, which were not, and an explanation. It should be stated that the Uniform Standards of Professional Appraisal Practice (USPAP) requires such a discussion in the body of every appraisal report.

COST APPROACH

When the appraisal business first started, the primary purpose of valuations was for placement of insurance, as well as provision of proof of loss in case of a fire. Prior to that time, insurance companies and those insured would almost always have a fight, arguing first what was lost, and second what the assets that were lost had been worth. By having an appraisal in advance—one that listed all the property *and* stated the value of that property—then in case of loss there would be no disagreement. The insurance company could be assured that premiums had been paid on all the assets, while the insured could know that the insurance company had agreed to the values and there would be no fight.

The early appraisers, in the 1890s and 1900s, literally listed every asset on a manual inventory sheet. Then the appraiser determined the value by looking at the *cost* new of those assets. Some professional skill was required to determine whether the specific asset had suffered any depreciation, and the cost of a new asset was reduced by the amount of depreciation. Thus, a lathe that cost $1,000 new would be valued for insurance purposes at $900 if it were objectively determined by the appraiser that 10 percent of the expected life had been consumed. There was virtually no professional judgment involved in listing the asset, with a full description including manufacturer and serial number. The only judgment was in determining whether the asset—assuming it was two years old and the lathe had a 20-year life—really had more or less than 10 percent depreciation. This was accomplished by physical inspection, looking at condition and maintenance history.

The key element was in identifying the asset itself and determining from the manufacturer what a new asset of like kind and performance would cost today (i.e., at the date of the appraisal). As long as there was little or no inflation (or deflation, for that matter) and that technology was not changing rapidly, this cost approach to valuation was accurate and easy to accomplish. Both the insurance company and the insured were happy, legal wrangling was eliminated, premiums were fair, and losses were settled amicably.

Just as a sidelight, to show how the cost approach was used, the author heard an "old-timer" describe the method applied to an office building. The appraiser would literally count the number of bricks on the outside of the building. He would then go to a brick supplier and determine the price per brick. Next, he would contact a firm of masonry contractors and determine the then current price per brick for laying. This would be repeated for each and every component of the building.

In effect, this cost buildup would have been identical to that used by each trades contractor developing a quotation for a bid on the entire building. As noted above, the only difference was that the appraiser had to allow for any depreciation, physical and functional, that had taken place since the subject property had been constructed, however many years ago.

It should be noted that this very detailed cost buildup is really no longer used in applying the cost approach. Rather, an appraiser today would determine the type of building (warehouse, commercial, manufacturing) and apply overall cost construction factors. A number of firms have standardized estimating manuals that show the cost per square foot for each type of building. This is further broken down by geographical location, because construction costs vary by locality depending on such things as local labor rates, construction codes, and material prices. The cost per square foot in Hawaii may be higher than on the mainland for all these reasons. The cost-estimating manuals adjust for these differences.

Thus, utilizing this approach to costing out a building may take less than a day, whereas the detailed analysis brick by brick could easily take a week or more. There have indeed been productivity improvements in the valuation field, as in so many others.

We have referred several times to the need for an appraiser, utilizing the cost approach, to determine depreciation from all causes. The cost of an asset new is the starting point in valuing an existing older asset. But just as an individual would pay less for a two-year-old car than for a new vehicle, so a prospective buyer would be expected to pay less for a two-year-old building or a two-year-old machine tool.

Why is an older asset worth less? Common sense suggests several factors:

- Higher maintenance expense
- Lower utility/performance
- Shorter remaining life
- Possible economic changes in the market for the product/service produced

Let's look at each of these separately. Understanding each of these ideas will then allow the reader to understand the thought process that an appraiser goes through in determining depreciation from all of these causes. The sum of these factors equals the total amount by which the *value* of the subject asset is *less* than the *cost* of a brand new asset. Remember that the cost of the new asset is determined from an independent source and can be verified. The subtraction for depreciation depends on the knowledge, experience, and skill of the appraiser.

The depreciation we are talking about here is *not* the same as depreciation expense shown on the financial statements. Depreciation expense on financial statements is usually based on an estimated life of the asset less an assumed salvage value, and then the amount is spread ratably over the life of the asset. Accountants make no attempt to relate current depreciation charges, or accumulated depreciation, to actual diminution of value of the asset. Depreciation accounting is strictly a mechanical application of an accounting convention, unrelated to real-world changes in value. As an example, most real estate is depreciated over 40 years. Yet look at the vast number of buildings still going strong after 50 years. Accounting depreciation and value are two entirely separate concepts.

DEPRECIATION

One reason that an older asset is worth less than a new similar asset is that it has *higher maintenance expense.* A three-year-old car is starting to require periodic repairs. Tires may have to be replaced, brakes need to be tightened, and so forth.

In figuring the total cost of ownership over the life of an asset, maintenance and repairs can easily approach the original cost of the asset. The older the asset, the greater the likelihood that there will be *increasing* maintenance expenditures.

Thus, in terms of cash outflows, if one acquires a five-year-old machine tool, more money will have to be spent in the next three years than if one bought a brand new machine. As an approximation, the present value (using discounted cash flow techniques) of the higher and sooner maintenance expense is a reduction in value as compared to the new asset.

Appraisers who specialize in machinery and equipment (M&E) develop expertise in examining all types of assets. They estimate the timing and dollar amount of anticipated routine maintenance plus the probabilities of unanticipated breakdowns. The degree to which a company has provided for routine preventive maintenance affects this professional judgment. Useful information on this aspect of value can usually be obtained by the appraiser from plant engineers, maintenance foreperson, and even the workers who utilize the equipment.

Another type of depreciation that has to be measured in the cost approach is the *lower utility/performance* from the older equipment. The best way to look at this concept is the personal computer (PC). Several years ago an Intel 486 computer was state of the art. It was faster and could outperform all existing PCs. A 486 could handle the most sophisticated software, including large spreadsheets and databases.

Ten years later, a 486 computer with its original complement of software will perform exactly as well today as it did then, at least as long as one uses only the original software. Essentially, there is no maintenance expense for electronics and even mechanical disc drives have a long life. So in determining the value of a 486 computer there really is no diminution in value solely from physical characteristics. Why then is a 486 today worth so much less than when it was new?

Two things account for the difference. The performance of the latest generation of PCs is a full order of magnitude greater. A 486 probably cannot even run on the Internet, or play high-graphics-intensity games. Further, given application of Moore's Law, the price of a new PC in absolute dollars is less than a 486 cost when new.

While there is a good market in used computers, and an appraiser would actually probably use the market comparable approach in valuing any PC, if the cost approach is used, substantial penalties must be assessed for functional obsolescence.

In terms of actually calculating functional obsolescence, a better example would be a process manufacturing facility. A well-maintained chemical plant will probably produce output at the same cost per pound today as it did when new. The latest plant design, perhaps larger in capacity, using less energy, and developing fewer environmental costs will have a *lower* cost per pound of output.

Valuing the older plant on the cost approach, the appraiser will obtain today's unit construction cost per unit of output. He will then determine the cost per pound of output utilizing today's technology. Comparing the cost per unit of output from the new plant with the cost per unit of output from the subject plant will provide a cost differential or penalty that the old plant suffers.

On a present-value discounted cash flow analysis, the appraiser will then determine the excess costs involved in running the old plant. The theory is that a prospective buyer could either acquire a new plant with low output cost or pay much less for the old plant and lose some of the benefit through the higher operating costs. How much less the old plant has to sell for, to equilibrate the two, represents the depreciation charge for functional obsolescence.

The third type of depreciation that an appraiser will take into account is the *shorter remaining life* of the older asset. Nothing lasts forever. Even with the best maintenance a 747 plane will probably not have a useful life beyond perhaps 30 years. That is not to say that a particular 29-year-old plane will stop flying at the end of year 30. But on a statistical basis, for a large fleet of planes, 30 years is probably the effective life. This is comparable to life expectancies for humans. A male in the United States at birth may have a life expectancy of 77 years, and a 65-year-old male may have a 13-year life expectancy. That does not mean that an individual who is 65 in 2003 will be dead in 2016.

Whether the total loss of utility is due to physical inability to perform the function for which it was designed, or because of functional obsolescence, the fact remains that most assets are replaced at some point in time. All other things being equal, investors would prefer to own an asset with a 20-year remaining life rather than an 18-year life. The longer the life, the more valuable the asset. The shorter the remaining life, the less valuable the asset.

Appraisers, therefore, must estimate the remaining life in order to determine the current fair market value (FMV). This requires judgment as to the physical condition of the asset, an estimate of any potential functional obsolescence and, as will be discussed immediately below, recognition that the ultimate life may be affected by external conditions. The estimate of the *real* remaining life of most assets requires both significant professional experience and a substantial amount of judgment.

At this point it is important to distinguish between the life allowed by the IRS for tax purposes and the real economic life an investor can reasonably expect. As a broad generalization, lives allowed for the purpose of computing tax depreciation are *shorter* than economic lives. Thirty or more years ago, the then IRS code, plus revenue agent determinations, were strongly anti-taxpayer. In fact, for the first 20 years after World War II the subject of tax lives and depreciation was perhaps the hottest tax controversy in business. As technology was rapidly developing, the abnormally *long* lives mandated by the IRS came increasingly to appear discriminatory. Following numerous political battles, over the next 25 years tax depreciation was greatly eased. Now, with the possible exception of personal computers, few corporate taxpayers are complaining about lives allowed for tax purposes. While not a hot political issue today, the pendulum may have swung too far. Put bluntly, tax lives are materially shorter than economic lives.

There is no law that says lives used for financial reporting must be the same as those used for tax purposes. In practice, however, most companies do use the same lives because of the simplicity. If different lives are used for book and taxes, the taxpayer has to develop an estimate of deferred taxes, either positive or negative. After several years, the bookkeeping becomes difficult, the tax schedules complex, and, worst of all, few investment analysts, much less individual shareholders, even begin to understand deferred tax accounting as required by generally accepted accounting principles (GAAP) in Statement of Financial Accounting Standards (SFAS) 109. It simply is easier to keep books and taxes the same.

But what is easiest is not the same as correct. The best evidence that tax lives are too short is found in the amount of fully depreciated assets still currently in use. In many situations, when appraisers perform a physical inventory of plant, property and equipment (PP&E) 12 to 20 percent or more of the assets actually still in use have been fully depreciated. Relatively few assets are disposed of before they are fully depreciated.

As a result of this discontinuity between tax lives (and hence book lives) and economic reality, book value (original cost less accumulated depreciation) is rarely the same as FMV. On occasion, the additional diminution in value of asset(s), due to functional or economic obsolescence, offsets the over-depreciation due to too short lives. Book value *can* be close to FMV, but if it is, it is usually a coincidence. Two different measurement systems will occasionally have the same answer just as a stopped clock is correct twice a day.

The final adjustment in using the cost approach to determine the FMV of an asset is to test for *economic changes in the market for the product/service produced.* Assume for sake of example that a special plastic injection-molding machine costs $100,000 new. Based on physical and functional depreciation there should be $10,000 of depreciation, resulting in an apparent net value of $90,000. Now suppose that the molding machine can produce only hula hoops, for which there is currently a very limited market. An economic analysis shows that the total sales would be $30,000 per year, raw materials would be $20,000 per year, and operating expenses were $5,000. Allowing nothing for selling, general and administrative (SG&A) expenses, there would be operating profit, pretax, of $5,000. How many people would invest $90,000 to obtain a pretax return of 5.5 percent? And this allows nothing for SG&A expenses.

In order for the machine to produce an economic pretax return of 15% (disregarding SG&A), an investor would not be able to pay more than $33,000 for the molding machine. This, of course, assumes that a 15 percent return is itself satisfactory. Under this set of assumptions, the $90,000 cost of the machine, less depreciation from physical and functional obsolescence, has to be reduced by an additional $57,000 for what appraisers call *economic depreciation.*

In other words, an investor would pay only $33,000 for the specific asset, irrespective of what it might cost new. A brand new machine that costs $100,000 is no bargain at $90,000 if one can obtain only a $5,000 profit from it. Irrespective of what it would cost new, a $33,000 machine might appear attractive if one could get $5,000 a year and was willing to settle for a 15 percent return.

In this scenario, the appraiser would determine that the FMV of the machine was $33,000. Under the cost approach the net value would have been developed as follows:

Cost new:	$100,000
Less physical depreciation:	7,000
Less functional depreciation:	3,000
Less economic depreciation:	57,000
Fair market value:	$ 33,000

In summary, the cost approach is best used for tangible physical assets, and for those assets places an upper limit on value. A rational investor would not pay more for an existing asset than he would for a new asset, with the latter depreciated down to the condition of the asset being appraised.

There is one further point that needs to be clarified. When there has been technological progress, do we start with the cost of a new asset that is *identical* to the asset being appraised, or do we utilize a *replacement* asset that has the same or similar performance characteristics?

INDEXING COSTS

Recall that in utilizing the cost approach appraisers start with the listing of the assets, then they go to the manufacturer or supplier and determine the specific cost new of each asset as of the valuation date. Usually, the valuation date is the current date, although occasionally appraisals are done as of an earlier date.

If one is valuing a large or complex manufacturing site, determining the cost new of each asset can be a time-consuming job, involving calls to numerous suppliers. Each call involves getting in touch with the correct person at the supplier, identifying the appraiser, usually having to describe the property being appraised, and then waiting for the answer as to what the same or a similar assets sells for today. Because appraisers charge based on time spent, not the value of the assets being appraised, this can be a costly procedure.

Often, appraisers will choose to apply one or more *indexes* to the *original cost*. An analysis of the statistical properties of indexes is beyond the scope of this book. The consumer price index (CPI) measures trends in prices of a total bundle of goods and services utilized by the typical consumer.

Just as the CPI measures retail prices, so there are many indexes that measure industrial prices. Many of these are prepared by the U.S. government, some are prepared by trade groups and commercial publishers, while in certain cases appraisal firms develop their own indexes.

A properly constructed index will accurately reflect the underlying change in prices over time. The problem with indexes, however, is that the assets themselves change. Very few things are static. There is often a discussion in the press regarding how the CPI should handle changes in automobiles. The base price of a new model Chevrolet may go up one year from $20,000 to $20,400, which is a 2 percent increase. General Motors, sensitive to the issue of raising prices, then argues that the new model has certain safety features that increased the price $300, so the real price increase was only $100 or 0.5%. How much did the price really go up, $100 or $400? There is no easy answer, but if there are a wide variety of items in the index there is a possibility that these technical problems can offset each other. Even if they don't exactly offset, at least if there is no bias in the preparation of the index, it can be used safely.

Applying cost indexes as part of the cost approach is very straightforward. As long as the fixed-asset record has the original cost of the asset, and the date (year) it was acquired, then application of the index to the file will provide a good estimate of what the total group of assets would cost today. Indexing is in fact a shortcut, but experience has proven that it works to the desired degree of accuracy.

Indexing works very well when the *original cost* and *original date of acquisition* are available in the computer file. Indexing does *not* work when the file contains allocated costs based on a subsequent purchase.

As discussed in Chapter 12, when a company is acquired, the buyer must allocate the purchase price over all the tangible and intangible assets. This involves determining the FMV of each asset. In practice, this is often accomplished through application of the cost approach, with the initial step being an indexing of the original cost to the then-current date.

Many companies then take the new FMV and set up a new fixed-asset record, with the date of acquisition being the merger date. This is fine for financial reporting purposes for the buyer, and is the proper way to do it for tax reporting. Effectively, a purchase of an existing business is no different from buying really new assets.

Problems will arise, however, if this new fixed-asset property record itself becomes the basis for a *second* allocation, assuming the entire business is sold for a second time, which happens more often than one might imagine. Cost indexes, in theory, should not be applied to allocated costs.

The reason is straightforward. A cost index relates increase in cost from one year to the next in a time series. If you have a price index for a numerically controlled milling machine, a standardized commodity, one can apply the index amount for five years ago to the product from five years ago and get a good idea what that milling machine would cost in today's dollars. But if the recorded amount is from an allocation five years ago, that amount represents the then-current value, reflecting physical and economic depreciation. Applying a *cost index* to a previous *value* amount does not provide a meaningful answer.

The only solution to this problem is for the buyer or acquirer of an existing business to *retain* the original cost and date of acquisition information. Most computerized fixed-asset or property record software can handle multiple inputs. The primary use of the original cost and date information would be for subsequent indexing, say for insurance purposes. Most insurance appraisals are kept up to date through application of indexes.

It costs very little to retain original cost and date of acquisition information on today's property record systems. The benefits are substantial. We strongly recommend this based on the cost/benefit tradeoff.

REPRODUCTION COST VERSUS REPLACEMENT COST

At the height of inflationary pressures in the late 1970s, the Securities and Exchange Commission (SEC) imposed a reporting requirement on publicly traded companies. It called for companies to report on a supplemental basis the replacement cost of their PP&E. Concurrently, the Financial Accounting Standards Board (FASB) imposed a reporting requirement that called for companies to price level adjust, or index, the *original* cost of their PP&E. Both requirements were a response to the then-prevalent inflation. The feeling at both the FASB and SEC was that investors and creditors who utilized financial statements were being misled. Depreciation computed on original cost was not enough to replace the assets; hence, income was being overstated.

Both the SEC and FASB requirements were repealed a few years later, after inflation had been brought under control and the utility of the information itself had been seriously questioned. What was wrong with both the replacement cost and price level–adjusted data? In a nutshell, investors found little use for either the theoretical cost of replacing assets that were not going to be replaced, or the cost today to buy the same assets even though they were not being bought again. It turned out that the theoretical problems with historical cost depreciation were less than feared, while the actual problems with price level and replacement cost were almost insuperable.

This brief introduction into replacement cost versus reproduction cost appears to be only of historical interest. But it does bring to the forefront two different approaches to determining today's cost. **Replacement cost** represents what it would cost to acquire comparable assets that are available today, that is, what you would obtain today if you were actually starting from scratch. It takes account of the latest technology. The new asset would provide the same or better utility as the existing asset. In a high-volume manufacturing situation, you might well replace three manual screw machines requiring three operators with one numerically controlled machine utilizing the services of only one operator. The one computer-controlled machine might cost a lot more than three of the manual units. The savings in operating expense would more than make up the difference in initial capital cost.

Ordinarily, in utilizing the cost approach, appraisers will consider the replacement cost as the starting point. The logic for this is that a rational investor wants to utilize the lowest current cost production in order to be competitive. Therefore, the value of the existing asset is related to the alternatives that are available in the market today (i.e., newer technology). That newer technology may have higher or lower operating expenses. This operating cost differential, whatever it is, will be captured in the appraisal analysis and will accordingly affect the value of the subject existing asset being valued.

Thus, to summarize quickly, the cost approach usually starts with the current cost of *replacement,* adjusts for physical and functional depreciation (plus economic, if appropriate) and thus determines the FMV of the subject. The basic concept is that the buyer of an existing asset faces a choice, either the asset under consideration or alternatives. And the alternatives in terms of *new* assets usually have been improved because of technology, for example, a modern refrigerator does not use Freon and runs with lower electricity usage. Both an old and a new refrigerator will keep food at the desired temperature, but the operating cost differential affects the value of the old unit. Nobody today would go out and buy an older-model, Freon, high-electricity-usage refrigerator even if one were available. The new refrigerator is a *replacement* for the existing model and the value of the older unit is affected by the cost characteristics of the replacement.

Now let us look at a major exception to the use of replacement cost information. In determining values for insurance, we explicitly look at the *reproduction cost* (i.e., a specific look at the same asset). The reason for this is that when buying insurance, your contract with the carrier requires them to "make you whole," but not to improve your position.

It is a fact that most losses covered by insurance are *partial losses,* not *total.* As an example, relatively few buildings burn down to the ground. Rather, fire damage is usually confined to a portion of the structure. This means that the insurance company is now responsible for putting the building back into the condition it was before the loss. So if the building had been constructed with plaster walls, that is what has to be reproduced; even if sheetrock is currently used in new construction, as long as the rest of the building has plaster, then the fire damage has to be rebuilt in like kind.

In determining values for insurance purposes, appraisers must be careful to utilize cost of reproduction, not cost of replacement. Often, an appraisal firm will provide two separate reports to a client for the same property, one based on cost of reproduction for insurance and one based on replacement cost for FMV purposes, say financial reporting. These two reports would definitely have different values. It is therefore incumbent on the reader of *any* valuation report to review what the appraiser said the purpose of the report was. Every appraisal report states that, usually right on the first page.

If a company has good PP&E computer records, showing date of acquisition and original cost, it is relatively easy to update that annually (or once every three years) for insurable values. This is because cost indexes deal with current prices of the same assets. The very difficulties that make it hard to update *values* through application of indexes make it easy to update original costs through indexes for insurance purposes.

PROPERTY RECORD ATTRIBUTES

So far in this chapter we have discussed developing asset values through the cost approach. We have stated that appraisers usually start with the computerized record of PP&E. It was only fairly recently that companies were able to keep their property record system on a PC. Prior to that, property record systems were mainframe only. Such systems were expensive to buy, expensive to maintain, and difficult to modify, for example, if the tax law changed.

The advent of PCs changed this, and now most companies have PC-based property record systems. Accounting departments can now control the PC systems, as contrasted to the old mainframe system that required substantial management information systems (MIS) involvement. We now have greater flexibility and ease of use.

In Chapter 14 we discuss property record systems in more detail. The one point we want to make here is that there is often widely varying data in a firm's property record system. What happens is that over time various accountants have had the responsibility for inputting new data, and removing records for assets disposed of. No two accountants handle fixed-asset information the same way. Sometimes a large capital expenditure project will be entered as "remodel building—$4,367,886." Five years later, just what does this mean? Sometimes there is an entry "50-ton press—$105,000" followed on the next line by "install press—$15,000." The total cost of the press was obviously $120,000. But then on the next page there is an entry on a single line "40-ton press—$60,000." Does this include installation? Is it a new or a used press? What has happened is that in years with high income, and to minimize taxes, companies will expense as much as they can. Then in a bad year they will capitalize everything under the sun.

The point is that property record systems themselves are often relatively inaccurate. Before relying on them, an appraiser has to make a physical inspection of the assets, usually on a sampling basis. Often, a dozen of the very largest dollar items are reviewed carefully, to determine the degree of reliance that can be placed on the record. As discussed in Chapter 14, if the record is too bad, the only solution is a physical inventory. But if the record, while inaccurate, is within reasonable limits, appraisers will often utilize it, adjusting only for major errors.

UNIQUE ASSETS: LAND AND FINE ART

Can the cost approach be applied to truly unique assets? The answer is clear and unequivocal: no. Take as an example a piece of fine art, say a Rembrandt etching. There is a specific market in fine art, etchings, and even one focused solely on Rembrandt etchings. Dealers and collectors frequently buy and sell these prints. They often come up for sale at Sotheby's and Christie's auctions.

These do *not* represent the cost of reproduction, much less the cost of replacement. Rembrandt is dead, and no matter how much the Metropolitan Museum or Bill Gates (or both together) were willing to pay, nobody today can get Rembrandt to produce another etching. The market for such works of art is strictly limited to the examples that are extant. If you own a

Rembrandt etching and want to know what it is worth, or you wish to buy such a work and want to know how much it would cost, you have to go to an appraiser of fine arts, a dealer, or one of the auction houses. Depending on condition and current demand, they can estimate the value within perhaps 10 to 20 percent.

Where people get confused is that the *price* of a piece of fine art is what it will currently sell for in the open market; it is not the *cost* to acquire a *new* Rembrandt etching because the latter is impossible. The terms *cost* and *price* are sometimes used interchangeably, but in valuation we use price for existing assets, and cost for new assets.

Specific parcels of land are individually unique, but there are often very close substitutes. Thus, in a new subdivision, one lot may have a view of a lake, while the lot across the street has a view onto the golf course. The lots are different and may sell for different prices. If there are 20 lake lots and 20 golf lots, there may be very little difference in price or value among each of the lake or each of the golf lots. Every single lot has specific differences (e.g., distance from clubhouse or number of trees), but because of the large number available, these differences may have virtually no effect on the price.

Now take a look at a truly unique piece of land. It is a small corner lot on 34th Street in New York City. The Macy's store is built around a small store owned and operated by someone else. Obviously, when the site was being assembled, the owner of the corner lot, thinking Macy's *had* to buy the parcel, held out for a *very* high price. At some point the developer said "Hell, no!" and simply built around the holdout lot. Before the deal closed, the owner of the small lot had a very valuable piece of real estate, albeit not as valuable as he thought. Today, completely landlocked, the parcel is probably worth a lot *less* than it was before Macy's started to build.

The point is that while every single parcel of land is unique in one sense, the actual impact on value may or may not be significant, depending on circumstances. This is why attempts at computerizing the valuation of commercial and industrial real estate have usually failed. Computers simply cannot capture the judgment inherent in the valuation of land and buildings.

Computer databases do exist on the *cost* of construction of buildings and real property. But computer databases cannot capture the unique aspects of any single parcel of land, primarily because the value of a specific parcel of land is a function of what is around it and what it can be used for. Only with the somewhat theoretical concept of filling in water (think Netherlands) can land be built or created. Thus, land values, representing a unique asset, must always be derived from the income approach or the market comparable approach.

SUMMARY

The cost approach to value is perhaps the easiest to understand because almost everyone is familiar with the concept of cost. If you can buy something for $1,000, that is its cost, so that can also easily be its value.

Problems come in, requiring experience and expertise, when the asset available in the market differs from the asset whose value we are trying to determine. The cost of a replacement asset usually places an upper limit on the amount that the subject asset could be sold for. Prospective buyers always have a choice, and they are unlikely to pay a premium for an existing asset that presumably is used, as contrasted with a new asset.

Further, with the advances in technology, newer assets are usually more productive, using less energy or material or labor content. These factors all lead toward the conclusion that existing assets may have lower values than an outside observer might expect. However, assets physically last a lot longer than is assumed by accountants, so fully depreciated (financial depreciation) assets still have economic value.

The cost approach is primarily used by appraisers in allocation of purchase price in a merger transaction, and in insurance valuations. It occasionally is used in valuing an intangible, like an assembled workforce, but can never be used for fine arts, antiques, and land. For those assets, the market approach is used by appraisers.

CHAPTER 6

Income Approach to Value

The income approach is the most appropriate method of valuation for many business enterprises as well as intangible assets. In the final analysis, an investment in any asset is worth no more than the present value today of the income to be derived in the future from that investment. The income to be derived consists of cash flows (i.e., dividends, cash for reinvestment, salaries to the owner, and so forth), plus the cash received as and when the investment is actually sold.

In valuing a business, using the income approach, an appraiser looks in detail at the income and cash flows expected to be received from an investment in the subject property. The question is then asked, "How much would investors in the marketplace be willing to pay for the income stream that the subject property will throw off?" The appraiser looks to see what *rate of return* investors are receiving from other investments currently available in the market; this willingness of investors to pay for a stream of income has to take into consideration the *risk characteristics* of the subject enterprise or other asset. Professional judgment is required to adjust for any unusual or nonrecurring items in both the subject asset and the publicly traded investments used as the basis of comparison. This is the theory and will be elaborated on in more detail in this chapter.

The income approach is highly dependent on the assumptions utilized by the appraiser or analyst. Often, small changes in estimates of future results can have a magnified effect on the valuation. For this reason, in assessing a valuation utilizing the income approach, be sure to check the reasonableness of the assumptions. Any professionally prepared valuation will clearly specify the key assumptions. Often, in fact, an appraiser will test the sensitivity of the assumptions and indicate the effect on the valuation of a change in one or more of the key assumptions.

MECHANICS OF APPLYING THE INCOME APPROACH

In valuing a specific business, the mechanics of the income approach are straightforward:

- The appraiser first develops an income projection, usually in conjunction with the management of the entity.
- This income projection is then adjusted to become a cash flow forecast.
- Depreciation of fixed assets and amortization of intangibles are added back to net income. Offsetting this is a subtraction for required capital expenditures.
- Working capital requirements associated with increased sales have to be subtracted from income to arrive at net cash flow.
- The projection period, often five years, does not mean the firm goes out of business at that point. The standard way of handling this is to *assume* that the business would be *sold,* intact, at the end of the five-year time horizon to another third party.

This approach (as shown in Exhibit 6.1—Base Case) to valuation provides a series of annual cash flows for each future year of the analysis period. For the (five-year) forecast period these are net operating cash flows during the period. At the end there is a one-time inflow upon the assumed sale of the business.

To derive the net present value it is then necessary to discount, back to today's dollars, these cash flows at an *appropriate discount rate.* This is because a dollar in the future is worth less than a dollar today. Put a different way, if you have $.89 and can invest it at 6 percent, you will have $1.00 two years from now. Thus, $1.00 two years from now is only worth $.89 today, assuming that money is worth 6 percent.

The choice of discount rate may be a critical element in the valuation process, and we discuss in this chapter the methods appraisers use in deriving the rate to use.

STRENGTHS AND WEAKNESSES

Many security analysts in brokerage firms develop very elaborate discounted cash flow (DCF) models, which is what was described above. The projections can range from the very simple (e.g., revenues, cost of revenues, SG&A expenses, and taxes) to the very elaborate. For complex

Exhibit 6.1 Sample Corporation: Base Case

WACC	15.3%
EBITDA EXIT MULTIPLE	5.5

Year	(Base Year Sales)	1	2	3	4	5
Net Sales	$ 46,122	$ 46,122	$ 48,429	$ 50,850	$ 53,392	$ 56,062
EBITDA		3,567	3,987	4,441	4,930	5,457
Depreciation		1,098	1,051	1,002	962	929
EBIT		2,469	2,936	3,439	3,968	4,528
Taxes @ 40.0%		988	1,175	1,376	1,587	1,811
Debt Free Net Income		1,481	1,762	2,063	2,381	2,717
Add: Depreciation		1,098	1,051	1,002	962	929
Less: Capital Expenditures		(461)	(484)	(508)	(534)	(561)
Less: Increase in Working Capital		—	(507)	(533)	(559)	(587)
=Free Cash Flow		2,118	1,821	2,024	2,250	2,498

Total Free Cash Flow (Years 1–5)	$ 10,711
Total Residual Free Cash Flow	$ 30,013

		1	2	3	4	5
Discount Factor		0.931	0.808	0.701	0.608	0.527
Discounted Free Cash Flow		1,973	1,471	1,418	1,367	1,316

Present Value of Free Cash Flow	$ 7,545
Present Value of Residual Free Cash Flow	14,729
Total Discounted Free Cash Flow Before the Addition of Nonoperating Assets	22,274
Add: Nonoperating Assets	576
Debt Free Business Enterprise Value	$ 22,849

Key Operating Assumptions:

		1	2	3	4	5
Net Sales Growth		0.0%	5.0%	5.0%	5.0%	5.0%
EBITDA/Sales		7.7%	8.2%	8.7%	9.2%	9.7%
Depreciation/Sales		2.4%	2.2%	2.0%	1.8%	1.7%
Capital Expenditures/Sales		1.0%	1.0%	1.0%	1.0%	1.0%
Working Capital/Sales		22.0%	22.0%	22.0%	22.0%	22.0%

companies, analysts will sometimes prepare separate projections for each line of business and then sum up these separate schedules. Within the line of business the projections can be as simple as gross dollars of revenues through elaborate forecasts of prices and volumes of each product. Thus, an analyst of the steel industry could try to project the demand for each type of steel by tons, and selling prices per ton for each product category. Cost of sales similarly could be an assumed total dollar amount or be as complex as trying to predict energy costs, labor costs, and raw material costs. Sales, general and administrative (SG&A) expenses are not usually projected in as much detail, and a percentage relationship between sales volume and expenses is usually assumed.

Interest expense and taxes on income do not usually provide much of a challenge to the analyst, and historical experience is usually relied on, at least in the absence of specific facts to the contrary.

If all the assumptions, both explicit and implicit, in the analysis are reasonable, and supported by historical experience, the DCF methodology is accurate and provides useful values. It should be stated once again that the income approach to value is highly dependent on the quality of the assumptions, as discussed in Chapter 9. Depending on the model, sometimes relatively small changes in one or two of the variables can have a significant, almost disproportionate, impact on the final answer.

As an example, for a "risky" investment, in which the appraiser feels it appropriate to utilize a high discount rate, small changes in the first two or three years will affect the answer much more than comparable changes in years nine and ten. This is because at high discount rates, above 30 percent, the present value today of a dollar 10 years from now may be only 5 to 7 cents. Thus, a slight change in the assumptions regarding sales, or operating profit, in the first two or three years will dramatically affect the results.

If the reliance on key assumptions is a weakness of the income approach, and it is, then the strength is that this is how most investors evaluate most prospective investment opportunities. If I buy this stock today, how high do I expect it to go; if it achieves that objective, what kind of rate of return will I have earned? Similarly, in buying an entire business, as opposed to shares of stock in a publicly traded firm, a prospective buyer asks the identical question. In valuing a division of a company being put up for sale, the seller asks, "What could the buyer expect to earn?" That then becomes the starting point for the negotiations.

To sum up, the income approach to valuation actually is no more than the application of sound business principles as taught to future MBAs in any business school. The cost approach to valuation is similar to the work performed by cost accountants, while the market comparable approach to valuation is used by individuals when setting a selling price on their car or house. The basic principles are easy to explain and understand, but as one commentator put it, "The devil is in the details." Looked at that way, it is the appraiser's task to delve into the details. What separates a good appraisal from a poor one is the care and accuracy with which the details are examined.

INVESTOR CHOICES AND RISK

There is an implicit assumption in every valuation utilizing the income approach. The assumption is that:

- Prospective investors have numerous other investment opportunities.
- The alternative investment opportunities have varying characteristics, including the amount and timing of the future cash flows.
- The alternative investment opportunities have different risk profiles.
- By adjusting for the timing of the future income and cash flows, as well as the risk of receiving those cash flows, one can put all the alternative investment opportunities on an equivalent basis.

Let's look at how realistic these assumptions are. To the extent that they reflect economic reality, the income approach to valuation is a sound methodology.

Prospective investors have numerous other investment opportunities: In considering investment opportunities we not only are talking about buying shares of stock in NASDAQ or on the New York Stock Exchange (NYSE). Alternative investment opportunities represent all businesses with approximately the same size and geographical and industry characteristics. By definition, there is never an identical alternative. Nevertheless, it is reasonable to assume that investors who have capital available will be presented with far more investment proposals than they have resources. Many venture capital firms receive literally thousands of business plans every year. Business brokers—and there are hundreds, if not thousands— each have numerous companies for sale. In short, there is a large market for business enterprises, with many participants as both buyers and sellers.

The market for businesses is not nearly as efficient as the NYSE, where price changes of 10¢ per share will move thousands of shares in just minutes. Buying or selling a business takes a lot more time than executing an order on the big board. Selling a business involves negotiations that are both time consuming and may arrive at a final price based less on underlying value than on negotiating skill. Nevertheless, at any point in time, there are thousands of businesses for sale, and prospective investors have numerous alternatives available.

The alternative investment opportunities have varying characteristics, including the amount and timing of the future cash flows: As mentioned, there are never truly identical businesses, which is why the income approach is necessary. A two-year-old consulting firm has a different future growth pattern than a well-established firm doing business for 20+ years. Compensation levels may differ significantly, capital expenditures are likely to be dissimilar, the economic characteristics of the customer base of each firm are probably different, and so forth.

Assume you are a roll-up firm and have a choice of buying one of three such consulting firms. How would you evaluate the three widely varying opportunities on a quantitative basis? The answer to this question was developed in the 1950s relative to capital budgeting in the petroleum industry. It was here that the DCF methodology was developed and first applied. For the first time, corporate management could evaluate whether it was better to invest $100 million in constructing a pipeline or $150 million in building a refinery. On the assumption that the firm had insufficient capital to undertake both at once, and the company wanted to maximize its value, it wanted to choose the one with the highest net present value. The DCF methodology provided workable answers in comparing what on the surface might be considered an "apples and oranges" comparison.

The same DCF methodology developed in the 1950s is still being used today. The only difference is that the calculations done then were manual and very tedious. Today, anyone with a PC and a spreadsheet program can run 10 different scenarios (assumptions) in less than a day. The mechanics of the income approach, using a DCF methodology, can be learned by any business graduate in a couple of days. Learning what numbers to put down on the spreadsheet, however, may take a significantly longer time to learn.

The alternative investment opportunities have different risk profiles: Buying 100 shares of Ford is not the same as buying 100 shares of General Motors, and neither is equivalent to buying shares in Microsoft or Oracle. In fact, as discussed in the market comparable approach to valuation, there are never identical investments or identical business enterprises. Each company and each investment has its own characteristics, history, and prospects. Companies have different management, resources, competitors, and outlooks.

As a consequence, while investors might disagree individually in how they evaluate Ford as compared to General Motors, and both as contrasted to Microsoft and Oracle, taken as a whole the *market* places an overall assessment on every investment opportunity. While hard to pin down precisely, nonetheless investors can judge how the market in its entirety evaluates each specific company and each specific business opportunity.

The basic generalization, with which most observers agree, is that the *higher the risk, the greater must be the potential return* to offset that risk. It is true that a diversified portfolio can minimize expected risk, but when we are valuing something, it is in terms of that specific business, *not* an overall portfolio. Evaluating risk is far from a science, and it is beyond the scope of this chapter to go into the theoretical niceties of betas, portfolio theory, diversification, and so on.

An appraiser's task is to try and determine the risk characteristics of the specific business being valued and evaluate how the market would respond to that risk profile, looking at the market's evaluation of similar (not identical, since there are no identical investments) businesses. Then, the appraiser utilizes a discount rate that hopefully reflects the market's reaction to that type of business.

Venture capital investors focus on start-up and other highly risky businesses. Maybe only one or two out of 10 firms they invest in will become winners. Going in, they look to see if it is possible that the company *could,* at least conceivably, return 25 to 50 percent return or more. Venture capital investors need those high returns because they know that the one or two winners have to pay for the eight or nine losers. Going in they do not know which will be the winner(s) and which the losers, thus requiring that every single investment at least have the potential for being a winner.

At the other end of the spectrum would be a building with a 25-year lease to an Aaa credit, say a post office leased to the U.S. Postal Service. The dollar return is fixed and the chance of nonpayment is remote. Since many investors want a high degree of certainty, are uncomfortable with risk, they are willing to accept a low return, perhaps 8 percent a year, on the post office lease.

Most investments should have their cash flow discounted at rates between 12 and 20 percent. Rates above that imply highly risky business ventures with perhaps a low probability of ultimate success. This would include, of course, start-up business ventures with no real history of actual cash flows.

It must be repeated that the choice of discount rate by an appraiser is a critical element in determining the final answer. By the same token, this is the area that requires the greatest degree of professional judgment. It will always be easy for a critic to question the appraiser's choice of discount rate. While some appraisers try and quantify this through elaborate analysis, at the end of the day the choice of discount rate is purely judgment.

As stated elsewhere, the professional opinion of an appraiser is sought only in situations in which the answer is not intuitively obvious to all observers. That different appraisers might have differing judgments and hence different answers is to be expected. Lawyers on opposite sides of a case make different arguments. Physicians disagree as to whether radiation or surgery is preferable for prostate cancer. The very essence of professional judgment, almost irrespective of what profession, is that judgment is being provided, not certainty. In the final analysis, the reader of an appraisal report has to ask himself, "Does the answer make sense?" If so, it is a good appraisal. If it does not make sense there is little alternative but to disregard the value(s) presented.

By adjusting for the timing of the future income and cash flows, as well as the risk of receiving those cash flows, one can put all the alternative investment opportunities on an equivalent basis: The essential element of a DCF approach is that it correctly distinguishes between a dollar to be received today and a dollar to be received in five years. When state lottery winners are announced as having won $10 million, although it will be paid out $500,000 a year for 20 years, this schedule is not the same as handing the winner a $10 million check today. If money can be invested at 8 percent, then only $4.9 million would have to be paid today to the winner. In other words, the lottery winner's ticket is worth only $4.9 million, not the $10 million that appears in the headline.

The DCF approach accomplishes both requirements, of adjusting for risk and adjusting for timing of cash flows. The risk adjustment is done through choice of the discount rate and the timing adjustment is accomplished by laying out the future cash flows year by year. The farther-out flows are discounted to a greater degree than the near term, effectively putting everything on an "apples-to-apples" basis.

FASB AND EXPECTED VALUE

The DCF approach described above, which forms the heart of the income approach to valuation, is ordinarily performed as shown. Recently, the Financial Accounting Standards Board (FASB), in its Concept Statement No. 7, has suggested an alternative approach.

The DCF methodology utilizes a single set of cash flows into the future, and one discount rate that attempts to adjust for all the myriad risk factors affecting any estimate of future results. The FASB argues that when dealing with the future there is uncertainty about the cash flows themselves. Sales may be better than expected or worse. Expenses may be higher or lower. Technology and competition may affect the project favorably or unfavorably. In short, there are almost an unlimited number of *possible* outcomes. Trying to capture all of these possibilities in a single projection of cash flows, and then applying a single discount rate is, the FASB feels, overly simplistic.

As an alternative, the FASB now requires analysts to set out several different possible outcomes, again in terms of prospective cash flows. They then ask that a probability be assigned to each possible outcome. For example, if you had a new start-up Internet firm, there could be a 15 percent chance of great success, 20 percent chance of moderate success, 40 percent chance of breakeven, and a 25 percent chance of failure. Of course, each of the four scenarios would be laid out in terms of prospective cash flow for the period of years being analyzed. Then, according to the FASB's approach, one would discount each of the four scenarios at a *risk-free* rate, presumably the rate at which U.S. Treasury securities (considered risk-free) are trading.

Under the old approach an appraiser would have a single estimate of cash flows, and a judgmentally derived discount rate that hopefully captures all the elements of risk. The new approach weights the probabilities of alternate outcomes and the discount rate no longer matters. However, the new approach still requires professional judgment in:

- Laying out reasonably possible alternatives
- Assigning probabilities to the potential outcomes

Does it really make any difference whether the professional judgment is involved in choosing the discount rate, or alternatively in choosing the probabilities? The FASB approach does have one advantage. By laying out alternative scenarios it makes the appraiser, and the reader of the appraisal report, think more logically about the various things that could happen in the future. With a single estimate of future events, the one thing that is virtually certain is that the projection will not come to pass exactly as specified, inasmuch as no one can foresee the future.

But there is a real question if the FASB multiple scenario/risk-free rate approach provides *better* answers. Because nobody can predict the future, and any DCF analysis deals with the future, there is bound to be error. Is it better for the error to be in the discount rate or in the probabilities of each scenario coming to pass? Theoretically, the FASB approach is probably superior, but 40 years of utilizing the standard DCF approach has bred a degree of comfort and understanding in appraisers that it will take years to overcome.

WHOSE PROJECTIONS TO USE

At this point, given that the FASB approach to valuation is far from "generally accepted," we are left with the traditional single-best-estimate of future cash flows. The question often arises, "Whose projection(s) should we use?" The alternatives, for an appraiser, are to use the client's own projections, or instead to develop her own. Which is better, from the perspective of a reader of an appraisal report?

There is no good answer to this question. Depending on the circumstances, either party (appraiser or client) can provide a superior assessment of future performance.

The *client* often has self-interest in the outcome of the valuation; as a broad generalization, therefore, one might be skeptical as to the objectivity and hence reliability of the projection. However, at least for a well-established business, the *appraiser* may not have as close knowledge of the company and the industry as the client. What the appraiser gains in objectivity may be offset by less knowledge of the industry dynamics, including competition.

In a perfect world the client would prepare the three- to five-year projection from which the cash flow would be derived and the appraiser would independently verify the underlying assumptions. The problem is that in dealing with the future which of the two parties is to say definitively that sales will grow 5 percent a year rather than 6 percent. Yet such a seemingly small difference will often have a significant impact on the final valuation. So if the client says he thinks sales will grow at 6 percent compounded and the appraiser feels more comfortable at 5 percent, more likely than not the client's choice will be utilized, assuming the client is looking for a higher value. Of course, the reverse is likely to be true when lower values are desired, say for an estate tax valuation. Then the client will argue for a low growth rate and the appraiser may feel a higher rate would be more supportable.

At the end of the day, it is the appraiser who has to sign the report, whose professional reputation is at stake. Thus, the appraiser should take final responsibility for the forecast and cash flow projections. The appraiser may well rely on the client, but ultimately cannot shrug off responsibility by saying, in effect, "Well, I don't really believe the projections but that is what the client wanted me to use." The one advantage of the FASB's approach is that by utilizing multiple forecasts and assigning probabilities to each, the reader of the report can more easily make his own judgment.

The real problem with projections and the use of the income approach to value comes with start-up firms such as Internet businesses. Promoters, entrepreneurs, management, and venture capital investors all usually have an interest in high values. In turn, the high values come from optimistic projections of future sales revenue. In practice, and this is one of the SEC's chief targets, such companies usually try to maximize the amount of reported revenues. In other words, not only are the projections optimistic, the financial reporting of historical performance takes a very aggressive position.

Appraisers have a difficult time dealing with valuations of start-up firms because of the absence of historical performance against which the projections can be tested. Assume such a situation in which there is no objective basis with which to test management's projections, and an inability of the appraiser to develop his own independent projections (e.g., a new one-product pharmaceutical firm whose product is still in Phase 3 testing). If it works as anticipated, and no competitive product appears, sales can be huge. If it flunks the Phase 3 test, the product, then the product line and/or the company, may have little value.

In such a situation the best alternative is to use the client's projections, and the appraiser then must clearly state the real risk factors. Obviously, in such an example the discount rate will be high, a reflection of the perceived risk. Nonetheless, in a situation in which there are only two possible outcomes that are mutually exclusive, (i.e., the drug is either a big success or a total failure), no discount rate can properly reflect the uncertainty of the outcome. Full disclosure is the only answer, and that has to be the appraiser's responsibility to ensure that the written report clearly lays out the circumstances.

CASH-FLOW PROJECTIONS: FIXED COSTS

Developing a good cash flow projection involves making a number of somewhat subjective judgments. As discussed above, the single most important thing is that the projections be realistic. The underlying assumptions on sales revenue have to be based on sound analysis of the market, customer reactions, and competitive conditions.

All too often, analysts forget to take into account what competitors will do in response to their actions and plans. So, for example, if Amazon developed a new business model of selling books on the Internet, it would have been reasonable to project fast-growing sales because of the benefits to customers. And, in fact, Amazon's sales did grow rapidly. The analyst at the time should also have taken into account the response of the bricks-and-mortar book retailers like Barnes & Noble. Amazon was not left to be the sole provider of books over the Internet. Competition arose, and the impact was felt in competitive pricing and perhaps a focus on sales volume rather than profits. Thus, Amazon's profits took far longer to arrive than might have been expected had there been no competition.

The second area of projections that needs careful scrutiny is in expenses. It is time to lay out King's Law. This Law states:

There are no *fixed* expenses. All expenses are *variable*.

Analysts and cost accountants refer to the phenomenon of increasing profits in the future, as sales increase and expenses remain fixed, as the hockey-stick syndrome, or alternatively as a J-shaped curve. Either way, the assumption is that while volume goes up, certain expenses will not increase at all or will increase much more slowly. This means that in a start-up situation there may be low or even nonexistent profits today, but just wait until next year and the curve will be steeply upward to the right. Examples of so-called fixed expenses include rent, the president's salary, and depreciation.

The fact is that if a company increases its sales, it will require more space and hence increased rent. If the company grows, the president will expect increased compensation. If the computers and office furniture or production equipment for the company expands, then additional capital equipment is required (e.g., a factory), which automatically increases depreciation. In short, there are no fixed expenses. Period.

The implication of this is that all too often projections prepared as the basis of an income approach to value understate future expenses. This is not to say that increased volume won't translate into better profitability. Increased volume is highly desirable. It is just that experience shows that, despite assumptions that management will hold expenses in check, SG&A expenses inexorably rise in absolute dollars. Further, they probably do not decrease over time as a percentage of sales.

If this phenomenon did not exist, then most companies should be making ever-increasing profits. After all, sales volume usually does increase in most years. The reasons why profits do not keep growing are clear. Expenses go up at approximately the same rate as do sales. Thus, profit *margins* are not necessarily significantly higher for larger firms than for smaller firms. Yet this real-world phenomenon is not necessarily utilized in many corporate forecasts. And when appraisers then use those corporate forecasts, they may be making unrealistic assumptions about future profit potential.

Some sales increases consist of larger orders by existing customers of existing products. Holding everything else constant (i.e., customer base and product base), it is perhaps reasonable to think that the accounting department, human resource department, and engineering department expenses will be fixed, and that selling and marketing expenses likewise will grow much less quickly than sales.

However, most increases in top-line sales revenue do not come from more sales of today's products to today's customers. Rather, sales increases are from new products or an additional customer base, or both. Proponents of activity-based management (ABM) start out with the basic assumption that all costs are variable and can be traced to specific products and customers.

While outside the scope of this book, interested readers are urged to go to one of the many good books on ABM. Particularly useful is *Implementing Activity-Based Management in Daily Operations.*[1] The main lesson to be learned from ABM is that if you introduce new products or sell to new customers, expenses are going to go up. It is inevitable, so get used to it.

CASH-FLOW PROJECTIONS: TERMINAL VALUE

Most business enterprises go on until they are bought out. Occasionally, of course, a company fails and goes into bankruptcy. But in the vast majority of cases, companies have what, at any one point in time, is an indefinite life.

The DCF methodology projects results into the future. How far can we look? Most appraisers are comfortable with a five-year outlook, and in many circumstances a 10-year horizon is supportable. But looking out beyond 10 years involves so many assumptions that the projected results may become unsupportable.

The solution, now accepted as standard, is to assume the business is sold at the end of the projection period. The sale price is estimated based on expected then-current operating results. The price *multiple,* to be applied to the forecast cash flow or earnings, is usually related to one of two things. Either current multiples (e.g, $7 \times$ EBITDA or $16 \times$ P/E), or projected multiples are used.

Current multiples are readily available. But *projected* multiples have to rely on the judgment of the appraiser. We have found only one reliable source of projected multiples from an outside neutral and unbiased source. This is from the *Value Line* service. Their analysts explicitly make projections of price/earnings multiples three to five years out. These multiples are available separately for each of the 1,700 companies covered by *Value Line,* as well as on a composite industry basis for most of the approximately 90 industry groupings utilized by that service.

Using the *Value Line* future multiples provides a degree of objectivity that is superior to one that may appear to be pulled out of the air by some analyst or appraiser. This is not to say that the *Value Line* estimates turn out to be correct three to five years later. But at the time they are issued, they are the best that is available.

CASH-FLOW PROJECTIONS: INCOME TAX

Another element in the income approach that an appraiser has to take into account is the income tax rate. Some companies, and some industries consistently have above average, or below average, effective tax rates. However, most appraisers do not try to anticipate changes in corporate tax rates or specific tax circumstances. Rather, they use a composite rate that reflects both federal and state income taxes, allowing for the deductibility of state taxes on the federal return.

At the present time, most appraisals use something between 38 and 40 percent, applied to pretax income. The margin of error is relatively low. Any increase in precision from a detailed examination of the components of income (tax versus book depreciation, foreign tax credits, etc.) would in turn require a tax professional to make the analysis and calculations. Just as appraisers are not environmental engineers, so also are they not tax attorneys or accountants. A flat 39 percent tax rate is good enough in almost all circumstances.

CASH-FLOW PROJECTIONS: WEIGHTED AVERAGE COST OF CAPITAL

One of the most critical elements in applying the income approach is the choice of discount rate. Many appraisers attempt to derive the discount rate from the weighted average cost of capital (WACC). This is a somewhat sophisticated topic from financial management theory and is best reviewed by readers of this book in a textbook.

Suffice it to say that the basic assumption is that there is a cost of debt, and a separate (higher) cost of equity. Debt cost is derived from comparable issues in the public market. So, for example, if a BBB-rated company's debt is currently selling at 7.5 percent, and the subject company being valued would be rated BBB, then the appraiser uses a 7.5 percent cost for the debt component of the capitalization.

The derivation of the equity component is more complex. In essence, the appraiser attempts of equate the risk characteristics of the subject company with those of other publicly traded firms. Alternatively, the analyst starts with a risk-free rate (ordinarily, the U.S. Treasury borrowing rate) and adds elements for the fact that the subject is not publicly traded, the volatility of the business (beta) relative to other firms, the size of the company, and so forth. There is a complex mathematical buildup, which is often shown in the report and provides an appearance of objectivity and precision.

Suffice it to say that when all is said and done, there is still significant professional judgment in the equity cost finally selected. The report may give an appearance of precision, but careful examination of the cost buildup will show that the appraiser or analyst at some point made some very specific choices based on professional judgment.

The final element in deriving the WACC is the assumption about the optimum or expected debt/equity ratio. The WACC is going to be lower (thus arriving at a higher value) to the extent that the calculation assumes more low-cost debt and less high-cost equity. Again, the choice of the debt/equity ratio is a matter of professional judgment.

DEALING WITH SUBCHAPTER S CORPORATIONS

At this point, a comment about Subchapter S corporations is relevant. Subchapter S corporations are effectively taxed as partnerships and do not pay corporate tax. The individual shareholders pick up a pro-rata share of the firm's earnings in their own personal tax return. The big benefit of an S corporation is the tax savings arising from elimination of the usual double-tax burden on so-called C corporations.

The question arises, in valuing an S corporation, whether it is appropriate to value the pretax cash flow, or whether a theoretical 39 percent tax rate should be applied anyhow. Appraisers differ in their approach, and there is certainly no one correct answer.

We tend to favor application of an income tax even for S corporations, because the most likely buyer of an S corporation is likely to be a C corporation that does pay tax. Thus, from the perspective of most potential buyers taxes will be a real-world cost element. It is only reasonable therefore to assume such a tax rate.

Only if the purpose of the appraisal is to value a small block of stock, one that will be reacquired by the company or another existing shareholder, is it appropriate to value the future earnings and cash flow on a pretax basis. Obviously, not applying income taxes tends to raise the present value of the business. Offsetting this, to some extent, is the fact that most S corporations are relatively small; such firms tend to have relatively high costs of capital and hence a higher discount rate.

SUMMARY AND CONCLUSION

The income approach to value is generally used as one method in valuing business enterprises, and is the only method usually applied in valuing intangible assets such as trade names and patents. Given good assumptions about future events, and an appropriate discount rate, the income approach provides very supportable answers.

However, every forecast of the future is subject to potential error. The DCF methodology is sensitive to the choice of discount rate and the assumed cash flows. Thus, readers should scrutinize the assumptions inherent in every income approach to see if they pass the basic smell test.

Assuming the assumptions are reasonable, readers who wish more should ask the appraiser to provide tests of sensitivity to the key variables. It is impossible to specify in advance just which elements are significant, a small change in which will materially affect the answer. Nonetheless, most DCF analyses do have one or more such elements and they are not difficult to identify.

ENDNOTE

1. *Implementing Activity-Based Management in Daily Operations,* John A. Miller, John Wiley & Sons: New York, 1996; and *Activity-Based Costing: Making It Work for Small and Mid-Sized Companies,* 2nd ed. Douglas T. Hicks, John Wiley & Sons: New York, 1998.

CHAPTER 7

Market Comparable Approach to Value

The basic assumption underlying the market comparable approach is that a measure of value is to see what other similar companies or comparable assets are actually selling for. In a new subdivision perhaps four houses have been resold in the last three months; each of these houses was on a one-fourth-acre lot and had four bedrooms. Each of the houses sold for between $280,000 and $290,000. Assuming the quarter-acre four-bedroom house we are trying to appraise has no unusual characteristics (e.g., better landscaping), then our house *should* sell for $285,000±. People will pay no more for a specific asset than other similar assets are currently selling for.

At this point we are not concerned about the *cost of replacement* of the house. Nor are we interested in the potential rental income that the house could generate. If the *market* says an asset is worth a certain amount, in effect prospective buyers and sellers have already encompassed this information into their bid and ask prices; in this situation the cost and income approaches may be superfluous.

In the final analysis the value of *every* asset is what someone is willing to pay for it. Every appraisal, every valuation report, is no more than an estimate of what the appraiser thinks somebody else would pay for the asset. Some people can do a better job than others in developing that estimate. But at the end of the day it takes an actual transaction—in which cash changes hands—to demonstrate conclusively what the *real value* was or is. In the absence of such a transaction an estimate of value is just that—an estimate.

To the extent that there is an active market, with numerous transactions of similar assets, one can come up with a close estimate of the price at which a transaction would or could take place. The key point in understanding the market comparable approach to valuation is that, other than for financial assets like stocks and bonds, there is rarely an *identical* asset. Assets like cars and houses are frequently very similar, but most assets are essentially unique.

IS THERE A MARKET?

In applying the market comparable method, the first step is to determine the relevant market. No matter how offbeat it may seem, there are markets for virtually every type of asset.

A commercial dispute between the buyer of a company and the former owner of the business ended up in court. The company in question sold electronic office equipment, primarily imported from the Far East. In addition to selling new machines, there was a substantial business in spare parts for repair. The seller had consistently written off to expense the purchase of spare parts. Just prior to selling the company there was a change in accounting and they "wrote up" the value of the spare parts inventory. Thus, the buyer was suddenly faced with paying $5 million more than they had anticipated, based on the previously supplied financial statements.

There were several legal issues dealing with the contract language and the surprise accounting entry. In addition, there was a real question whether the parts inventory was even worth $5 million. An appraisal company was brought in to determine the real value of the spare parts as of the date of the sale.

The point here is that there turned out to be an active market for spare parts for this category of office equipment. Old machines were being refurbished in Florida (because of low labor cost) and then sold in Latin America. Because of the wide variety of equipment from many different manufacturers, the people who performed the refurbishing had a difficult time obtaining replacement parts.

The appraisal company identified this market, contacted several participants and determined that typically dealers would pay approximately 15 percent of the list price for such parts. The selling company had valued the spare parts at 100 percent of list price. Further, many of the parts were not new, having been stripped from machines that were not repara- ble. Finally, many of the parts were for obsolete models that would never be repaired.

The appraiser determined that the fair market value (FMV) of the spare parts inventory, based on the market comparable approach, was no more than $500,000 as contrasted with the seller's estimate of $5 mil- lion. Because of the numerous accounting and contract language is- sues involved, the appraised value simply became one item in the final court decision. The point was that even for something as obscure as spare parts for electronic office equipment, there was a thriving market.

Application of the market comparable approach requires, as the first step, determination of the relevant market. For a single-family house, the market is the local residential community. For a warehouse, it may be an area within a 20-mile radius of the city. For a large shopping center or a 2,000-acre in- dustrial park, the relevant markets may be statewide or even regional.

Next, one has to understand the depth of the market. An occasional busi- ness deal is not nearly as important as frequency of transactions. When there are numerous transactions, it is far more likely that assets very simi- lar to yours will have been sold, making the comparison more reliable. In- frequent transactions are more complicated. As an example, suppose you have a 50,000-square-foot warehouse with 16-foot ceilings. The most re- cent transaction was for a 40,000-square-foot building with 18-foot ceil- ings. How important an effect on value is the 2-foot difference in height? Is the larger building worth more or less per square foot than the smaller one? Obviously, some sorts of adjustments have to be made, and the nature and magnitude of those adjustments probably requires significant profes- sional experience and judgment.

In discussing the depth of a market, auctions represent a very good ex- ample. Usually, a group of prospective buyers with similar interests are assembled and assets appealing to those buyers are put up for sale. There are two broad types of auctions. The first is when a business is being sold, perhaps in a bankruptcy liquidation. The buyers will be a combination of used equipment dealers plus end users, that is, people in the same line of business who can take the individual assets and use them directly. The fine arts auction houses, Christie's and Sotheby's, represent the other type of auction. There the auctioneer takes the responsibility both for assembling the items to be put on sale and for advertising the sale to attract the buyers.

Auction prices are an excellent source of market information. Assuming a lack of collusion among the buyers (sometimes alleged in fine art auctions), the final price realized for each lot represents a true indication of a willing buyer and a willing seller, the terms used in the standard definition of fair market value. Appraisers often utilize auction prices in application of the market comparable approach to value.

One disadvantage of auction prices is that auctioneers in recent years have instituted a buyer's premium: Simply put, a 20 percent buyer's premium is a commission added by the auctioneer to the highest price realized. So if the final bid is $1,000, the buyer actually pays $1,200, of which the seller receives $1,000 and the remainder is profit to the auctioneer. Further, auction houses usually charge the seller a commission, often of at least 10 percent. So in this example the seller would receive $900 and the buyer would pay $1,200. This represents a 25 to 33 percent difference between the bid and asked price. If an appraiser is trying to value specific assets, should he utilize the $900 or the $1,200 amount? It certainly makes a difference which is used, so which is correct?

As discussed in Chapter 3, this is the issue of premise of value. If one is determining the value of assets that will be sold, the relevant price is the $900 to be received upon sale. If one is determining the cost to acquire the assets, perhaps for a value-in-use report for financial reporting and accounting, the $1,200 is more relevant. Put this way, these concepts are clear and straightforward. It should not be a surprise for the reader to learn that these concepts are often mixed up by those not in the appraisal business. It is the same differential that exists between the price that a used car dealer will pay to acquire your car and the price asked for the same car when it is sitting on the lot, or the loss in value that occurs the day you take delivery of a new car. Dealers in all asset categories must have a profit margin, and application of the appropriate level of discount or premium is part of what a professional appraiser provides.

MAKING ADJUSTMENTS TO MARKET PRICES

"No two assets are ever identical." Other than financial assets and commodities, which are fungible, this statement is true. This is the primary weakness of the market comparable approach. No two used cars are identical, in terms of age, condition, and mileage. No two houses are truly identical. No two machine tools are identical. No two business enterprises are identical.

Therefore, in applying the market comparable approach one has to determine the ways in which the subject asset *differs* from the reported transactions. Then, as appropriate, adjustments have to be made. For this section we will look at three types of assets for which such adjustments are made, and show how an appraiser goes about performing this analysis. These will be real estate, machinery and equipment, and securities of closely held companies.

REAL ESTATE

Unlike the stock market, where millions of shares of Microsoft or Compaq are traded every single day, there are relatively few actual transactions completed in a particular local market. Appraisers have to gather facts about the actual sales of commercial and industrial property that have taken place within the last three to five years. Basically, the larger the parcel of land and building being appraised, the fewer will be the number of comparable transactions. Thus, there may be 10 sales of five-acre parcels within two years, but only two transactions within five years of 200-acre parcels.

If the assignment is to value a specific 20-acre parcel, it is difficult to draw meaningful conclusions from only two data points. What the appraiser does in that situation is to look at transactions of parcels ranging perhaps from 20 to 500 acres. The appraiser will look at the per-acre price and see whether there is a correlation with parcel size.

Another adjustment is made for the time of the sale. In a particular market area prices may be rising, slowly or quickly. However, in case of economic trouble, prices may actually be falling. So a sale that took place three years ago has to be adjusted in relation to both inflation and market direction.

Another adjustment will have to be made for zoning. To the extent that the potential use is limited by zoning restrictions, the price of any parcel of land will be affected. Thus, if there are five transactions being analyzed, the appraiser has to look at the zoning of each of the comparables and adjust accordingly.

As another example of adjustments, an appraiser looking at land sales will have to determine the effect of location on land value. The well-known popular phrase about real estate, "Location, location, location" is still valid. This is perhaps the most important yet most difficult adjustment that has to be made. How much of a premium attaches to interstate highway access? Is proximity to a railroad siding an asset (for a warehouse) or a liability (for a residential development)?

The fact is that there is no standardized approach to these issues. Every parcel of real property is different. Every real property valuation is unique. All an appraiser can do is apply standard techniques to the actual situation. Knowing what questions to ask, and where to develop the data is half of the solution. Understanding the answers and drawing meaningful conclusions is the other half. The first can be taught, the latter only learned on the job over time.

Entire textbooks have been written regarding the valuation of real estate, so in this section we can only describe what an appraiser does in utilizing the market comparable approach. Two more points should be mentioned. How do appraisers handle special purpose property? How do appraisers handle environmental problems?

SPECIAL-PURPOSE PROPERTY

An important aspect of the valuation of real property on a market comparable approach is how appraisers handle truly unique or special-purpose assets. Here the concept of "highest and best use" comes into play. The idea is that property should be valued based on whatever will maximize the value. As an example, at one point a large former hospital that was now vacant had to be valued. Because of surplus medical facilities in the area and state rulings, the one thing the building could *not* be used for was a hospital. Yet the total design, including services, insulation, layout, and so forth was designed explicitly for use as a hospital. How to value this?

In this case the appraiser had first to decide just what the building could be used for, given its layout, zoning, and so forth. Alternatives considered were a hotel, apartments, dormitory, and nursing home. Based on the location, the dormitory use appeared optimal, and the property was valued as a dormitory. The next step was to look at dormitories and college housing since the property was located in a major college community.

Because much of the original cost of the building was of no value, and even was a hindrance, the value of the subject building as a dormitory ended up as much less than if a brand new dormitory were to be built. This allowed for the needed costs of reconversion, removing operating room lights and so forth. The point of this example is that even a highly specialized property can probably be used for some other purpose, albeit with a severe cost penalty.

Let us reiterate something mentioned earlier in the book. Every appraisal is done at a point in time, for a specific client, with a specific purpose in mind. The appraisal report must specify, right up front, these points. So in the case of the hospital to be valued as a dormitory, the appraiser's report would have had the following on page 1 of the report:

> You have asked us to determine the fair market value of the land and buildings currently known as Local Hospital, as of June 1, 20xx. The purpose of the report is to determine the value of the property, assuming it cannot be utilized as a hospital, for which it was built. Rather, after inspection and research we have valued the property as a dormitory, based on what we consider to be its highest and best use.

ENVIRONMENTAL PROBLEMS

In the current era, environmental problems are a fact of life in valuing real estate. Since no two properties will ever have identical remediation problems, there will never be a comparable environmental problem. By definition, appraisers are not environmental engineers. Appraisers do not and will not estimate the cost of remediation, inasmuch as this is a highly specialized profession, requiring knowledge of applicable laws and regulations, plus the specific engineering know-how as to what can and should be done to comply with the requirements.

If visual inspection indicates that environmental problems are present, appraisers will explicitly recognize that there is a problem and obtain an estimate of the cost to cure it. Further, whenever they are valuing real property, even if not visible, appraisers will typically *ask* if there are environmental issues. The owner of any property that is for sale, or potentially for sale, will likely have had an environmental study performed by environmental engineers.

Appraisers, in valuing real property with environmental concern, will determine the FMV of the subject property *without* any problems. They will then *subtract* the cost of remediation, as determined by the environmental consultant. If the property would be worth $2 million cleaned up, but the cost of remediation is estimated at $500,000, then the FMV of the property, as is, is $1.5 million. What if the cost of remediation is *greater* than the value of the property even after it is cleaned up? A 10-acre parcel without environmental problems could be worth $200,000 but as is cost $300,000 to clean up!

The fact is that property can have *negative* value. Some people have trouble dealing with this concept. The fact remains that the cost of remediation can often exceed the value of environmentally contaminated property. It is unlikely that a willing buyer could be found who would have to pay more to clean up than the property was worth once it was cleaned up. So what really happens is that the present owner has a strong incentive to do nothing. Ordinarily, remediation would be necessary only if the property were to be sold. So with negative value, the present owner has a strong incentive to *do nothing*. By *not* selling, the cost to remediate will not be incurred.

The following is a direct quotation from an actual appraisal report and shows just how the issue of environmental liabilities is handled:

> Valuation Research Corporation is not an environmental consultant or auditor, and it takes no responsibility for any actual or potential environmental liabilities. Any person entitled to rely on this report wishing to know whether such liabilities exist, or their scope, and the effect on the value of the property is encouraged to obtain a professional environmental assessment. Valuation Research Corporation does not conduct or provide environmental assessments and has not performed one for the subject property.

In this era it should not be surprising that environmental liabilities, real or imagined, often affect the value of real property. Appraisers, however, are not expert in determining whether environmental problems exist. Neither are they able to estimate the cost to perform required or expected remediation. Nonetheless, the existence of environmental problems affects value both directly and indirectly.

The *indirect* impact of environmental problems is a lot harder to quantify. Assume prospective buyers were faced with two otherwise identical properties, one on which the asking price was $500,000 and there were no environmental problems. The other was being offered for $400,000, with a signed contract from a remediation firm to clean the parcel up for $100,000 on a flat-fee basis.

The out-of-pocket cost would be the same for the two parcels. Which would the buyer most likely choose? Simply phrasing the question this way provides its own answer. Even with remediation, a parcel of land that formerly was contaminated is going to be less desirable. Suppose additional environmental problems turn up in the future? Suppose regulations change and the degree of remediation required changes? Suppose more sensitive tests in the future show new contamination? And so forth. A parcel requiring remediation is worth less irrespective of the current estimated cost for such remediation.

How much less, and how to determine the amount, is far more difficult to answer than it is to ask the question. It would seem that at least a 10 percent penalty should be placed against the remediated parcel, simply to reflect the risks inherent in such a situation.

MACHINERY AND EQUIPMENT: DEALERS AND AUCTIONS

The market comparable method of valuation for machinery and equipment ('M&E') in some ways is easier to apply than for real estate. A certain model Cincinnati milling machine is standard whether it is located in California or Maine. Serial numbers accurately determine the age of the equipment. What cannot be determined, except by inspection, is the physical condition and maintenance history. But the rated output is going to be the same for each example of that milling machine, and so, in like condition, two different machines will essentially be interchangeable.

There are used equipment dealers for virtually every type of equipment, whether restaurant stoves or medical x-ray. Those dealers know their own market, know what is in demand, and know what users are willing to pay for used equipment, depending, of course, on condition. In setting a price, they work backward; they estimate their own costs for storage and transportation, plus profit margin, and that determines essentially what they are willing to pay to buy a specific piece of used equipment from its present owner.

Manufacturers who need additional milling machine capacity have a choice. They can go to Cincinnati Milacron and order a new machine, or they can go to a dealer and buy an in-stock used piece of equipment. Assuming reasonably transparent markets, the selling price of the used equipment is going to reflect the age, condition, and functional capacity of the old item, relative to the cost and functional utility of the new machine.

Thus, in determining the value of M&E, the first place an appraiser goes is to dealers in that type of asset. In fact, to get a feel for the market, appraisers will usually go to several dealers and compare their prices, just as a car buyer would do. In valuing M&E, one is more often valuing a complete factory rather than a single piece of equipment. Consequently, the condition of one specific asset is less important than the overall weighted average of the total complement. Obtaining current prices on a wide range of types of say metal working machines will provide reasonable results even if one specific asset is in poor condition.

Why are dealers willing to spend the time providing all this data to an appraiser? After all, in the short run the dealer will not transact a sale or purchase of additional equipment, certainly not with the appraiser. The answer is that a good dealer likes to keep his finger on the pulse of the market. Providing current prices for a wide range of equipment also lets the dealer know what assets are located where. In effect, the appraiser provides a means of contact and communication between the dealer and either prospective sellers or purchasers.

An alternative source of information on M&E is from auctions. There are auctioneers who specialize in liquidation of businesses. These specialized auctioneers will go to a specific location and sell everything on site, after having advertised the sale widely. Or, alternatively, a dealer will accumulate certain types of assets at his own location and then hold a sale. The prices realized at auction are an excellent reflection of the current market. The one difficulty in looking at a prices realized list a month later is that the appraiser does not know the specific condition of the specific asset that came up for sale. But with model and serial number, the age of the asset sold is determinable and reasonable assumptions can be made.

As mentioned in an earlier chapter, an appraisal is an opinion of value as of a specific point in time. The reason for bringing this up is that the market for used machinery and equipment is subject to all the factors that make up supply and demand. As an example, a client asked the appraisal company to value a large and very expensive piece of equipment that was going to be leased. The lessor wanted an estimate of the FMV at the end of the lease, so the first place to start was the current value for used equipment of that type.

The dealer called indicated that he would not pay anything for the asset, and in fact had a dozen of the exact type available for sale. The last thing he wanted or needed was one more! It turned out that a major automotive manufacturer had just shut down a factory and disposed of all the equipment including a dozen of these very specialized metal working machines. At that point the future FMV of the subject asset, assuming it were to come off lease, would appear to be almost zero. In fact, at that point in time the asset was almost worthless. Of course, the purpose of the appraisal was to provide comfort to the lessor as to the value five years in the future. So the appraiser could reasonably assume that within five years the present overhang on the market would have been absorbed and the leased asset would again have a decent fair market value.

Another situation was more difficult to resolve.

A dragline is a huge piece of equipment utilized in strip mining. A mineral company had leased a dragline that was just now coming off lease. The lease document called for the lessee to have the right to purchase the asset at its then current FMV. The lessor came to an appraisal company and asked it to determine the value of the asset.

The best geological estimate was that there were three to four year's worth of reserves in the ground, at which point the mining operation would have to cease. The market for the product was almost 100 percent export, and the current buyer of the mine's output was having political and economic troubles.

Nonetheless, the output was being sold and paid for; further, the output, which was a component of fertilizer, was a necessary input to the buyer.

Further complicating the situation was the fact that the dragline was so large that simple transportation to a location, and subsequent erection, was itself a multimillion dollar job. At that moment, a virtually identical drag line was disassembled and available at a dealer location, but would cost a lot to move and install in place of the leased asset.

If the lessor did not arrive at a deal to sell the asset to the current user, the cost to disassemble the dragline, and simply move it would be large. And with another virtually identical asset already on the market, the likelihood of selling it was remote.

However, without a dragline the mine would be worthless. The only economical way of scooping out the mine's contents was with a dragline. There was only one practical solution to both parties. Continue to utilize the dragline at its existing location for the next three years until the mine was empty. But what was the dragline worth?

The leasing company argued that if they took out their asset it would cost the mine several month's production, plus many millions of dollars to go out and buy the other unit for just three year's output. So the dragline had real value to the mine operator.

The mining company argued that the dragline was virtually worthless to the leasing company because there was no real demand for such an asset, inasmuch as the one already available was not selling. Further, it would cost the leasing company a lot to disassemble and remove the existing asset.

In this situation the arguments of each party made good economic sense. Should the dragline be valued on the basis of continued use? In this case it was worth quite a lot. Or should it be valued on the open market? In that case it was worth very little.

The answer the appraisal company gave was that "it all depends." Both values were provided, and it was left to the parties to negotiate. The final answer, as might be expected, was that the parties split the difference, each unhappy with the final result.

The moral of this story is that a single asset can have different values at the same time, depending on the assumptions. That is why even a market approach to valuation has to be looked at very closely. Just what is the relevant market is itself a relevant question.

We have mentioned several times that the value of an asset is a function of the purpose for which the asset will be used or for the purpose of the valuation. An insurance valuation based on cost of reproduction differs materially from the FMV, assuming the same asset will be sold to a dealer.

Even in the market comparable approach the *difference* between valuing an asset installed in place and for sale to a third party can be as high as 50 to 70 percent or more. The following cost elements are present when an asset is installed, but are lost if the asset is to be sold to a third party:

- Freight in
- Engineering design
- Erection/installation
- Testing and initial run-in
- Sales tax

If a company has bought an asset, whether new from the manufacturer or used from a dealer, the above costs often must be incurred. Yet upon deinstallation they are totally lost. Further, from the perspective of the next buyer, they have no value. Even worse, it costs money to take a machine down and make it ready for sale to a dealer or other third party.

This phenomenon is particularly true for manufacturing assets.

Our firm recently had a valuation issue involving leasing of a chemical plant. A substantial portion of the total cost was related to the design and installation of miles of piping and related chemical production assets such as pressure vessels, valves, and so forth. The cost was high, but the value was also substantial because the plant was very profitable. However, for purposes of the lessor, they wanted to know what the asset(s) would be worth at the end of the lease period if the lessee did *not* renew the lease or buy out the assets.

There were several other companies that would be interested in acquiring the plant, as is and where is. So we could determine the FMV on a going concern basis, and it fully met the lessor's requirements. However, the client's public accountants also wanted to test the lease for financial reporting. For this purpose, they insisted not on what the total plant would sell for as a business, but what the assets, *per se,* would realize if they were sold separately. As a going concern, the plant was worth $100 million. Torn down, the assets would be worth only $15 million, although this did include the estimate of disassembly expense. This is a somewhat extreme case, but nonetheless reflective of the point that even the market comparable approach has to be considered quite carefully.

A rule of thumb might be that there is at least a 25 percent and up to a 50 percent difference in value between assets in place and ready for use and what those same assets could realize in a sale—either to a dealer or at auction. Deinstallation costs, transportation to the new owner, time value of money until the dealer can resell the asset, and a profit margin all add up to a significant amount.

Typically, lenders want the bottom line liquidation amount, just in case the borrower cannot repay the funds. But the borrower usually argues that this is unfair and penalizes him. As long as the business has positive cash flow, the value in use probably is the better number. But the lender is also right in insisting on knowing the lower value, because that is what will be received if he has to look to the assets themselves as the source of repayment.

PUBLICLY TRADED SECURITIES

There are few valuation issues related to using market prices for publicly traded securities. If you are developing a personal net worth statement, and own 200 shares of AT&T, a look at today's *Wall Street Journal* gives you the closing price. Sometimes, people will utilize an average of the high and low price for the day, but more often it is the closing price. The assumption in valuation is that you could pick up the phone and have the broker sell the stock at the closing price.

There are three issues that should be discussed. Depending on the magnitude of the block of stock being valued, they may or may not be material. These are;

1. Commissions owed upon sale;
2. Bid versus asked price;
3. Blockage, related to very large transactions

A number of years ago, when stockbroker commissions were both fixed and high, it cost a substantial amount of money to sell even New York Stock Exchange (NYSE) securities, much less NASDAQ or over-the-counter stocks. In the era of Internet brokers this no longer is a real valuation issue. For fees ranging between $5.00 and $30.00, one can sell at least 1,000 shares of any stock. In fact, some observers have commented that individuals actually pay less commission than do large institutional investors. (Offsetting this may be the availability of very profitable initial public offerings [IPOs] to those same institutional investors, IPOs that are not usually available to individuals.) Essentially, we can disregard commissions in valuing publicly traded securities.

At any one point in time there will be a bid price and an asked price for every traded security. The size of this spread, as it is called, is a function of the volume of transactions. Actively traded securities, with numerous brokers as well as buyers and sellers, have very low spreads, often as little as five cents or less. With decimalization this has dropped to literally pennies per share.

However, for less popular stocks the difference between the bid and asked price can be as much as $1.00 per share. So if a stock closed at $8.00, the bid might be as low as $7.00. But only the last transaction price is listed in the newspaper, so there could be a 15 percent diminution in value if one tried to sell the portfolio. In valuing a portfolio, therefore, which implies what the assets could be sold for, it could be important to utilize only bid prices, which could be lower than what shows in the newspaper. Current bid and asked prices are available on the Internet from most of the brokers. Obtaining specific bid *and* asked prices for an earlier date is very difficult, but probably not necessary very often. Spreads, per share, do not vary much; utilizing today's spread against quoted transactions shown in a past issue of the newspaper should be sufficient for most purposes.

Finally, we come to the issue of blockage. The theory is straightforward. If you are buying or selling 100 shares of AT&T, Compaq, or Microsoft, you are not going to affect the market at all, since literally millions of shares of each company trade every day. Even a purchase or sale of 10,000 shares is unlikely to change significantly the then current bid and asked prices.

For every company traded there is a point at which a prospective purchase or sale is going to move the market. Mutual funds and other institutional investors find this phenomenon particularly troubling. The manager of Magellan Fund, with perhaps $100 billion under management, is required to have a very large investment in each portfolio stock if there is going to be any impact on overall results. If 1 percent of the fund ($1 billion) moves up 10 percent, the total return of the entire portfolio goes up by only .001.

A $1 billion investment in AT&T for example might involve 50 million shares just to reach the $1 billion level. Now imagine going to a dealer or market maker and say, "I'd like to place an order to buy 50 million shares of AT&T." If 2 million shares change hands on an average day, it is going to take at least a month to accumulate the 40 million shares. Alternatively, if the portfolio manager wants the total position filled more quickly, other dealers and investors, seeing what is happening, are going to raise their asked price. Even if there are no fundamental changes at AT&T, the imbalance of demand over short-term supply is going to raise the price. Even for actively traded securities, a large buy or sell order can move the stock 5 percent or more. Then when the time comes for the 50 million shares to be sold, the process reverses. This time the portfolio manager will have to settle for 5 percent less than the previous market.

For low-volume stocks, the phenomenon is identical; it just takes fewer shares to move the market. Thus, getting back to the original point, if one is valuing a substantial block of stock in a publicly traded firm with low average daily volume, it is appropriate to apply a discount for the existence of the blockage factor.

The same thing holds true when a buyout firm is trying to acquire control of a target company. Buyers have to pay a premium for control.

CONTROL PREMIUM

The concept of paying a premium to obtain control of a business enterprise seems straightforward. The reverse of this, the concept that a minority interest in a business enterprise that someone else controls should be valued at a *discount,* seems equally straightforward. Yet application of these concepts often causes confusion.

Let us start with the control premium. It is a familiar story. Company X offers to buy the stock of publicly traded Company Y in a tender offer. This means that Y's shareholders are offered the opportunity to sell their stock at the price offered by X. Such tender offers are open for a limited time frame, and are usually contingent on the X receiving a certain minimum number of shares, usually at least 50 percent of the outstanding stock. This ensures that the shares tendered by Y shareholders, if accepted by X, will provide X control over company Y.

Almost invariably, X has to offer a *premium* over the market price on the day before the tender offer is announced. This assumes lack of a leak prior to the tender offer when so-called insiders may have illegally bought the stock or tipped off their friends. Needless to say, the Securities and Exchange Commission (SEC) frowns on this. So, assuming a fair and open market, why would Company X have to offer more than the market price?

There are certain advantages to controlling another business. You can install yourself or your colleagues as management. This permits you to pay compensation and other perquisites commensurate with your value to the company. If you control a company through its board of directors, you can set its investment policy, determine dividend levels, determine financing strategy, and, in general, run the company. Given the universal feeling among corporate management that bigger is better, doubling the size of your own company through an acquisition of another firm is often very attractive.

Getting back to the tender offer and the required premium, what happens if Company X offers to buy Company Y's shares at yesterday's closing price? Perhaps 5 percent of the shareholders may offer their shares, but essentially there is no incentive for Y's shareholders to do anything. Any of them who had wanted to divest could have done it easily *without* the tender offer. And, presumably, the rest of the shareholders were satisfied with their ownership position.

Further, if Company X makes the tender offer, it has to go into debt and borrow money to acquire the shares. Now suppose there is a tender offer with little or no premium. Company X soon will have accumulated perhaps 5 or 10 percent of Company Y. What will Y's management do? Probably fight back. What can X do with 10 percent of Y's stock? It does not provide control; X can not vote Y's management out of office and take over the company. In fact, what X owns is an expensive block of stock in a company with hostile management.

If you are going to attempt a takeover through a tender offer, you *must* obtain that magic 50.1 percent shareholding that provides true control. There is only one practical way of convincing existing shareholders to sell their stock. Because Y's shareholders will perhaps have to pay an unexpected capital gain tax, and they will certainly lose the benefit of future appreciation in Y, some incentive must be provided. That incentive is the *premium* over yesterday's closing price quoted in today's *Wall Street Journal.*

With a sufficient premium, existing shareholders in Y will be motivated to tender their shares, pay any capital gain tax, and forgo future potential from their existing commitment to Y. Absent a premium if you are a Y shareholder, why do anything?

If the premium offered is sufficient to acquire the 50+ percent control of Y, then from X's perspective that premium has to be considered the value of obtaining control over Y. The bottom line is that *all* of Y is worth more than the sum of the individual shares.

VALUING A MINORITY INTEREST IN A CLOSELY HELD COMPANY

While the NYSE and NASDAQ are very efficient markets on a day-to-day basis, it is often forgotten that the share prices quoted each day do *not* represent control of the individual firms. Rather, the daily prices represent a *minority* price. To obtain majority control of any company requires paying a *premium,* and that is what happens in a tender offer.

Statistics on mergers and acquisitions (M&A) have been kept for a number of years. One figure that is regularly captured is the premium offered by the buyer of a publicly traded target. These statistics on premiums offered are available by industry by year. While there is tremendous variation, ranging from nominal to 70 percent or more, typically tender offers involve a premium of 30 to 40 percent. If this average holds true, and let us call it for the sake of simplicity 35 percent, this means that buyers have to pay 35 percent more than the then market price to obtain control.

Put a different way, the market tells us that *control* of another company is worth *35± percent.*

Now let us look at a *minority discount.* The concept of a discount for lack of control, or a minority holding, is used in practice in valuing closely held businesses. If we have the value of 100 percent of a business enterprise, which implies control of that business, then a minority interest in that business should be worth somewhat *less* than a *pro rata* share of the total.

For a closely held (nonpublicly traded) company, say a local family-owned trucking company, would you, as a nonfamily member, like to be a 5 percent owner? You would not control the business policy. You would not control management salaries or dividends. You would have no say over capital expenditures, or even potential acquisitions, much less sale of the business itself. You would receive only any dividends that the board of directors chose to declare. If the earnings were in practice paid out to family members on the payroll, so there was little net income reported, what could you as a 5 percent owner do? In practice, not much!

The fact is that the economic position of a minority owner in a private business enterprise is not a strong one. One can read about corporate democracy and the rights of all stakeholders (including shareholders). In practice, the corporate world follows the Golden Rule: "He who has the gold makes the rules!" He who has control runs the company for his benefit, not yours.

Given these economic facts of life, let us see how an appraiser goes about valuing a minority interest in a closely held business, using the market comparable approach to valuation.

Step one is to identify other publicly traded firms in the same industry as the subject company. There are databases that sort all publicly traded firms by industry, and it is a matter of inputting the right code and quickly the appraiser receives a list, often quite a long one. This list is then scrutinized to determine the half dozen or so firms that are most closely related to the private firm being valued.

The appraiser looks at characteristics such as size, market, distribution channel, asset characteristics, and so forth. A final selection is made and certain operating performance indicators are calculated. These would often include return on sales; return on assets; debt/equity ratio; sales, general and administrative (SG&A) expenses; gross margin; growth rates; capital expenditures; and so forth.

These performance indicators are related to the current price of the publicly traded security. Average performance indicators are developed for the half dozen publicly traded comparable firms. These performance indicators are then applied to the subject company. So, for example, the following was developed for valuation of a service business:

Valuation to sales	0.5×
Valuation to earnings before interest, tax, depreciation, and amortization (EBITDA)	4.7×
Valuation to EBIT	5.6×
Valuation to assets	1.5×
Valuation to equity	4.1×

These multiples are applied to the subject company's results, and a separate value indication is derived from each. It is then up to the appraiser to correlate the answers, utilizing experience and professional judgment. So, for the sake of example, 0.5× sales might provide a value indication of $5 million, while 4.1× equity would provide a value indication of $6 million, and 4.7× EBITDA would suggest a valuation of $5.75 million. While averaging the preliminary value indications may appear reasonable, often more weight is given to sales, asset base, or earning power.

In this example, assume that the appraiser determines the value of the subject company, based on the information from publicly traded firms, to be $5.5 million. With 500,000 shares outstanding, this equals $11.00 per share on a minority basis. In other words, the business enterprise value might be some 35 percent *higher* if someone were to offer to buy the entire firm.

The concept of the minority discount, for lack of control, is often applied directly to values derived from the Income Approach. Recall that the income approach, utilizing a discounted cash flow analysis, looks at the total income of the enterprise, and hence the value derived is that of the enterprise as a whole.

If one is interested in the *per share* amount, then one has to apply the appropriate discount, simplified here as 35 percent. In practice, the application of a specific minority discount is ultimately a matter of professional judgment, related to the specific circumstances of the subject firm.

MARKETABILITY DISCOUNT

In valuing privately held businesses using the market comparable approach, many people lose sight of an important factor. In the example above, the so-called performance indicators derived from the publicly held firms were just that—publicly held. Now if the owner of a minority interest wants to sell, one way to accomplish this is for the company as a whole to go public, that is, have an initial public offering (IPO).

As indicated, it is often hard to sell shares in a privately held company, or even find a buyer for the firm as a whole. Having an IPO is always an alternative, at least for firms of a certain size. But having an IPO is not a cost-free alternative.

There have been studies on the cost of going public, and to a certain extent it is a function of how one defines *cost*. However the significant cost elements, each of which must be incurred before going public, include legal and accounting fees, printing, underwriting expense and fees, and filing fees with SEC. On top of all this, although perhaps hard to measure, is the management time that must be committed to the entire IPO process. This can easily take six to nine months or more, and then the final stock offering is totally dependent on the underwriter's perception of the market.

By and large, underwriters do not like to incur risk. They do not want one of their offerings to fail. So, in a down market, they will make the prospective seller wait. Unfortunately, too long a wait then makes all the legal and accounting information laid out in the prospectus out of date. The company may have to go through the exercise a second time.

Thus, in looking at the cost of selling a company or the discount to be applied for lack of marketability, the appraiser will take into consideration all the out-of-pocket costs, the management time, and finally the time value of money. You can sell 100 shares of ExxonMobil in one minute. You may have to incur 15 percent costs and wait a year to sell a trucking company.

CORRELATING THE ANSWERS

As can be seen from the discussions in this and the previous two chapters, there are several different ways of arriving at the value of an asset, whether it be a business enterprise, a trademark, or a piece of machinery. Theoretically, at least, one would hope that the different approaches to value might arrive at very similar answers. And they usually do arrive at similar values, but not identical answers. So, if an appraiser has been able to apply all three approaches to value, she will likely be looking at three different numbers. If one of them is way out of line with the other two, this is an indication to review the work and revisit the assumptions. But assume that they are all within 15 percent of each other.

Clients usually want fairly precise answers, not a range. It is incumbent on the appraiser to arrive at a single answer by applying judgment as to how to weight the preliminary value indications from the three different approaches. While it may appear repetitive, the only answer we can give is that this is the kind of judgment that an appraiser makes and for which she gets paid.

Because of this requirement to correlate answers from separate analyses, it is always possible that if two *different* appraisers are given the same assignment, that they will come up with somewhat different answers. In our experience, most appraisers believe that if they are within ±10 percent of another appraiser, that there may be little basis for choosing one over another.

The author was involved in a lawsuit between two partners. The court had ordered the partnership dissolved. Each side hired its own appraiser, and the hope was that if the answers were, as one might have expected, within 10 percent of each other, that the parties would use that as the basis for one to buy out the other.

The business had been bought three years earlier for some $6 million, in an arm's-length transaction from a knowledgeable and sophisticated seller. The business had lost money for each of the subsequent three years. It was still operating in the red, and the partner running the business had had to personally guarantee loans to meet the payroll. The other partner wanted no part of further investment, and simply wanted out, albeit at a price his partner would not agree to, hence the court trial.

Each side presented its expert appraiser. One side argued that the business was now worth $21 million. The other said it could be anywhere between zero and $1.5 million. The judge ruled that the value was $1 million.

How can you explain an expert's report at $21 million, when the business had been purchased for $6 million and had consistently lost money since then? Here the two experts were in disagreement, not by 10 percent but by 2,000 percent. The judge, recognizing that the one side was simply reaching, in the hope that the difference would be split, came down on the side of economic reality.

Because no appraisal is likely to be more accurate than ±10 percent, this sometimes allows clients to encourage the appraiser to go to one end of the range or the other. It must be admitted that, within the range specified, some appraisers do go to the upper or lower limit. But if as an appraiser you try to "push the envelope" and you lose (e.g., claim the business is worth $21 million), the entire valuation becomes suspect.

Many appraisals are challenged, either by an adverse party or in court or by the tax authorities. In the final analysis, only if an appraisal report will stand up in court should it be relied upon. Clients who push their appraiser too hard risk losing everything.

CONCLUSION

In Chapters 5, 6, and 7, we have demonstrated how appraisers actually go about doing their work. Whenever possible, appraisers are supposed to use all three approaches to value. When they cannot, the requirements are that they state why they did not use one or more of the approaches.

Sometimes, prospective clients ask appraisers which is the best method. If there is a good market for the asset(s) in question, most appraisers would respond that the market comparable method is the most supportable. However, as discussed above, the degree of comparability among seemingly similar assets is often illusory upon close examination.

The cost approach is very supportable, to the extent that there have not been significant technological or economic changes in the market, and that one can fairly evaluate the physical condition of the subject asset(s). The downside is that a reasonable investor might not, in fact, invest today in those assets, thus making the cost approach somewhat artificial.

Finally, the income approach represents effectively the thought process of investors. It suffers from the great disadvantage of requiring estimates of future events. Everyone knows that predicting the future is fraught with error, and the answers from the income approach are no better than the underlying assumptions.

Having laid out the strengths and weaknesses, we can summarize by saying that an appraisal is an expression of opinion. If you trust the appraiser, you can rely on the answer. If you do not trust the appraiser, get a different answer. It might not be as supportable, but in the short run it might make you, the client, happier.

CHAPTER 8

Can Value Information Be Objective and Independent?

Many an executive, lawyer, and accountant have said something to the effect: "You can get any answer you want from an appraiser." While this is a canard on the basic integrity of appraisers and the appraisal process, one hears it so frequently that there may be an element of truth to it. The purpose of this chapter is not to defend the integrity or accuracy of all appraisers and all appraisal reports. But in more than 30 years, the author has seldom come in contact with the type of results implied by the quote.

Valuation is not an exact science. We and other appraisers tell clients that if two independent appraisers are given the same identical assignment, with similar assumptions (e.g., the business is valued as a going concern or the business is valued in liquidation), then the two reports *should* be within 10 percent of each other. While it is rare for a client to hire two appraisers for the same assignment, it does happen, and more often than not the two answers are fully comparable.

The reason is that the appraisal process is straightforward, and if two people independently follow the same approach, one would expect the final results to be similar.

Where there can be vast disparities is in lawsuits in which the two parties are already fighting each other. Each side instructs the appraiser, either directly or more subtly by winks and nods, that the higher (lower) the answer, the better.

Invariably when this happens, particularly in a lawsuit, the vast differences between the appraisal reports can be traced directly to the *assumptions* inherent in any appraisal.

The author was retained by a major law firm on behalf of a client who was involved in splitting up a partnership. The major asset was a newspaper that the parties had acquired for $6 million (numbers somewhat disguised). The newspaper had lost money for three straight years and the one partner did not want to put in any more funds, while the other partner was running the paper.

The two parties ended up in court, and the judge said that he would determine the value of the newspaper, giving each side the opportunity to hire an expert who would prepare a report. Two reports were given to the judge, followed by oral testimony and cross-examination, which took place in court in front of the judge.

One party, who wanted to be bought out at a high price, hired an appraiser who stated with a straight face that the newspaper was now worth $21 million. This represented a threefold increase in value in three years, during which time the property had suffered substantial operating losses.

The basis of the argument was essentially that the partner managing the property had in fact mismanaged it; second, that newsprint prices for the foreseeable future would be very low; and third, that other newspapers with comparable circulation were selling at multiples of revenue and readership that might justify the $21 million.

The other side looked at the projected cash flows, which at best were going to be breakeven, assuming newsprint prices remained at current levels. Second, the purchase price three years earlier had been totally at arm's length from a newspaper chain that itself could not run the paper at a profit. Finally, there was a question whether cash could be made available even to meet the payroll.

The conclusion of value of this second appraisal was between zero and ±$1.5 million. The judge was faced with two reports on the same property, one at essentially $1 million and the other at $21 million!

Frankly, in circumstances like this one, it is no wonder that judges and others can say to themselves that appraisers cannot be trusted and that you can obtain any answer you want.

But let's look at the two appraisals a little more closely. How reasonable is it to say that a paper bought at arm's length three years ago, from a knowledgeable and willing seller—in this case, a chain of newspapers— could *appreciate* in value while losing money steadily? Frankly, it was so unreasonable that the judge found for the plaintiff and valued the paper at $1 million.

Note that he did not split the difference between the two values. This is, in fact, one cause of such disparate valuations. The feeling is that if a judge or arbitrator is going to split the difference, then the higher (lower) your figure is, the more likely the final decision will be palatable. If your figure is reasonable and the other side's is not, and the decision ends up in the middle, then with hindsight you should have stretched as far as you could.

However, if both parties believe that the decision will be objective and based on the soundness of the assumptions, the realism with which the valuation was developed, then one would not expect to find such wide disparities as often occur. In such a situation the best solution would be for both parties to hire one appraiser, agree to split the fee, and ask him to do his best. This approach also has worked well; the ultimate test of this is when both parties think the appraiser's answer is wrong and both are mad. If both sides are unhappy, this means that the correct value was probably found.

PROFESSIONAL STANDARDS

The title of this chapter is framed as a question: "Can value information be objective and independent?" At this point we will answer the question directly and then elaborate.

Not only *can* valuation information be objective, independent, and accurate, but all appraisers who belong to the American Society of Appraisers ('ASA'), or whose organization belongs to the ASA *must* follow professional standards. These standards are referred to as '*USPAP*,' which stands for the Uniform Standards of Professional Appraisal Practice.

We do not need to go into detail regarding USPAP, because the book contains some 100 or more pages of detailed requirements. The real pressure behind adoption of USPAP came from the savings and loan crisis of the late 1980s; banks and savings and loan (S&L) organizations lent way too much on a number of properties. Their excuse, when the loans failed, was that they relied on appraisals. It turned out that, just as one example, five men would get together in someone's home. They would buy and then sell the same parcel three or four times at ever-increasing prices. Each sale would be recorded as a transaction in the county courthouse.

Conspirator 1 would thus buy a five-acre parcel for $50,000. He, in turn, would sell it to conspirator 2 for $80,000. A week later, conspirator 3 would go to the courthouse and report he had purchased the parcel for $100,000. Buyer 4 would find the parcel so attractive that he paid $125,000 within days. Finally, investor 5 would go to a bank and say he wanted to finance purchase of the parcel at $150,000 and needed a $120,000 loan, which represented an 80 percent loan-to-value. An 80 percent loan-to-value mortgage on empty acreage in a good location might be a reasonable amount for a bank or S&L to lend. However, to satisfy regulatory requirements, the S&L needed an appraisal in its file justifying the $150,000 value, because the purchase price, by itself, was insufficient proof that the land was worth that much.

In those days the appraiser would go and look at the land, and then report that the land was worth $150,000, because there had recently been a series of transactions showing great appreciation (from $50,000 to $125,000) and the latest transaction at $150,000 seemed reasonable. So the appraiser would sign a report stating that the fair market value (FMV) of the land was $150,000, the borrower would get his $120,000 mortgage, and pay off the original $50,000 real arm's-length purchase price, which was the only place cash had actually changed hands. All the other transactions, of course, had been only on paper.

Not too surprisingly, the loan was not paid off, and the bank took back the parcel to sell it and was disappointed to receive no more than $50,000, the amount of the first and only real transaction. The bank then had to report a $70,000 loss. The bank or S&L then told the regulators, and shareholders for that matter, "We relied on the appraisal!" Multiply this scenario by thousands of transactions, many for much larger amounts, and it is easy to see how the S&L crisis cost hundreds of billions of dollars.

What was wrong with this picture? Where did the appraiser go wrong? In many instances there may have been collusion between the appraiser and the participants in the scheme. There are no rules of ethical behavior that can preclude fraud.

But, more commonly, the appraiser would assert that he had "checked recent transactions" and that the latest $150,000 price was "in line with" trends in the market. The fact that the trends themselves were phony was asserted to be irrelevant. The appraisers' defense at the time essentially was that they were following generally accepted appraisal procedures, which called for checking prior transactions. Obviously, this was not enough. Something had to change.

What changed was that, according to a revised version of USPAP, appraisers now not only had to check recent transactions, but if the date(s) of the transaction were recent, further investigation was required. One more loophole was closed in this instance. In fact, the USPAP requirements were greatly modified to close out any number of such loopholes.

Provision is made for certain USPAP requirements to be waived, but if the appraiser chooses to do so he must so disclose in the body of the appraisal text. As a result, any appraisal report developed in accordance with USPAP should be reliable or must disclose any and all deviations.

The lesson here is that in case of question the reader of the report should inquire whether the report was prepared in accordance with USPAP. If so, one can be confident that at least minimum standards of professional competence were observed.

DIFFERENCES IN APPRAISAL REPORTS BETWEEN APPRAISERS

If all appraisers follow the guidelines set forth in USPAP, then how can appraisal reports still have such wide spreads in value? The truth is that every client who orders an appraisal knows in advance what answer he is looking for. He *wants* a certain result. In over 30 years, we have rarely met a prospective client who says, "I would just like to know what this asset is worth."

There is *always* a purpose for which an appraisal is required. So if one party is buying, and the other selling (as when a partnership is split up relying on a "buy/sell" agreement), one side wants a high number and the other a low number. A totally neutral observer, paid by a court or by agreement between both parties, *can* arrive at a neutral and fully supportable answer, one that may please neither party but can truly be described as fair market value. But this situation, in which the parties agree in advance to be bound by a third party, is rare.

Far more frequent is the situation in which the parties are negotiating with each other and each is looking for support for his position. This is true in tax controversies, financial reporting (company versus the SEC), financing (borrower versus lender), and any time property is to change hands.

When parties are looking for support for their own self-interested position, it is natural to think of the appraiser as comparable to an attorney, one who acts as an advocate. Further, in case of a dispute in which each side hires its own appraiser, each appraiser is being paid by his client. It is natural to support your client's position, to hope that his position prevails and therefore to do everything possible to make this happen.

In short, can an appraiser really be "objective"? Can an appraiser really be "independent"?

In case of a lawsuit, or even a dispute that has not reached that level of disagreement, it is possible for any competent appraiser to be objective, albeit very difficult to remain truly independent.

OBJECTIVITY

Can an appraiser be objective and at the same time be responsive to his client's needs? Objectivity, in this case, involves making realistic and supportable assumptions. As discussed elsewhere, most appraisal reports ultimately are based on evaluations of future business and economic conditions. Thus, when two appraisers arrive at vastly different conclusions, invariably it turns out they are assuming quite different future outcomes.

Now nobody can foretell the future with certainty. There always is a degree of uncertainty when looking forward. We are essentially dealing with probabilities. There is a high degree of probability that the sun will rise in the east tomorrow morning. The probability that a promising new product, currently only in research and development (R&D), will capture a 50 percent market share is very much lower.

For example, a realistic assessment of the probabilities of the new product being a commercial success can be seen in Exhibit 8.1.

The company wants to demonstrate that the product, even though it is still in the R&D stage, has significant value. The objective could perhaps be for financing purposes or to make the financial statements look better for an initial public offering (IPO). Appraiser 1, working for the company, might look at the above schedule and conclude that with a 20 percent possibility of complete success the product should be valued at the full $5 mil-

Exhibit 8.1   Valuing R&D Through Probability Analysis

Probability	Market Share	Value
40%	None	None
20%	5%	$ 500,000
20%	15%	$1,500,000
20%	50%	$5,000,000

lion. Perhaps there would be a comment within the narrative report to the effect that there was some uncertainty regarding the commercial success.

Appraiser 2, coming in for the lending institution, would look at the same fact situation and say, "Let's be conservative and value the product at zero, inasmuch as the single highest probability (40 percent) is for the product to be a failure.

Now at this point you could have two appraisal reports, each of which is "objective," but one is at zero and the other at $5 million. Just to make it more complicated still, one could weight the probabilities by the expected value and arrive at a $1.4 million figure.

All we are trying to show is how by changing the *assumptions,* in this case the assumed probability of success, the answer can change dramatically. Note it is not the case that one answer is right and the other two wrong. It depends on the assumptions and the reasonableness thereof.

To sum up this section on objectivity, appraisers and appraisal reports can have the appearance of objectivity, and in fact be objective, yet have widely differing answers.

RESOLVING DIFFERENCES

As we indicated, the primary cause of differences between or among appraisal reports is the use of different assumptions. A reader of an appraisal report is entitled to ask for the sensitivity of the key assumptions. For example, if the appraiser has chosen to discount future cash flows at 15 percent, the report should at a minimum indicate why that rate was chosen. Ideally, the report should also indicate the amount by which the answer would change if a higher or lower discount rate were utilized.

Similarly, if future sales projections are the key value driver, then the appraisal report must indicate why the selected growth rate was utilized. Again, ideally at least, the impact of slower or faster growth rates in sales could be disclosed.

In many appraisals there are dozens of assumptions regarding future sales, cost of sales, expenses, interest rates, and tax rates, not to mention working capital requirements and capital expenditure requirements. It is entirely possible that literally hundreds of alternative solutions could be prepared, utilizing most of the possible permutations and combinations. Nobody can cope with 100 alternate projections and no appraiser would include these in his report.

It is the appraiser's responsibility to make the choices of assumptions he thinks are most reasonable, and describe why he made the choices he did. Then he *should,* although this is not always done in practice, indicate how much the answer as to value would change if the top two or three key variables fluctuated by some amount or percentage.

Sometimes, financial analysts will prepare three different scenarios and label them *optimistic, conservative,* and *most likely.* It is not uncommon to find out three years later that the so-called conservative projection actually was overly optimistic. Nonetheless, providing three alternates is useful.

Appraisers are trained to provide a single-point estimate of value or sometimes a narrow range of values, for example, "In our professional opinion the fair market value of the parcel of real estate is fairly stated at $950 to $975,000." Even when a range is given, it is almost always a narrow range.

But there is nothing in appraisal rules or experience that precludes the appraiser from describing in the report the effect of changing the important assumptions by certain amounts or percentages. Almost always, if the appraiser calculates the impact of changes in assumptions, only a few of the assumptions change the resultant value by a significant amount. These few key assumptions and their sensitivity can and should be disclosed.

Now, if two different appraisers are valuing the same asset, although they are working for different clients, the two reports still will differ in terms of the final value shown. But each of the reports should find that the same few variables are important and disclose that if assumptions regarding those variables were changed, the answer would also change.

As we said initially, nobody can foretell the future. So if two different appraisers have different answers and have clearly written their reports, it should be relatively easy for a third-party reader of the two reports to come to a conclusion as to which of the two sets of assumptions is more realistic. The skill and persuasion with which the report(s) are written will ultimately persuade the reader who is more likely correct.

INDEPENDENCE

Under the requirements of USPAP, appraisers must be independent of their client and of the property being appraised. For example, an appraiser cannot hold a financial interest in an apartment building, and then prepare a report stating that in his opinion the value of the building is $750,000. A bank lending officer could not trust the report if he knew that the appraiser's own financial interest was involved.

If the appraiser had the interest and did not disclose it, that would be equally serious, if not more so. It is true that in the 1970s and 1980s, during what is now referred to as the savings and loan crisis, many appraisers were in fact in collusion with the principals of some of the real estate transactions. When this came out, as it inevitably did, public opinion rightly believed that such behavior was wrong and should be prevented. Hence, the ethical standards enunciated in USPAP simply preclude any such investment.

One valuation firm's standard report states:

> In accordance with recognized professional ethics, the professional fee for this service is not contingent upon our conclusion of value, and neither Valuation Research Corporation nor any of its employees have a present or intended material financial interest in the subject company appraised.

The term *material financial interest* is used to suggest that if one of the firm's employees happens to own 100 shares of a large multinational publicly traded firm that such an ownership interest does not compromise independence.

The other aspect of the disclaimer, which is standard throughout the appraisal profession, deals with contingent compensation. Why can't appraisers earn a success fee, the way investment bankers do? If a company is paying $1 million property tax because the local assessor says the property is worth $75 million, shouldn't the appraiser be rewarded if he can persuade the assessor the actual value is only $50 million and the property tax would be reduced by one third? Lawyers take on all sorts of cases on a contingency basis, as do those who help companies find financing.

What is the difference between valuation and these other professions? Why can't appraisers work for a contingency fee?

The answer gets back to the *objectivity* discussed above. Can one be truly objective if the outcome (i.e., the believability of the appraisal report) determines whether the appraiser gets paid or not? We said that there is always judgment necessary in any valuation, judgment representing the best professional estimate of future occurrences. Nonetheless, that judgment is supposed to be objective, not slanted in advance to accomplish a specific purpose.

If, in practice, an appraiser really was being paid either a percentage of the value determined by some third party (e.g., the dollar amount of a mortgage) or paid totally on successful completion of a deal (e.g., final sale of a parcel of real estate above some agreed minimum), the other party would have no reason to believe the appraisal. In effect, if an appraiser and the appraisal report are supposed to be professional, then the integrity of the process will be totally compromised by contingency payments.

Compare for a minute a sales representative for Merrill Lynch with an appraiser. If you receive a call from your broker who says, "Buy ZYX at $40, it's going to $60," you know this is not an appraisal, but a sales pitch. However, assume an appraiser tells his client, for tax purposes, that a block of stock in the client's firm is worth $5.00 per share. Neither the share nor the underlying company is publicly traded, and the client relies on the appraisal report in filling out his tax return. How could the Internal Revenue Service (IRS) agent believe the appraisal if the agent knew the appraiser would get paid only if the agent accepted the valuation?

In the final analysis, an appraiser must command credibility. It appears incompatible to have the value of an asset, set forth in an appraisal report, be a function of the salesmanship of the appraiser. We do not mind if a car salesperson earns a commission only if the car is sold; we can discount whatever self-serving statements he makes about the car and the deal he is offering. But if an appraisal report is supposed to be objective, the appraisal profession and the Uniform Standards of Professional Appraisal Practice have agreed that fees for service should be based solely on time spent on the valuation. Contingent payments or payments based on a percentage of value are strictly prohibited.

LITIGATION

Litigation involving valuations is relatively limited and usually involves one of three types of issues:

1. Tax controversies involving securities, for estate and gift taxes
2. Property taxes
3. Business disputes, including bankruptcy and corporate dissolutions

It is outside the scope of this book to try and provide detailed guidance regarding valuations of securities for gift and estate taxes. Suffice it to say that, generally speaking, taxpayers look for low values, resulting in lower taxes. The IRS is invariably on the other side, typically arguing that values should be higher, inasmuch as this will bring in more revenue.

Thus, when the owner of a closely held business dies and estate tax is due (or before death with gift of the shares to relatives), the valuation dispute revolves around the issue of how much the total business is worth. Appraisers will first value the business in accordance with generally accepted valuation principles. Then there will be a further dispute as to whether the specific block of shares being valued is a minority block that does not have control. If so, a discount is appropriate, at least as compared to a majority interest with control.

The parties will also argue as to how much of a discount should be applied because the business is not publicly traded. With three variables involved (the business enterprise value itself, the minority discount, and the marketability discount), it is easy to see that there is a lot of room for dispute.

With estate taxes at or above a 50 percent rate, relatively small differences in value can have a large impact on the amount of tax due. No wonder these disputes between the taxpayer and the IRS sometimes end up in court. As a generalization, the courts often tend to split the difference between the IRS position and the taxpayer position. However, the better the appraisal submitted by the taxpayer, and the more support provided, the more likely the court is to find for the taxpayer. Thus, the recommendation is that if a tax dispute is contested and an appraisal report is required, then the taxpayer should insist on a realistic appraisal, one that he thinks is truly correct.

Coming in with a much lower value, even though theoretically such an amount can be supported by assumptions that *could* happen, is probably not a good idea. The hope is that the court will split the difference and by having an extreme value the final answer arrived at by the judge will be nearer the desired result. However, our experience suggests if an objective and realistic valuation is presented the first time, the IRS is more than likely to accept the answer.

The truth is that in most tax disputes there are a number of open issues and the parties ultimately settle on the basis of overall equity. This means that the IRS may settle valuation issues if the appraisal report is very strong, simply because they realize that if the whole matter goes to trial, they could lose on that specific open item.

In short, realistic valuations are preferable in tax disputes, as compared to extreme positions with a hope that a compromise will be reached. Better to have the correct answer the first time, and then insist that the valuation matter be resolved on the strength of the underlying support.

With respect to property tax disputes, the basic problem is that local assessors are used to using a cost approach to valuation. That is, they start out with the original cost at date of acquisition, and then apply cost trends through application of index numbers. Over a period of years this can lead to very high values that are totally unrelated to fair market value, defined as what a willing buyer might pay. As we discussed in Chapter 5, the cost approach states what it would cost today to replace the assets, not what those same assets are worth in terms of the present value of future cash flows.

The cost of replacing a factory (e.g., land, building, and machinery and equipment) can be high if inflation has been substantial. But if the product line capable of being produced in that plant has lost its market (e.g., "buggy whips"), then no matter how much the factory would cost to replace, its value is greatly reduced. Disputes about property taxes almost always involve whether an indexed approach to original cost properly reflects today's economic situation, taking into account technological changes in the production process, the cost of inputs (e.g., natural gas), and the market for the output. Here is a situation in which it is not necessary to have extreme values presented. More important is the rationale for not using historical cost indexed for price increases. If the taxpayer can get over the burden of proving that the cost approach is erroneous, there usually is little difficulty in reducing the assessment to the real FMV.

Disputes that end up in court regarding business valuations, whether they are related to a divorce, termination of a partnership, or disagreement about the value of a failed acquisition, are inevitably bitter. This is because a lot of money is usually at stake, combined with the emotional issues between the parties. Each side feels the other is trying to take advantage of it. Thus, if the dispute boils down to value, far more than the absolute dollars are being contested between the parties.

DIVORCE

The author's firm almost always respectfully declines to take on valuations dealing with divorce because the parties are so mad at each other it is almost impossible for them to agree on anything, including the future outlook for the family business. If the husband runs the company, and the divorcing wife owns half the stock, one side will argue that the business is going straight down into bankruptcy and is worth nothing. The other side then indicates the business is sure to be the next Microsoft and conservatively is worth tens of millions of dollars, if not billions!

In this situation the parties are so far apart that compromise or even reasonable assessment of the situation is difficult. Each party comes into court with widely disparate appraisals, and it is no wonder the judge makes some comment to the effect "You really can't trust appraisers." The truth is that the parties don't trust each other and request their own appraiser to take an ultra-extreme position. Whether a competent appraiser *should* be guided in that way by the client is an interesting question. But if you *know* the other side is taking an extreme position, it may seem best to "fight fire with fire." We do not subscribe to this philosophy, which is why we do not like to get involved in divorces.

With regard to business disputes, say in a failed merger or split up of a partnership, the parties may have no use for one another, particularly as the case drags out in the court system. But they do not usually have the bitterness found in a typical divorce dispute.

SUMMARY AND CONCLUSION

In most types of business dispute, the parties are far apart in their expectation as to value, but a reasonable and realistic assessment of the future outlook for the business is usually possible. Without trying to be repetitive, the best offense in a business dispute is to ask the appraiser to be as objective as possible and to fully support the key assumptions on which the appraisal report is based. If the assumptions cannot really be supported, the proposed values are probably too high (low).

Value information can be objective and independent. Nonetheless, readers of valuation reports should constantly keep in mind that the appraiser responsible for writing the report was being paid by his client, and the client undoubtedly had some goal in mind.

The best way to read an appraisal report is to see what are the key or crucial assumptions. Then stand back and ask yourself as a reader, "Are these assumptions realistic?" If the answer is in the affirmative, then the valuation report is supportable and can be relied upon. If the answer is no, then ideally one should be able to test alternative assumptions from the information given. If that is not possible, one should then get in touch directly with the appraiser.

When litigation is involved, and the determination of value affects the outcome, one is more likely to find that extreme positions are taken. The normal human tendency is to think that if my opponent is going to do something I will counter it in advance. Distrust breed distrust.

Even so, as a client, the best advice we can offer is to discuss with your appraiser the pros and cons of trying to come up with the correct answer the first time, as contrasted with taking an argumentative or advocacy position initially, and then being willing to compromise. If it were our decision, we would choose the best answer the first time, but the alternate is at least understandable.

CHAPTER 9

What Will Happen in the Future? Why Assumptions Are Critical in the Valuation Process

Appraisers can and do determine values on a *retrospective* basis. That is, in November 2002, we can be asked, "What was the value of this asset, perhaps a trade name, in January 1999?" This involves having the appraiser try and put himself in the position of a then current 1999 observer. Then, hopefully without using the benefit of hindsight, the appraiser can state with some degree of confidence, "If I had been asked in January 1999 I would have determined the value of the trade name to have been $x million."

At least when doing a retrospective appraisal, the analyst usually has some ideas as to how things actually turned out. That, of course, is the biggest single weakness of such an appraisal report. An adversary, often the IRS, can always object that the answer was clouded by the benefit of hindsight. Nonetheless, appraisers are often asked to go back in time and value an asset as of an earlier date. (An example of this would be in a merger, when the buyer now wants to sell a piece of the acquired business. In order to determine the current gain or loss, the original basis or cost must be determined. Often, in the original allocation, sufficient detail was not prepared and the unit being sold is only a portion of a larger entity. In effect, a new mini-allocation has to be performed.)

Having described a retrospective appraisal, it should be stated that most valuation assignments are as of a current date. The income approach to value may be the most frequently utilized in valuations. As discussed in

Chapter 6, the income approach relies heavily on an estimate of *future* cash flows. In turn, the anticipated cash flows are a function of expected future sales revenue, cost of sales, operating expenses, interest and taxes, capital expenditures, and working capital requirements.

It is impossible to use the income approach without being explicit about a whole range of assumptions that deal with the future. The one thing we do know is that the specific assumptions, with hindsight, are highly likely to have been wrong in one way or another. Nevertheless, despite any margin of error, appraisals and in fact *all* investment decisions depend on evaluations—guesses, if you will—of the future.

DEVELOPING ASSUMPTIONS ABOUT THE FUTURE

There are two schools of thought as to *who* should prepare the assumptions regarding possible future outcomes. One school says the appraiser himself should develop his or her own best estimates. The other school says the appraiser should rely on the client's projections.

The argument for the appraiser doing his own projections, making his own assumptions about the future course of events, is predicated on his objectivity. Company-prepared budgets or forecasts almost inevitably turn out to be optimistic. In fact, all one has to do is to go to the files in virtually any business unit and pull out the five-year plan prepared three years ago. Any resemblance between what actually happened and what was projected to happen is going to be coincidental. Many observers have referred to these internal projections as *hockey-stick* or *J-curve* (i.e., things will always get better out a couple of years).

What is meant is that perhaps the next 12 to 18 months are assumed to be flat, but then things are going to improve markedly. There is a human tendency to be optimistic, and no executive wants to be perceived as "unable to meet his numbers." Therefore, even if in the short term things may not show tremendous progress, at least in the midterm, future sales and profits will always show an increase.

The nature of the discounted cash flow (DCF) methodology utilized in the income approach to value is that results in the first four to five years will have a seemingly disproportionate impact on the final value answer. Therefore, if company projections show significant improvements in years two through five, the value of the project, product line, or business will be inflated.

If appraisers rely too much on company projections, there is a substantial risk that valuations will be too high and that readers of the appraisal report may be misled. One solution, of course, is for the appraiser to state clearly that he is using, and relying on, company projections. Sometimes, the appraiser will say, "We have utilized company (sales) projections which we have reviewed and believe reasonable." This puts the reader on notice, but also associates the appraiser with the answer.

An alternate approach in making projections about future events is for the appraiser to develop his own projections of revenues and cost of sales and expenses, as well as taxes, working capital, and capital expenditures. The advantage is that the appraiser is much less likely to be swayed by optimism, a feeling that if the number is not met the individual executive will lose his or her job.

A general manager who projected flat revenues for the next five years likely would feel that he was jeopardizing his career, inasmuch as every executive feels he has to show growth. Yet not all products or product lines do grow. Therefore, it is easier for an appraiser whose job performance is not at stake to make realistic projections.

The disadvantage of having the appraiser do the projections is that he is not necessarily as familiar with the industry, competition, product developments, and the internal business situation. His projections may not have bias, but they may also lack the detailed perspective an executive with 20 years' experience.

There is no good answer to this question of accuracy in forecasts. It is relatively easy to avoid bias if the appraiser performs the work, but a company manager may have greater insights into the dynamics of the market. At the end of the day, some forecast is necessary in determining value, and the combined best thinking of the company and the appraiser should be utilized.

A case study of the reliance on overly optimistic projections can be found in a recent court trial.

A company undertook a refinancing, and the banks requested a valuation to determine if the were solvent, to see if the value of the assets exceeded the liabilities at the time of the transaction. Unfortunately, some six months later the company was forced to file for bankruptcy protection. The company had become insolvent and the original lenders were now in trouble. The lenders went back to the Solvency Opinion prepared by a large well-known appraisal firm.

The report stated that, at the date of the report, in the professional opinion of the appraisal firm, the subject company was solvent. The value of the assets exceeded the value of the liabilities (including the new debt) immediately after the deal was consummated, and the cash flows should be sufficient to meet the obligations. With the company now in bankruptcy, needless to say, the appraiser's original opinion was now subjected to detailed scrutiny.

The basis of the solvency opinion was the appraiser's expectation as to the sales potential for the company. Actual sales had not begun to meet the projections utilized in the opinion, and in court the appraiser was asked what the basis was for his opinion about sales prospects.

The answer was enlightening. It turned out that the investment banker, in trying to sell the deal to prospective lenders, had prepared three separate projections. One was labeled "Optimistic," the second "Realistic," and the third "Conservative." The appraiser testified that he had used the *lowest* of the three projections, the one the investment banker had prepared that was conservative.

The opposing lawyer then asked the appraiser how he could explain that the "conservative" projection actually showed sales and profits at a level *higher* than the company had ever done in its history. In other words, "conservatively speaking," business was anticipated to go only one way—straight up.

The company representatives, when asked to comment on the investment banker projections, indicated that they had really not paid much attention to the projections. The company was just "interested in getting the deal done" and left everything up to the investment banker! The appraiser, likewise, had trusted the investment banker, who was only motivated to get the deal done, not necessarily analyze sales in detail.

In this situation, were the banks that lent money in the belief the borrower was solvent, and relied on the appraiser's solvency opinion, at fault? Presumably, the banks had access to the borrower's historical financial statements, and it would not have taken a lot of analysis by some credit analyst to identify the discontinuity between historical performance and projected performance. It is easy for the banks later to say, "We relied on the expert's [appraiser's] opinion." But a lender advancing tens of millions of dollars has to do its own due diligence. In this situation, it appears that there was more than enough blame to go around. The investment bankers wanted the deal to succeed, the lenders wanted the up-front fees, the borrower wanted to close the transaction, and the poor appraiser thought he was helping everyone out by being conservative.

There are two lessons here. First, read any appraisal opinion or report carefully, and with a degree of skepticism. Second, perform your own due diligence if a lot of money is at stake. Projections are at the heart of most valuations, and readers are entitled to question the underlying assumptions.

START-UP BUSINESSES

Appraisers are often asked to determine the value of newly formed businesses, particularly for the dual purposes of lender financing and equity investment. This type of assignment is particularly difficult because there is no history on which to draw.

Usually, when projections have to be made, there is at least some historical experience that can be used as a basis for the forecast. A business may have been growing at 4 percent a year, and significant new investment in capacity may now make it possible to grow 6 to 8 percent. A projection between 5 percent growth and 10 percent growth per year is going to at least look possible, and probably reasonable.

But when a business is only five months old, with just two employees and a "great idea," one cannot look at the three most recent audited years' results. They do not exist.

Yet owners of such new firms desperately need financing, debt or equity. Some of them feel that a report by an independent third party (e.g., an appraiser, will help them achieve their goals). How do you value a start-up firm? With difficulty.

The value today of almost any asset (other than unique items like antiques and fine art) is directly or indirectly related to the future cash flows that the asset can produce. If a company has positive and growing cash flow, investors will be willing to pay a lot of money for that business. However, if the business is going to have no future cash flows, it probably has little value other than in liquidation.

So if an entrepreneur has a business plan, and little else, can one realistically develop a value? The answer is "Yes, but.. .."

The issue then boils down to one of the believability of the business plan. Every business plan written shows high and increasing profits in years two or three and beyond. In one sense this is probably realistic because if investors cannot see that positive cash flow is possible, the business will not survive into year three. Investors will not put in money, and a self-fulfilling prophecy will have developed. Assuming the business will fail, the lack of investors will then cause it to fail.

But, of course, many new businesses do get off the ground and become successful. In fact, every successful business today was a start-up on its own day one. Statistics indicate, however, that maybe only one in five new businesses succeed.

So if an appraiser is presented with a business plan and asked to determine the value of the business, what is the solution? As might be expected in a chapter of this book dealing with the future and assumptions, the appraiser starts out with a very close look at the business plan.

While the appraiser should not be an actual or prospective investor in the business, the thought process has to be that of someone being asked to place his money in the business. As previously indicated, *every* business plan shows solid growth and ever-increasing profits after an initial start-up period. But in practice only one in five is going to make it. How do we know whether this is the one winner or one of the four losers?

The correct answer to this question, if known, would make any one of us rich. Looking back, why didn't our grandparents buy IBM in 1945 or our parents buy Microsoft in 1990? Wasn't it obvious? Yes, in hindsight it was, but at the time it was far from clear who would be a winner and who a loser.

The truth is that, today, we cannot tell tomorrow's winners from tomorrow's losers. It may be relatively easy to weed out the bottom 50 percent of the start-up ventures as doomed to failure. This evaluation can be based on common sense (e.g., lack of management, inadequate capitalization, already well-established competitors, and unrealistic expectations as to customer acceptance). These, of course, are but a few success factors. But if any of them are absent, the odds against success are long, and if two or more are missing, why get involved?

The much tougher call for an appraiser, or for a venture capital (VC) investor for that matter, arises when all the success factors *appear* to be present in one degree or another. The business plan makes sense. There are few, if any, competitors. Management has solid experience. Test marketing has been successful. The company is sufficiently funded so that this round of financing is not needed to meet next Friday's payroll.

In this situation all of the omens are favorable. But there is little actual business history, and the plans are just that—plans. Can we put a value on the business at this stage?

What we have done in this situation is to lay out the projections, indicate how we have tested them for reasonableness, apply a very high discount rate, and indicate the value *if* the projections come to pass.

How do we test the projections for reasonableness?

An entrepreneur came to an appraisal company and requested a value for his company's stock. The purpose was to issue options to existing and soon-to-be-hired employees. These options had to be valued at fair market value, both for tax purposes and for financial reporting if the company were to have an IPO.

The appraisers were presented with initial projections for revenues, as is almost always the case, that were almost astronomical, approaching $1 billion within four years. The projections assumed virtually immediate acceptance by all the businesses that would be affected; in effect, the entrepreneurs were forecasting a new industry and that they would end up with 100 percent of that market.

We were unable to agree to such aggressive projections and asked them to rethink their assumptions. Within days, they came back with new projections at 50 percent of the original, albeit numbers that were still very high. One more round of negotiations with management resulted in a revised forecast about 25 percent of the original, and one that if achieved would be quite satisfactory to all parties.

We now had a projection developed by management, with significant input from the appraiser. It showed losses in the first year, breakeven in the second year, and profits growing rapidly in years three and beyond.

To arrive at a value of the business, we applied a high discount rate, on the order of 45 percent. At that point the first year's loss is weighted heavily and the fifth year's profit is worth only 15 cents on the dollar.

We had a result that showed the company was worth a significant amount today. If things did *not* go according to plan, the value of the options was going to be purely academic anyhow. If the company did meet management projections, once the losses were behind them, the then high profits would make the options valuable. But because the valuation had been on a contemporaneous basis, before any profits had been achieved, the low option value was going to be supportable.

The initial low value for the business enterprise was going to be taken care of because we agreed that as the company met certain milestones we would perform another valuation, with a potentially increased valuation. In effect, the risk of the business, which caused us to use a very high discount rate initially, could be perceived as less risky as they met their goals and reached certain milestones.

Reducing the discount rate even from 45 percent to 40 percent raised the value of the business enterprise. A further reduction to 35 percent, combined with having losses behind them, would place the overall value at a level management was comfortable with, and one that could attract additional investors.

The real question, in valuing a start-up business, is how to select the appropriate discount rate. Just to review, the *higher* the rate used to discount future cash flows, the *lower* the present value. Also, the further out in time, the lower the present value. For example, the value today of $1,000 in five years and 10 years is as follows:

Discount Rate	5 Years	10 Years
10%	0.621	0.386
15%	0.497	0.247
20%	0.402	0.162
25%	0.328	0.107
30%	0.269	0.073
35%	0.223	0.050
40%	0.186	0.035
45%	0.156	0.024
50%	0.132	0.017
55%	0.112	0.012

The choice of discount rate is one of the crucial assumptions in any valuation. There are a number of scientific methods of building up the discount rate starting with the risk-free interest rate on U.S. government bonds, and adding various factors, including a risk premium, to arrive at the final rate. Another approach is to calculate the weighted average cost of capital (WACC) from information about publicly traded companies, including weighting for both traded debt and equity. The greater the percentage of debt, the lower the WACC.

These two approaches can produce comparable answers. Nonetheless, the final choice of rate used in any appraisal is based on the professional skill and experience of the appraiser. In the final analysis, the discount rate utilized has to be based on professional judgment as to the real business risk.[1]

When one is dealing with start-up firms, it often is most appropriate to utilize rates of return demanded by angel investors and venture capital firms. These high-risk investors typically look for returns of 30 to 50 percent and above, on an annualized basis.

The reason that experienced investors are looking for such high rates of return is that they know, from past performance, that maybe only one or two out of 10 investments will actually pay off. Four or five may essentially break even, and three or four will probably fail. Moreover, these odds against success are *after* the angel investor or venture capital firm has examined hundreds, if not thousands, of business plans. To obtain an overall perhaps 20+ percent return on their portfolio, these investors have to have a couple of "home runs," which means perhaps a 10- to 20-fold increase in value over a five- to ten-year time horizon for the lucky winners.

How much return will be based on the time horizon and the rate of return is shown below:

	Total Return	
Rate of Return	5 years	10 years
25%	3.05x	9.31x
30%	3.71x	13.79x
35%	4.48x	20.11x
40%	5.38x	28.93x
45%	6.41x	41.08x
50%	7.59x	57.67x
55%	8.95x	80.04x
60%	10.49x	109.95x
65%	12.2x	149.57x

What this shows is that if an investment goes up ninefold in five years, it will have earned a compound rate of return of 55 percent per year. If there is a 10-year time horizon, then a 40 percent annual rate of return will provide a 29x return on the initial investment. From this, it can be seen that if an angel investor or venture capital firm can find one or two real winners out of 10, and several more at breakeven or slightly above, the overall portfolio can do well. In practice, many of the funds offered by venture capital firms have done this well, and so have many individual angel investors.

The point of this discussion is that 30 to 50 percent returns are needed on individual investments, to offset the fully expected losses on the other investments. This is the whole concept of a portfolio, as contrasted with a single investment. In a portfolio, one big winner can offset many breakeven and losing investments.

However, having said all this, when an appraiser is asked to determine the value of a *single* company, not a total portfolio, he has to ask the same question that an investor would ask. "Can this company do very well, can it provide the type of return that venture capital funds are looking for?" Inasmuch as the VC funds hope that each investment can produce 30 percent, 35 percent, or even 45 percent returns compounded, then we as appraisers have to take this into consideration in choosing the most appropriate discount rate.

As can be seen, assuming a 30 percent discount rate, as contrasted to a 40 percent discount rate will significantly affect the final answer. There is no known scientific basis for selecting one over the other. A more risky investment will be discounted at perhaps 40 percent, a less risky one at a lesser rate. In our work, we have seen discount rates as high as 50 percent and higher, which explicitly assumes a very high level of risk. Actual investment experience, however, supports this assumption because a high percentage of risky businesses do fail.

While the appraiser is ultimately responsible for the choice of discount rate, and it does involve professional judgment, the reader of an appraisal report can be justified in asking the sensitivity of the final answer to a change in discount rate.

This discussion of risk and discount rates has focused on high-risk investments such as start-up firms. Much better established businesses often are valued using discount rates between 12 and 20 percent. The one positive statement we can make is that there is no single rule of thumb regarding discount rates. Look at it this way: If valuation were solely a mechanical exercise, then a simple computer program could value all companies. There must be a reason that many businessmen, lenders, investors, and tax authorities pay appraisers for their professional judgment. The truth is, every valuation involves judgment, and the choice of discount rate may be one of the most significant choices.

TIME HORIZON

Another choice that must be made by the appraiser is the time horizon for the financial projections. Many appraisers go out at least 10 years into the future, showing year by year all elements of the profit and loss statement. For each year of that 10-year period, the net cash flows (revenues less all expenses) are discounted back to today.

Stand back and ask yourself where were you 10 years ago and how have things changed in the interim. Most businesses have experienced significant change. If nothing else, 10 years of economic prosperity during the 1990s had never been seen in the U.S. economy. Nobody anticipated the arrival of the Internet and its impact. A swing from government deficit to surplus, along with concerns that "we are going to run out of U.S. Treasury bonds" would have been unthinkable. The list of changes goes on.

Now ask whether anyone can realistically forecast the economy, the political situation, international events, and technology over the *next* 10 years. A neutral observer would be forced to the conclusion that a 10-year time horizon is probably unrealistic. It is hard enough to know what will happen next year, much less in 10 years.

Even worse, most financial projections are actually constructed on the assumption that some growth rate, be it 3 percent or 10 percent, will keep on going for the total period of the forecast. A perusal of the 10-year historical summary in any company annual report will show that steady constant growth simply does not occur. In the few instances in which it does, and Emerson Electric comes to mind, many financial analysts then accuse the company of managing earnings.

Just a comment here. Why do financial analysts dislike a company whose management is believed to manage earnings? What is the purpose of management other than to earn money and to manage the business to accomplish this? Is a company that is well managed poorly serving its shareholders, creditors, and employees? Good management produces good earnings. Better management produces better earnings. Why shouldn't earnings that grow steadily and consistently over time be a sign of *good* management?

The reason may be that those external forces, which can neither be predicted nor controlled, affect most companies at some point or other. These external shocks may be favorable or unfavorable. Nevertheless, they do happen. Most companies have exceptionally good years, often followed by poor years. The one thing they do not have is straight-line growth.

Financial analysts—and appraisers are included in this category—are uncomfortable trying to predict when, if ever, these external events may happen in the future. It is far easier, if less accurate, to forecast straight-line growth at whatever percentage rate is chosen. One can even choose different growth rates for sales, cost of sales, and operating expenses. In fact, most projections assume that so-called fixed costs will remain fixed and not increase as fast as revenues, hence the phenomenon alluded to earlier that things are always projected to get better in years two, three, and beyond.

It is difficult to project the future, and the uncertainties increase geometrically with the length of time being projected. For this reason we believe that financial projections in a valuation report that go beyond five years are inherently uncertain. Who will be president five years from now? Will we have war or peace? If answers to these questions are hard to come by, and they are this then leads to the conclusion that 10-year projections have the potential to be misleading. Inaccurate forecasts will provide unreliable answers

There is an aura of certainty in a spreadsheet printed in a report. But there is one point we have tried to make in this section: The fact that a forecast is printed to four significant digits does not make it any more accurate. The shorter the period projected, the more likely future developments will confirm the accuracy of the assumptions.

TERMINAL VALUE

As discussed in Chapter 6, a discounted cash flow approach ordinarily will have a terminal value for the project or asset being appraised. This is because at the end of the period used to project future results, the business, or other asset being valued will *not* cease to exist.

We just mentioned that going out beyond five years is often difficult to support. Therefore, if the business will continue to produce revenue and cash flows in years six and beyond, how do we capture this? One way would be simply to accept the limitations of projections and yet carry out the projection over a 25- or 30-year time frame, assuming that few businesses last more than that time. Further, given the fact that income generated 25 years out into the future has a very low present value at say 15 percent (it is actually only worth 3 cents today), one could feel confident in stopping the projection after 25 years. But, if a 10-year projection is inherently unreliable, what can one assert about a 25-year projection except that it is likely to be even more unreliable?

A solution to this conundrum was developed many years ago and has worked very satisfactorily. The analyst makes a basic assumption that at the end of the projection period, the company, asset, or project will be *sold* outright to a third party, one not related to the current owner. This approach results in a cash inflow in year six, if a five-year time horizon was chosen. In other words, we show five years of operating results, assume the business will be put on the market at the end of year five, and assume it will be sold for cash in year six.

This provides for all the cash flows the company will generate. The assumed selling price at the end of year five will be a function of the then current operating results. It is, therefore, not the price at which the business would be sold today. The appraiser has to make the assumption as to the business conditions to be present five years hence. Then, based on the operating projections already developed, the assumed selling price can reasonably be estimated.

The publishing company *Value Line* routinely prepares estimates or earnings three to five years out into the future, as well as assumed price/earnings (P/E) ratios. We have found it highly supportable to develop our terminal values applying the *Value Line* P/E ratios to our estimates of year five earnings. It is not that *Value Line* necessarily has a better crystal ball than anyone else does. Rather, they do this routinely, week after week, for each of the companies they cover, presently over 1,700 businesses.

The *Value Line* estimates of future P/E ratios may or may not be correct, but they have the great benefit to the appraiser of being unbiased. Thus, if you are valuing a retail operation, and *Value Line* projects an 18× P/E ratio for retail businesses for the three- to five-year time horizon, utilizing that 18× ratio reflects an absence of bias on the part of the appraiser. It may turn out five years from now to have been wrong, but we are doing the valuation today, with today's best information. By relying on an independent and neutral third party for the P/E ratio to be applied to the estimate of future earnings, the appraiser has strong support.

Having said this, one caveat is in order. Because the year five earnings are going to be multiplied by a large factor, in this case the P/E ratio from *Value Line,* a small change in the year five earnings can have a big impact on the overall value. In practice, in many cases the year five terminal value will account for well over 50 percent of the final valuation, particularly at discount rates below 20 percent.

This puts a premium on reviewing the projections closely and seeing how realistic the growth trends are that were used. In fact, it would be desirable for the appraiser to at least comment on the sensitivity of the terminal value in order to provide the reader of the appraisal report this useful information.

ECONOMIC CONDITIONS AND OUTLOOK

As mentioned earlier, it is hard for an appraiser to forecast economic conditions two, three, or more years out. Nonetheless, either implicitly or explicitly, the appraiser or analyst is making some assumptions.

Most appraisal reports have a section in the front that deals with then current economic conditions. This is provided as a framework for the reader to understand the basis of the projections being made.

In the author's opinion, many appraisal reports waste too much space rehashing current economic conditions. Perhaps this helps a reader of that appraisal report, two or three years from now, to understand the framework of the then current analysis. However, much more important would be an explicit statement by the appraiser of the assumptions he is making regarding *future* or *projected* economic conditions. A five-year expectation that the economy and gross domestic product (GDP) will continue to grow at today's rate, say 3 percent a year, is more important than commenting on recent Federal Reserve moves or the latest twist in the balance of payments.

What has happened in the past is history. Appraisals deal with the future. Therefore, it is more important to state the economic assumptions for the future that underlie the projection than to explain the recent past. Many appraisers, however, do not subscribe to this view. The reader of any appraisal report should carefully review what is written; he can then choose to accept or reject the hypotheses put forth.

INDUSTRY CONDITIONS AND OUTLOOK

Appraisal reports also generally discuss the industry and the industry outlook for the company being appraised. In many ways, this industry analysis may be more important than the appraiser's discussion of general economic conditions. There will be a significant difference in valuation of a company with a strong competitive condition in a strong industry, contrasted with a weak company in a weak industry. This will be true irrespective of overall economy-wide conditions.

The appraiser has a responsibility to analyze the industry, industry growth potential, and the subject company's ability to compete. This involves an analysis of management, financial strength, product position, and customer acceptance, among other factors. Ideally, the appraiser will lay out the company, the industry, and the company's position in the industry in such a way that the reader of the report will be carried along by his logic and then agree fully with the appraiser's conclusions.

The only way for an appraiser to perform this function is to have done the work and researched the company and industry. In short, there is more to an appraisal than number crunching. This is why we look with skepticism at the $200 computer programs that purport to allow the user to perform a "do-it-yourself" appraisal. There are no shortcuts. The financial analysis should be a culmination of the valuation process, not the beginning.

SUMMARY AND CONCLUSIONS

Inherent in the valuation process is the need to look to the future. Today's value is a function of future cash flows, which in turn are functions of future operations. There is no escaping the need to evaluate the future. This is inherently difficult and certainly subject to error. Nonetheless, it has to be done.

If the appraiser has a responsibility to do his homework and come up with reasonable assumptions regarding the future, readers also have a responsibility. Readers must read the entire appraisal report, not just turn to the last page and look at a single number. That single number is the resultant of many variables. A good appraisal report will not only have reasonable assumptions, it will explain the logic behind the choices. Further, a good report will explain the sensitivity of the final answer to the important variables. One cannot state in advance which variables in the report will be important. What is certain is that in every appraisal certain essential assumptions will control the final answer. If the assumptions chosen are perceived by the reader to be reasonable, one can have faith in the value conclusion. If the reader disagrees with the assumptions, go back to the appraiser and ask him to either provide better justification or test the impact of alternative assumptions.

ENDNOTE

1. The Financial Accounting Standards, in its Concept Statement 7 proposes an alternative methodology. The analyst has to make a number of different projections, assign probabilities to each, and then discount the results using a risk-free interest rate. Judgment is still involved, but instead of a choice of discount rates, the analyst has to make a choice of probabilities. Few utilize the FASB approach.

CHAPTER 10

Hiring an Appraiser; Reading an Appraisal Report

The most common question an appraiser is asked before being retained is: "Have you ever appraised _____ before?" Fill in the blank with whatever type of asset or company the prospective client wants valued.

Implicit in the question is the assumption that if you are now being asked to value a drugstore, you will do a better job if you have previously valued *other* drugstores. Virtually every time an appraiser is approached, this is the first question, followed of course almost immediately by an inquiry as to the cost of the valuation.

Both questions are actually reasonable, and we discuss them in this chapter as well as the subject of expert testimony by appraisers in lawsuits. Finally, we discuss what may be the most important aspect, and that is how a reader should approach an appraisal report. Nine times out of 10, most readers go to the end of the report, look at the value, and mentally either agree or disagree with the answer. Only when there is a real conflict—between buyer and seller, revenue agent, and taxpayer—do the parties really scrutinize an appraisal report.

AN APPRAISER'S EXPERIENCE

How important is it for an appraiser to have valued the same or similar types of assets in the past? The answer that an experienced appraiser will actually give to this question from a prospective client is that it depends. If the appraiser is being considered in conjunction with a competitive proposal (i.e., another appraiser is also being considered), the answer depends on actual experience.

If the appraiser has, in fact, valued the same type or similar assets in the past, he will assure the client that his experience is significant and totally relevant. Put a different way, the client will be made to feel that he has come to the country's leading authority on the subject, that he is in good hands. This is similar to going to a surgeon for a heart bypass operation and reassuring yourself that the surgeon has performed the same operation literally hundreds of times. In medicine and many other professional situations, experience does count. You might not want a first-year associate at your law firm drafting up the purchase contract for a major merger transaction. In architecture, for example, there is a saying that until you have gray hair you won't get any clients of your own.

Assume in our scenario of a prospective client and an appraiser, the appraiser has *not* actually valued the same or a similar asset. The response will be, "Well, no, we haven't done *exactly* that, but we have done a lot of similar appraisals for clients who have had virtually identical requirements." So the appraiser with experience will brag about it and the appraiser without specific experience in that industry will claim it is not particularly important. Which is correct?

These words will probably come back to haunt the author at some point, but the reader deserves nothing less than the truth. *An experienced business appraiser can value almost any type of asset.* The key words in that sentence are "experienced business appraiser." This is not to say that an individual with six months in the valuation business, who has just spent the last two months valuing several drugstores, is necessarily to be relied on for another drugstore valuation. The experience relates to overall years performing a wide variety of valuation assignments.

Appraisal experience deals with valuation concepts and the application of those concepts in a wide variety of situations. Then, when a new opportunity arises, the appraiser brings his valuation experience to bear, not his knowledge of a specific industry.

These statements, as mentioned, specifically apply to *business* appraisals, that is, real estate, business interests, machinery and equipment, and business intangibles. If the reader is looking to value fine arts, antiques, jewelry, and collectibles, then it is much more important to have someone with *specific* industry expertise. Appraisal firms such as the author's, Valuation Research Consultants, do not even attempt to value fine arts, antiques, jewelry, or collectibles. We would refer people to Sotheby's and Christie's auction houses. Those firms literally have dozens of specialists, ranging from Chinese pottery to glass paperweights to seventeenth-century Dutch paintings, and everything in between. Essentially, in the fine arts field, the appraiser has to identify the asset as well as determine its value. He has to determine the quality, as, for instance, the specific grading of a diamond ring. Further, he has to distinguish a diamond from a zircon. Business appraisers don't have to identify a drugstore from a convenience store.

This is the principal difference between a fine arts appraiser and a business appraiser, in that the former has to perform two quite separate and distinct functions. He has to identify the object(s) being valued (e.g., is this an original Salvador Dali print or a copy?). Then he has to estimate the value based on the rarity, quality, and comparable transactions. As an example, to value an eighteenth-century armoire, the appraiser has to properly identify the piece of furniture, determine its date of manufacture, and decide if it is an original or a reproduction.

In contrast, a business appraiser does not need training or years of experience to identify a drugstore chain. He does need experience in order to value the chain, but there is never any question for a business appraiser, "Just what is this asset, and is it genuine?"

The difference between fine arts and antiques, and business valuations, is that the former deals with individually unique items. What is a specific Rembrandt painting worth? There are no others like it in existence; Rembrandt is no longer producing any new works. To value it, the fine arts appraiser has to be able to compare this painting with all the others that have sold, estimate who might be in a position to buy, and come up with a valuation judgment essentially based on "gut feel."

In the business world, if we are valuing a warehouse, there may be no warehouse exactly like this one in just this exact location. The truth is that a new warehouse *can* be built close by, and in terms of utility, there will be little difference. The cost of a brand *new* warehouse, land, and building will be one of the major parameters affecting the value of an existing warehouse under appraisal. The same cannot be said of antiques and paintings. No amount of money can get Rembrandt to paint another portrait.

These are the reasons that if you are having unique assets valued, you need to find someone who specializes in that specific area. Someone knowledgeable about coins may know very little about stamps and so forth.

Business assets, in contrast, essentially sell on investment value. Any business can be, and in fact is, evaluated in comparison with all the other potential investments available. In the business world, investors are looking for one thing, return on investment. If asset A will not meet their need they will go to asset B, and so on until they see something that meets their needs, is selling at the right price, and promises their required rate of return.

As a consequence, business appraisers have to understand the investment process, the required rates of return that investors demand, and the relative risks of different investments. With that background knowledge, and with sufficient inquiry and research, a competent business appraiser can, in practice, value almost any type of business asset.

There was only one situation in the author's experience in which an appraisal firm, regretfully, turned down a business opportunity.

A Ripley's Believe It or Not Museum came to an appraisal company, and asked them to value the business for insurance purposes. The premise of value in an insurance valuation is "What would it cost to replace the assets if they were lost as a result of a fire or other accident?" In other words, in case of loss the insurance company has to make the insured whole. In practice, therefore, the company insures the assets for what it would cost to replace them, and in case of loss the insurance company pays out that amount of money.

The museum had a number of truly unique items, like a replica of the Eiffel Tower made out of toothpicks and a shrunken human head from Peru. When the appraisal company management started to think about accepting the engagement, they came up with a serious problem. Just what was the cost to replicate a shrunken human head? You could hardly go out to your local native tribe in Peru and order one!

In fact, the appraisal firm determined that they could not develop a cost to replace these unique items, on a basis that would be supportable in case of an actual loss. They instead went to the prospective client and said that they could value the business on a financial basis, based on the ticket revenues from people who paid to get into the museum. In effect, this would be the business enterprise value of the museum, although not the specific value of any one item in the museum.

The client declined, saying that they really needed the valuation report for insurance, and the cost of replacement of the individual items was what was needed. This particular appraisal company passed on the assignment. History has not revealed how the client ever obtained the information they were looking for.

The author believes that if a client is interviewing an appraiser for a prospective engagement it is *not* important that the appraiser has ever valued specifically the same or even a closely similar type of business or asset. Far more important for the client is to understand the methodology that the appraiser proposes to apply, how much work will be needed, what the final report will look like, and how reliable will be the final answer.

INTERVIEWING THE APPRAISER

Appraisal assignments range in size and scope from one-day valuations of a single piece of equipment, or a local residence, through month-long assignments dealing with multinational acquisitions. There really are only two things that prospective clients need to know, and usually ask. First, can the appraiser or appraisal firm do the job? Second, how much will it cost?

Surprisingly, perhaps, the two are closely related. As discussed above, experience in a particular industry, or for any type of unique valuation, is not really necessary. Any competent appraiser can learn enough about a particular company, industry, or type of financial asset to express a professional opinion that will be supportable. The difference is that the more familiar the appraiser is with the type of asset under investigation, the less time will have to be spent to arrive at an answer.

A major national appraisal firm is capable of performing valuations for individual private residences, perhaps for sale, financing, or property tax appeals. There is nothing in the valuation process from precluding a Los Angeles–based firm from going to Omaha and determining the fair market value of a $400,000 home. The Los Angeles firm would come up with the right answer, but it might take them two professional days, plus any required travel to get a real estate appraiser to Omaha, determine current market conditions, look up comparable transactions, inspect the subject property, and talk to local real estate professionals.

A local Omaha residential real estate appraiser, an individual who works closely with one or more mortgage institutions and values 150 to 250 houses a year in Omaha, would be able to complete the assignment in less than a day. He knows the area, he already has all the comparable transactions in his file, and he has to do virtually no research. His fee for the mortgage appraisal would be maybe one tenth what the national firm would have to charge.

By the same token, if a local shopping center developer in Omaha needed an appraisal for a major insurance company planning to finance a new regional development, the local residential appraiser could not possibly compete. There are few major regional shopping centers in any one area. To understand the economics of a shopping center requires experience on a regional, if not national, level. They do not change hands very often, so comparable transactions are hard to come by. The financial projections and analyses are complex; a local appraiser might well never have performed this work before. Could he learn? Certainly, he could learn. But it would take an inordinate amount of time and research, and in the end the insurance company lender might not be comfortable with the final report.

Appraisers charge clients strictly on the basis of the time spent, not on the value of the asset(s) being valued. The time involved for a particular job will be a function of the appraiser's experience in that industry or for that type of appraisal. Thus, all other things being equal, if two appraisal firms bid on the same engagement, the one with more experience in that industry may have a competitive advantage.

Suppose a client requires an allocation of the purchase price for a biotech firm it has acquired. It calls in three appraisal firms and asks each to quote. The firm with previous biotech experience estimates it will take 12 days of professional time. The other two firms estimate it will take 14 or 15 days, including two or three days to familiarize themselves with the specific part of the biotech industry represented by the acquired firm.

If all three firms utilized the *same* fee per day, then obviously the experienced firm would have the low bid, and in this situation would obtain the engagement. However, there is nothing precluding one of the other two firms from bidding the work at a *lower* per diem rate. Thus, the first firm might quote $18,000, which is equivalent to $1,500 per day. The second firm, utilizing the same $1,500 per day, would quote $22,000. The third firm, knowing it was at a disadvantage but still wanting the engagement, could bid $1,200 per day for a total quote of $17,500.

The client would see only three proposals with total dollar fee estimates, since appraisal firms rarely if ever disclose their man-day estimate. If the client wanted the low-cost bid, he would choose the third firm, with a $17,500 quote. That firm would then find the engagement less profitable inasmuch as more days would have to be devoted to ac-

complish the work. However, that represents a *business decision* by the appraisal company, rather than any reflection of lower quality.

The fact is that any of the three firms can do the work, and it really depends on who wants the engagement the most. Many prospective clients request competitive bids and there is no reason to avoid them, except for one aspect.

If an appraisal company has performed several different engagements for the same client, there develops a knowledge on the part of the appraiser as to just what kind of information the client wants. The appraiser knows how aggressive the client wants to be in their tax strategy, how much time is a constraint, and so on. Close working relationships, in other words, do have some benefit, and many firms do not want to deal with a different group of professionals every time.

Until recently, many firms chose to utilize their independent audit firm for valuation assignments. As mentioned above, because there was already a close working relationship with the auditor, the client felt comfortable utilizing the same firm. This was usually decided on a noncompetitive basis, with the audit firm simply told to "go and do the necessary work."

From the perspective of independent appraisal firms, those not associated with an accounting firm, this particular decision process had the effect of excluding them from a certain number of business opportunities. Also, because of the lack of competitive bids, the client often paid a higher professional fee, on a per diem basis, than they might have received competitively. Somehow, on balance, competitive bidding tends to keep fees down.

The Securities and Exchange Commission (SEC) looked at the entire area of auditor independence. As part of its findings, the SEC determined that audit firms should *not* do appraisal and valuation work for their own audit clients if the resultant valuations were to appear in the financial statements. The major accounting firms can still perform valuation work in association with tax-planning strategies, where the work is immaterial, and in other areas not associated with financial reporting. It is still too early to determine whether this SEC rule will reduce appraisal fees by making more work open to competition. Although an accounting firm cannot perform valuation work for its own audit clients, it certainly is permitted to compete for valuation assignments with all other prospective clients for whom they do not perform independent audits.

Should companies use independent appraisal firms, or is it better to go with the name and reputation of a Big Five accounting firm? The author admits to a bias in answering this question. Trying to be objective about it, probably either an independent appraisal firm or a Big Five firm can do a totally professional job. Independent firms tend to be smaller, which means clients deal with the senior management, as contrasted with the accounting firms that have much more of an organizational pyramid, with lower-level staff doing much of the work.

The one thing that a Big Five firm can do is cut the appraisal fee as a loss leader, hoping at some point to possibly obtain future work such as consulting assignments. By and large, the independent appraisal firms perform only appraisals and do not offer, and cannot perform, other professional services. Some appraisers are getting into providing financing for their clients. The major investment banks that provide financing will often perform a valuation for their client as part of the underwriting.

There always has to be a suspicion of a conflict of interest. If the financing transaction is going to have a large fee associated with its successful completion, how independent is the valuation going to be? Similarly, several business brokerage firms provide valuations for prospective clients, hoping to get them to sell the business based on the high value determined in the appraisal. Again, there may be a conflict of interest.

As already mentioned, the author comes from a background of strictly independent valuation work, with no conflicts of interest, and feels that this is best for the client and the appraiser. Obviously, others feel otherwise. Enough said.

REVIEW APPRAISALS ON REAL ESTATE

For most ordinary valuation issues, a straightforward appraisal is sufficient, assuming the appraiser appears to have a reasonable background and experience. There are certain situations, however, in which appraisal reports are reviewed by other appraisers. Occasionally, there will be a court case for which the appraiser must be qualified as an expert.

Particularly for commercial and industrial real estate transactions, major lenders will hire an outside appraiser to determine the fair market value, but then have another appraiser review the initial appraisal report to verify the assumptions, methodology and comparable transactions that were utilized. Keep in mind that it is the borrower who pays for the appraisal, even if the lender chooses him, and has the report directly sent to the lending institution; in such situations, the borrower may end up paying for two appraisals on the same property. Borrowers are entitled to ask the cost of such work before agreeing to it.

The review appraiser, usually an experienced professional, does just that (i.e., reviews the other appraiser's work). Somewhat like a second medical opinion, the review appraiser looks at the detailed support in the first appraiser's report, tests the assumptions for reasonableness, and finally applies his own experience. There is a natural conflict between the borrower, who wants the highest possible value, and the lending institution, which wants to err on the side of conservatism, just in case things do not work out.

Inasmuch as it is the borrower who is paying for the appraisal report, the lender may feel that the valuation could be biased. Realistically, the appraiser gets most of his referrals from the lending institution, so any bias will probably be against the borrower. Nonetheless, because of the history of bad appraisals in the S&L crisis, lending institutions are under pressure from the regulators to have good appraisals in the file, and if the loan goes bad to find out where the appraiser(s) went wrong. So from the borrower's perspective, the maximum loan that will be allowed, the so-called loan-to-value ratio, is likely to be in favor of the lender. With two separate approaches, and each with a conservative bias, the banks and insurance companies are going to be protected.

EXPERT OPINIONS

When there is going to be a court hearing or trial involving valuation, the lawyers on each side will, with their clients' approvals, hire an appraiser to act as an expert witness. In this type of situation attorneys like to have appraisers who have testified before. That sounds reasonable except from the perspective of an individual appraiser.

How does an appraiser obtain testimony experience, if it requires prior experience to be hired? Obviously, this is a Catch-22 situation, resolved only when some brave attorney is willing to take a chance on an individual who has not previously testified in court.

The standards for qualification as an expert witness are somewhat technical. Opposing attorneys may try to attack an individual as not qualified by education, training, and experience. Those who have taught, written, and spoken on valuation issues usually have little problem qualifying.

There is a class of appraisers who make their primary living by testifying as expert witnesses. In other words, they are "professional" expert witnesses in valuation. Such individuals are certainly familiar with court techniques, depositions, and cross-examination. They may not, however, have had much experience in the trenches performing actual day-to-day valuation assignments for business clients. Such varied experience may, in the long run, be more valuable and provide greater credibility. After all, if an individual is perceived—rightly or wrongly—as a "hired gun," can a judge or jury really view such a person as truly objective and independent?

Our observation is that broad valuation experience should beat narrow expert witness experience. Some attorneys may not agree, but in the final analysis the client paying the lawyer's fee, and the expert's fee, probably will have relatively little input into the final selection.

IRS REQUIREMENTS: REVENUE PROCEDURE 59–60

In 1960, the Internal Revenue Service laid out some requirements for appraisal reports if they are to be considered seriously as evidence in any sort of tax issue. The following are the requirements:

Revenue Ruling 59–60 requires that in valuing a closely held business a number of factors be considered. These include:

(1) The nature of the business and the history of the enterprise from its inception.

(2) The economic outlook in general and the condition and outlook of the specific industry in particular.

(3) The book value of the stock and the financial condition of the business.

(4) The earning capacity of the company.

(5) The dividend-paying ability of the company.

(6) Whether or not the enterprise has goodwill or other intangible value.

(7) Sales of the stock and the size of the block of stock to be valued.

(8) The market price of stocks of corporations engaged in the same or a similar line of business having their stock actively traded in a free and open market.

In point of fact, these requirements have generally been accepted by appraisers, and it is a rare valuation report that does not at least discuss each of the issues. The one requirement for closely held firms that is often, on a direct basis, irrelevant is number 5, dividend paying ability. Most privately held firms try to avoid dividends because of double taxation. What the IRS is really getting at, however, is prospective cash flows, and as discussed in Chapter 6 in the income approach to valuation, cash flows are critical.

READING AN APPRAISAL REPORT

Most readers of this book will have occasion at one time or another to receive an appraisal report. These can range in length from three or four pages, which is considered a letter report, to several hundred pages in the case of a detailed allocation of purchase price for a multinational business.

As mentioned earlier, many readers search the final report only in order to locate the final answer, consider whether it appears reasonable, and file the report away. This is not wrong. But an additional 10 minutes spent reading certain parts of the report will pay dividends in terms of understanding the answer(s) and providing the basis for discussion with the appraiser.

Most appraisers routinely provide their clients with a draft of the report, which then provides the basis for answering questions prior to making the report definitive. It is at this draft stage that clients should spend some time and ask the tough questions.

In every appraisal report there is some point at which the appraiser must use professional judgment. No matter how many comparables the appraiser has found, no matter how detailed the cost buildup, no matter how precise the income projections and choice of discount rate, at some stage you, the client, are paying for judgment. Think of your doctor who orders x-rays of your stomach. The radiologist takes a picture and then has to interpret or read the film. The film is objective; the reading requires judgment. Similarly, the appraiser can amass all the data in the world, but at some point has to evaluate it and draw conclusions.

This need for professional judgment is why *every* appraisal report can be questioned by someone who does not like the answer. There is no such thing as a "bulletproof" appraisal. In a straightforward real estate valuation assignment, the actual transaction prices of all the other transactions can be available and can be 100 percent accurate. Nonetheless, the subject property is never identical to any of the other comparable transactions in terms of size, location, and timing. The appraiser has to correlate the given information and arrive at a judgment. As indicated earlier, most competent appraisers should come within ± 10 percent of each other. But if one is 10 percent high (from the real value) and the other is 10 percent less, there will still be a 20 percent spread between the two. Any good lawyer can try to use this difference to impeach one or the other appraisers.

The answer is straightforward. While appraisals are often concluded with a single point estimate of value, all parties should understand that absolute precision is impossible and will never be achieved. Einstein figured out the *exact* speed of light. Nobody, however, can figure out the *exact* value of a parcel of undeveloped land to the penny.

Thus, in reading an appraisal report, always ask yourself where the appraiser applied judgment and what the impact would be if that judgment were changed. Maybe it is a key assumption about the future, maybe it is an estimate of future sales price, or perhaps a comparison with other transactions that were not identical. One cannot specify in advance where the potential soft spot is going to be. The fact is that every appraisal report has one or more such soft spots.

That does *not* mean any appraisal is wrong. It just means that a human being, the appraiser, did the best job she could. She applied her experience and judgment to the available information and drew her conclusion(s). We are not saying that all appraisals are right or that no appraisals can be relied on. More than 100 years of experience with valuations by the appraisal profession has more than proven their worth and utility. We are saying that a careful review of any appraisal report will make the reader a much better informed consumer, to paraphrase the slogan of Syms, a well-known clothing firm.

CHAPTER 11

Providing Value Information to Shareholders and Analysts

This chapter is written exclusively for investor relations (IR) managers who deal with shareholders, creditors, and security analysts. Certain of the material herein replicates material elsewhere in the book. But since the rest of the book is primarily written for financial executives, accountants, and attorneys, and presupposes a background in accounting, we have chosen to provide material that may be unnecessary for the primary audience. Nonetheless, the discussion regarding the usefulness of value information to shareholders, creditors, and analysts should be of interest to most readers.

Investor relations managers continually have one important task ahead of them, and that is to help the market maximize shareholder value. Of course, the company's chief executive officer (CEO) and chief financial officer (CFO) are also interested in shareholder value and through their actions, as operating executives, plan and execute strategies that accomplish this. The IR manager's task, perhaps of equal importance, is to communicate to the street what the company is doing, that is, its operations, its strengths (and weaknesses?), and its operating plans. Sometimes lost sight of is the need also to communicate information about the company's *assets,* assets that may not always appear on the traditional balance sheet.

For example, pick up almost any annual report and you will find the following statement from the chairman, "Our employees are our most valuable asset . . ." Right. So, let's go to the financial statements and see just how valuable those employees are. Oops. Can't find them in the balance sheet or statement of cash flows, much less the income statement. Maybe the chairman was wrong. Does this mean the workforce has no value?

It is apparent that the employees, as an integrated workforce, have tremendous value. Just ask any human resource manager given the task of recruiting for a call center or for software designers. In fact, the press often has articles about high-tech firms on the West Coast buying other firms just to obtain the workforce. It costs money to hire and train good employees; when already accomplished, this represents an asset that is valuable.

Why don't financial statements disclose this value? Would it help investors to know the value of a firm's workforce? From a different perspective, if there are subsequent layoffs, doesn't the asset decrease in value? Analysts are always trying to understand a company better, to obtain knowledge of the firm's dynamics. What is more important than the quality of the workforce?

In addition to the workforce, there are several other categories of intangible assets that have value, but are rarely if ever disclosed to shareholders and investors. Pharmaceutical companies are used to receiving questions about research and development (R&D) projects. The fact is that information on R&D projects in process can be quantified and disclosed.

Consumer goods companies spend million, if not billions, of dollars to promote brand names. These names have values, often increasing over time. These brand name values can be quantified and disclosed. Along the same line, most successful companies have developed selling and distribution channels that would be extremely hard to replace. These, too, have value, can be quantified, and can be disclosed.

In this chapter, we discuss how publicly traded companies, for purposes of disclosure, can develop, on a supportable basis, the values of *all* kinds of intangible assets. We then show how this information can help analysts obtain a better grasp on a company's competitive position. Finally, we discuss the implications of the Financial Accounting Standards Board's (FASB's) recently announced decisions on accounting for goodwill and determining whether it is impaired.

It is not necessary for a company to run intangible values through the income statement and show them on the balance sheet. Values of intangible asset can be, and in our opinion should be, developed offline and then disclosed as supplemental information in the management discussion and analysis (MD&A) section.

Intangible asset values cannot be audited effectively, and this is why certified public accountants (CPAs) have resisted for so long in dealing at all with self-developed intangible assets. But the fact that CPAs do not like dealing with intangible assets does not mean that IR managers should disregard them.

The better job an IR manager does in disclosing asset values, both tangible and intangible, to analysts, the more highly rated will be his or her company. If the efficient market theory stands for anything, it is that information is encompassed quickly into share prices. How can the street give credit for a company's assets if the company itself refuses to say what they are and what they are worth?

ACCOUNTING RULES

For IR executives not familiar with accounting rules, here is a very brief summary. For further explanations, discuss this with your controller and ask her to explain further.

The financial statements prepared by a company and filed with the Securities and Exchange Commission (SEC), and then distributed to shareholders and analysts, are prepared in accordance with generally accepted accounting principles (GAAP). Unfortunately, there is no one place you can go to and read all of the GAAP, were anyone so inclined. But accountants over the years have developed GAAP to the point that, although there are differences and disagreements, most companies and most accountants understand the requirements of GAAP. In the final analysis, the SEC is the arbiter of what companies do, although it is the FASB that sets the actual rules.

The basis of GAAP is so-called historical cost, which means in practice that companies record as an asset on their books only those assets for which they paid cash, and which can be identified by a vendor invoice. This then allows the CPA to audit the financial statements and trace any asset shown back to the original underlying transaction. This system works well for inventories, land, buildings, machinery, and equipment (i.e., tangible assets). In every case the company bought something concrete, the auditor can look at it, touch it, and count it. It can be valued in relation to the original cash outflow.

This system works well given two key assumptions. One is that price levels don't change much (i.e., low or no inflation). Second is that most of a firm's assets are tangible in nature. When USX builds a steel mill or CSX lays railroad track, these conditions are met. But when Microsoft develops Windows software or Procter & Gamble (P&G) advertises Ivory soap, where does the auditor go to look for the asset, verify that it exists, count it, and value it? It is probably an impossible task. Nonetheless, most investors would rather own the right to the brand name Ivory soap, or have the master code for Windows, than have another steel mill or another 1,000 miles of track.

In short, GAAP was developed before the era of software and brand values. In its present form, GAAP simply cannot cope with the intangible, but nonetheless real, assets underlying most companies in this new economy. Present interpretations of GAAP *require* companies to charge off to current expense *all* investments in developing and supporting a brand or trademark, as well as R&D. GAAP permits companies to capitalize only the *cost* of developing software, not its real value in the marketplace.

These limitations of GAAP are well understood by corporate financial managers, yet there is great resistance to change. Among the arguments in favor of the *status quo* are the following:

- Right now companies obtain a tax deduction for expenditures on advertising. Putting a value on brand names, and showing them as an asset, might increase current taxes due.
- While it is relatively easy for accountants to determine the *cost* of developing software, and then auditing that cost determination, it is much harder to determine the *value* of the software. Accountants are used to dealing with costs, they are not used to dealing in values.
- Research and development is inherently risky and perhaps only 50 percent (or even less) of projects ever become commercially successful. What happens if you place a value on Project X and it then fails? You will have to write it off, and no CFO likes unpleasant surprises (i.e., write-offs of unsuccessful projects).
- Values change over time. Under GAAP, any *increase* in value would show up as income. This might be considered good news. But GAAP is a two-way street. Any *diminution* in value of an asset would have to be disclosed as a *reduction* in income!
- Finally, accountants and auditors are conservative by nature. Aggressive extroverts go into marketing or even IR; they do not go into accounting. Today's accountants and auditors grew up with today's GAAP. They know it. They understand it. They are comfortable with it. "If it ain't broke, don't fix it" is a motto most accountants understand and support.

ROLE OF SECURITY ANALYSTS

Security analysts may or may not have an accounting background. Nonetheless, they are presently bound by the rules and strictures of GAAP to the extent that this is all the financial information they have available to work with. Security analysts could, *if they choose,* make any adjustments they wish to the financial statements of the companies they review. But right now they do not have access to anything but GAAP financial information.

Particularly now, with the SEC's recent shutting down of private discussions with management, analysts effectively can work *only* with the financial data provided by the company. As mentioned, that information, at least in today's environment, is prepared in accordance with GAAP, filed with the SEC, and disseminated to analysts, creditors, and shareholders in the identical format. Such information today does not disclose intangible asset values.

What we are saying is that if companies provided *supplemental data,* outside of the GAAP financial statements, this would allow analysts to draw their own conclusions. Analysts could then choose to utilize information about intangible asset values as they wish. Just as an example, P&G in its chairman's letter *could* state, "We believe the Ivory trade name is worth approximately $1 billion, up from $900 million last year."

Some analysts might come to the conclusion that P&G was worth $100 million more than it was a year ago. Other analysts would say, "Gee, the Dial soap trade name went up $125 million this year; it looks like P&G is falling behind." Still other analysts would probably disregard the information.

In short, it is hard to tell in advance just how analysts will use any information given to them. But if a company does *not* disclose its valuation of its brands, or its R&D, or its workforce, or its distribution channels, or its subscriber base, how can an analyst be expected to take this information into account in valuing the company?

Information about a company's intangible assets is necessary to really understand the firm, its business, and its competitive position. In the absence of this information, analysts are essentially being asked currently to make vital decisions and recommendations without all the facts.

It is interesting that, when asked, many analysts do *not* want companies to disclose this kind of value information, particularly about intangibles. The reason is that the good analysts feel they already have a real competitive advantage; their understanding of the "big picture" of a firm is developed over time. They feel, rightly or wrongly, that they already understand the intangible assets of the company they are following, and if the company developed and disclosed this data the experienced analyst could lose his edge.

By the same token, the less skilled analysts probably do not know how they would evaluate information provided them about intangible asset values, at least at first. They feel overwhelmed with the amount of data already being presented as part of GAAP and throw up their hands at the thought of any more information.

As a result of these twin pressures, analysts are not clamoring for information about intangibles, and financial managers are uncomfortable thinking about providing it. After all, if P&G estimated the value of Ivory as $1 billion and it was later proven wrong, someone might sue P&G. The threat of lawsuits regarding the somewhat imprecise determination of values is a real issue, but beyond the scope of this chapter.

CAN INTANGIBLE ASSETS BE VALUED?

The answer to this is a clear and resounding *YES*. In point of fact, any company that has been involved in a merger and acquisition (M&A) transaction treated for accounting purposes as a *Purchase* (as contrasted with a *Pooling of interests*) has already been forced to determine the value of the intangible assets of the acquired company. Companies sometimes bundle all of the intangibles together into some sort of heading like "Goodwill"; nonetheless, under GAAP for the last 30 years buyers have been determining the value of all acquired intangibles.[1]

What they have *not* done is determine and disclose the value of the intangible assets of their *own firm*. Right or wrong, GAAP today says you *must* determine the value of acquired intangible assets in a purchase transaction and *cannot* put the values of those same types of assets in your own company on your financial statements.

But saying you cannot put the value of your intangible assets in your balance sheet does not mean that a company is forbidden to determine these values and disclose that information separate from the audited GAAP financials. In short, a company *can* disclose anything it wants, as long as it is not misleading and has been prepared in good faith.

So there are two issues:

1. Can values be developed reliably for intangible assets?
2. If so, *should* companies disclose this information outside of the audited GAAP statements?

Our firm (and all the other professional appraisal firms) does this kind of intangible asset valuation routinely. In fact, our firm's major competitors are the valuation groups of the Big Five accounting firms, the same firms that have to certify that their clients' statements are prepared in accordance with GAAP. Put another way, even the Big Five accounting firms develop values for intangible assets and certify that they are accurate and comply with GAAP.

However, in the absence of an M&A transaction, neither our competitors nor we routinely determine the value of intangible assets like R&D, workforce, distribution channels, and brand names. Only in the case of a merger do these asset values come to the surface, and only for the acquired company. If a company has primarily grown through acquisitions, and those transactions were treated as purchases for accounting purposes, then the firm's balance sheet probably reflects fairly well all its values. However, if a large company buys a smaller firm, one that is one tenth its size, then it is likely that only 10 percent of the real values will be disclosed in the financial statements. In short, there is a real discontinuity in GAAP that requires some intangible assets to be developed and disclosed and precludes all others.

The methodology for determining supportable values for intangible assets exists today. After all, the Big Five are themselves routinely developing such data for their clients, as well as auditing that information. Finally, the SEC routinely looks at how a company allocates the purchase price to intangible assets, as well as the lives used to amortize those assets. So if the information is good enough for the Big Five and for the SEC, it should be good enough for companies to develop for their own internally generated assets.

WOULD COMPANIES BENEFIT BY DISCLOSING INTANGIBLE ASSET VALUES?

The answer to this question is a matter of judgment. Each company, each IR manager, has to make this decision in the context of its own unique circumstances and attributes.

The basic principle underlying GAAP is that companies should disclose information that will help investors and creditors *understand and predict future cash flows,* based on information presented about the past. Will knowledge about current intangible asset values, and changes in those values from year to year, lead to *better* projections by analysts?

Do IR managers want the analysts who follow their company to understand the business? Does better understanding lead to better coverage?

It would appear highly desirable, in terms of knowledge, for analysts, as well as creditors and shareholders, to learn about any undervalued assets.

This is particularly true if the asset in question is severable, that is, could be sold to someone else. An example of that would be a brand name. Liquor companies, as an example, often buy and sell specific brands of gin, vodka, or whiskey. Thus, analysts would be able to determine if a company is earning a decent return on its brand values or whether it would be better off by selling the brand and reinvesting the cash elsewhere.

There are other intangible assets, such as the value of its workforce, that cannot be converted readily into cash. Nevertheless, by putting a value on the workforce, all the costs of hiring and training its staff, as the firm is growing, will be shown as the real asset referred to in the chairman's letter. If the company does have to have a layoff, and the workforce does shrink, then it is only appropriate to disclose to analysts that the particular intangible asset referred to has shrunk in value.

Values are a two-way street. They can go up and they can go down. On the way up, it appears highly desirable to highlight the increase in value generated by a growing and profitable company. If a company subsequently has difficult times, earnings and sales go down, then disclosing that the intangible assets have concurrently gone down may not be all that detrimental. In the worst case situation, analysts are likely to say in their report, "Well, the company's intangible assets decreased this year (or are going to decrease next year) but it is a noncash charge so don't worry about it."

We cannot predict exactly how analysts will use this information about the value of intangible assets. But if a company takes the initiative and discloses its own estimate of intangible asset values, there may be some very favorable responses from analysts and shareholders.

Just a final word about the cost of developing this information. It is probably a lot less than one might imagine. The fact is that if the information is not going to be audited, that is, subject to detailed review by auditors and the SEC, there is room for a greater degree of estimation.

Admittedly, determining values for intangible assets requires judgment. It is more of an art than a science. So, just as an artist can paint a broad-brush painting, or a very detailed portrait, so can an appraiser determine a broad estimate of value or a detailed report accurate to the last decimal place.

In our judgment only the former would be needed for initial disclosure. Approximate estimates of the value of key intangible assets have to be better than nothing. Right now, these assets are being shown as worth zero (i.e., nothing). As one brilliant analyst put it, "It's better to be approximately right than precisely wrong!"

ACCOUNTING FOR GOODWILL AND INTANGIBLE ASSETS

In new accounting standards 141 and 142, the FASB has recently changed the rules governing business combinations (e.g., mergers and acquisitions). Pooling of interest accounting has now become a footnote in books on the history of accounting. All merger transactions have to be treated as a purchase. Chapter 16 deals with implementation issues of SFAS 141 and SFAS 142.

After a lot of discussion, it appears that the current accounting requirements will push companies in the direction of trying to maximize the amount of goodwill, and minimize the dollars allocated to other intangible assets. So things like an assembled workforce, and a customer list, will either not be valued at all or given minimum valuations. Brand names have to be valued on the balance sheet, but not amortized unless their value is impaired.

As discussed above, this new FASB requirement appears to fly in the face of reporting the best possible information to shareholders. But there is a motivation for companies to go in this direction. Under the FASB rules, companies do not have to amortize goodwill to expense every quarter. Reported earnings will now be much higher than they were before; the more goodwill, and less value assigned to a workforce or brand names, the better the company will look—at least in the short run.

We cannot comment on the efficient market hypothesis, which assumes that investors are smart enough to look through reported earnings and deduce what is really going on. So putting more dollars in goodwill, rather than assigning it to the workforce, will only make reported earnings look better. Since it does nothing for cash flow (amortization of intangibles does not affect cash), more sophisticated analysts really will not care one way or the other about the FASB's directions.

GOODWILL IMPAIRMENT

The crunch comes, under the new rules, as the massive amounts of new goodwill now have to be tested each year for impairment. Impairment is defined as occurring when the fair value of a business unit that has goodwill is less than the sum of the fair value of all the assets in that business unit. As a simplified example, assume a company has only one business unit, and the assets are carried on the books at $1 billion. The asset total includes $150 million of goodwill from a prior acquisition, and the goodwill stays on the books until the impairment is discovered. Now assume that the company has 20 million shares outstanding, and the stock is selling at $75. The market value is $1.5 billion, well in excess of the asset values, and there is no impairment.

Now what happens if the stock price goes down to $45 per share? The market value is now $900 million, below the value of the assets. The only way to get the value of the assets to equal the new lower value of the business as a whole is to take an impairment write down of goodwill of $100 million. This $100 million charge to earnings could easily wipe out operating earnings for the year. In turn, as reported in the business press, the company will show us a firm that lost money for the year.

This will be true even though the goodwill impairment charge was non-cash, and had nothing to do with day-to-day operations. In fact, to add insult to injury, the stock price could have gone down because of overall market conditions, not related at all to the company's own operating results. Then you add a large write-off, wiping out reported earnings, and what will happen to the stock price? The stock's market price could go down further, triggering *another* second write-off. And none of this was related to how good a job management had done for the year.

RECOMMENDATIONS

The FASB has developed its requirements in such a way as to motivate firms to maximize goodwill and minimize dollars assigned to other intangible assets. Avoiding future goodwill impairments may actually have a higher priority than maximizing current reported earnings; that is, assigning dollars to short-lived intangible assets will incur an amortization charge every quarter. But in doing that, there will be much less chance of a single large impairment write-off.

If it is true that sophisticated analysts pay little attention to amortization of intangibles, in fact adding it back to reported income to arrive at EBITDA, then this approach may actually turn out to be more investor friendly.

Determination of actual values inherent in a business, and then reporting those values—if necessary, in footnotes, in MD&A, or even in the chairman's letter—is preferable to blindly following the FASB's strictures as called for in GAAP. Companies must follow GAAP if they are to file with the SEC and receive a clean opinion from their independent auditor. There is nothing precluding companies, however, from providing *additional* information elsewhere in their shareholder communication.

Recommendations

As an appraiser, the author may well be biased in his views. Nonetheless, developing and disclosing the value of a company's assets has to be beneficial in the long run. Blindly following accounting rules that do not reflect economic reality can be in no one's best interest.

ENDNOTE

1. This requirement is called for in APB 16 and APB 17.

CHAPTER 12

Allocation of Purchase Price: Tangible Assets

One of the most common purposes of an appraisal is to allocate the purchase price of a company over the specific assets acquired. Since the purchase price hardly ever equals exactly the fair value of the individual assets, the difference is treated as goodwill. Some companies want to minimize this amount, while others prefer to put more in goodwill and less in other asset categories.

As we saw in Chapter 2, the historical cost model of accounting requires that a company show on its books the acquisition cost of assets purchased. What they paid for an asset is captured as the original cost, and that dollar amount is subsequently depreciated. This sounds simple until it comes time to handle the bookkeeping for a business combination (i.e., a purchase of another company).

Assume Buyer B purchases all the assets of Target T for $10 million. If only a one-line entry were made on the balance sheet of B—that is, Target T, $10 million, there would be no problem. The problem is that T is now going to be run as an operating business, with sales, cost of sales, depreciation, inventory, and payables. In short, T's operations are going to be consolidated with the financial and operating results of B. In turn, this requires that B break down T's assets into each element (i.e., cash; receivables; inventory; and property, plant and equipment [PP&E]). Even that may not be too difficult.

But what happens if the value of all those assets mentioned above adds up to only $9 million? B paid $10 million and can find only $9 million. Accountants have developed a solution for this problem. The missing $1 million is called *goodwill*. It is an intangible asset that is based solely on accounting conventions. One cannot go out and buy goodwill on a stand-alone basis. If you have it on your balance sheet you cannot sell goodwill by itself. Does goodwill even exist? Philosophers who delight in pondering the question regarding the noise when a tree falls in a forest with no one around have spent many man-years debating the nature of goodwill.

For readers of this book, suffice it to say that goodwill is very real, in the sense that it *must* be recognized and accounted for, irrespective of whether it is a real asset or not. In practical terms, goodwill is a real-life problem that must be solved.

Why is it a problem? The answer is simple. Goodwill on a firm's balance sheet does not stay there forever. Something has to happen to this asset. Theoretically, this time period for goodwill amortization should be the life of the asset (i.e., however long the goodwill has continuing value).

That goodwill has value, in the sense of being something that a willing buyer will pay for, is without question. The courts and the Internal Revenue Service (IRS) have for years agreed that goodwill represents something the buyer will pay for, simply a reflection of the fact that the acquired business has customers, a workforce, a product, and, in short, is in business with a profitable future. This contrasts with an idea in the mind of an entrepreneur for a great business, but one that is not yet started, that has no product, no customers, and no income stream.

By buying an existing business, one acquires the location, facilities, and customer trade of that organization. Two examples come to mind. Perhaps the easiest example is a professional services firm. Such firms, say a management consulting firm, have very little in the way of assets, other than a skilled workforce and a history of client satisfaction. A second example would be a physician who sells his practice; there will be a small amount of equipment, but the real asset is the patient base and patient records, which ensure that most people will return to the office (at least the first time) and see the new physician. In the case of the management consulting firm, the client base and assembled workforce are the real assets, not the office furniture and fixtures. In the case of the physician practice, the real asset is the patient records and the likelihood that patients will return even to the new doctor who bought the practice.

If the purchase price for a management consulting firm and a physician practice was based on the future income stream anticipated from the business, say 1 to 1.5 times annual revenues, this purchase price will be way above all the identifiable assets (e.g., receivables, inventory, and PP&E). The difference between the purchase price based on future income and the small amount of real assets is goodwill.

At first glance, the calculation of goodwill is easy. Take the purchase price of the business (however arrived at) and subtract all the assets you can see. The difference is goodwill.

AMORTIZATION OF GOODWILL

Prior to 2001, GAAP, in the United States at least, required that goodwill be written off over its life, but in no case over more than 40 years. Thus, if there were $1 million of goodwill, the minimum amount to be written off each year was going to be $25,000. But if a 10-year life was determined to be correct, then $100,000 per year had to be written off.

What appeared objectionable to acquirers was that this write-off, whether $25,000 per year or $100,000 per year, had to be charged to expense. Therefore, it showed up on the profit and loss statement. At the end of the year, the company's profits were going to be $25,000 to $100,000 less than they would have been without the goodwill amortization.

This accounting treatment, mandatory write-off of goodwill, was a very controversial subject. Having paid a lot of money to buy another business, the buyer was faced with the possibility that future income statements would show no income, just losses. Service businesses, as well as high-tech businesses, typically have very few tangible assets and lots of goodwill. The more goodwill, the greater the charge to expense each year. The greater the charge to expense, the worse management looked in terms of performance. Good managers produce profits. Poor managers report losses. How could you be a good manager if you have a huge anchor, goodwill amortization, dragging you down each and every year?

Managers who wished to grow their business faced an unpleasant choice. They could forgo making acquisitions and have no charges each year for goodwill amortization. Or they could make the acquisition(s) and pay the price of a seemingly endless series of charges that made them look bad.

Adding fuel to the fire, look at cash flow. As discussed in Chapter 2, most investors are *supposed* to be interested in cash flows. Yet corporate management acts in the belief that reported earnings per share are more important than cash flow. How do we know this? Because rational managers of publicly traded firms, when faced with allocating the purchase price of an acquisition, consciously chose to place as many dollars as possible in goodwill, that had a long write-off. When offered the opportunity to place a major part of the cost of a purchased firm on machinery and equipment with a 5- to 10-year life, they often opted not to do this and instead chose goodwill with a 20- to 30-year life. The effect of this choice was to reduce tax deductions, consequently reducing cash flow, albeit with reported earnings per share *increased* in the short run.

How could this happen? Many businessmen think that allocating the purchase price of an acquisition is an exact science. Give the same assignment to three appraisers, or accountants for that matter, and they will come up with the same answer. Wrong. As has been discussed elsewhere in the book, valuation is much more a matter of professional judgment than it is a science. The following case study is representative.

A very large U.S. diversified manufacturer bought a business that had two facilities in Europe and one plant in the United States from another company. The product lines of the new acquisition, essentially automotive components, were related to the new owner's business, but served slightly different markets and customers.

The two European facilities were profitable, but the U.S. plant was old, inefficient, and suffered from poor quality. In turn, this led to customer dissatisfaction. Unfortunately, some of the customers of the U.S. plant also were customers of the parent company for other products.

Despite heroic management efforts, the U.S. plant could not be turned around, and the three units taken together were barely profitable. Compounding the problem, research and development (R&D) efforts were separately undertaken in Europe and the United States, and some of the product and process developments were used in all three locations. In short, the business was more or less integrated within itself, but was diverse in relationship to the parent company.

The only solution, after about four years, was to sell the three-plant business to another firm, one that specialized in the basic product line. A buyer was found, and a mutually satisfactory price agreed to.

The sales contract called for the buyer to allocate the purchase price among the assets acquired, with the understanding that the seller would use the same allocation—absent some significant difference of opinion. It should be noted that the IRS requires buyer and seller to agree on any allocation, to avoid having contradictory positions taken that would adversely affect tax revenues.

In the case at hand, the buyer contracted with a major reputable appraisal firm and after a detailed evaluation presented its conclusions. Keep in mind that the total purchase consideration had already been established and the only issue was to determine how much of the purchase price related to the U.S. operation and how much to the European plants.

The appraiser turned in the preliminary report and it showed that the majority of the purchase price, totaling several hundred million dollars, was assigned to the U.S. facility, and the balance—much less than 50 percent—to the European plants.

From the buyer's perspective (and they had hired the appraiser), the answer was excellent. Placing too many dollars against the foreign assets would cause future tax issues dealing with foreign tax credits. Because the buyer was primarily a domestic manufacturer, the U.S. facility was going to be the crown jewel, while the two foreign plants simply were considered part of the deal.

When the seller saw the draft of the appraisal report, they went ballistic. Putting the bulk of the purchase price against the U.S. asset meant that far fewer dollars were treated as gain on the foreign plants. The seller had unused foreign tax credits that could be used only by showing a profit on the sale of the foreign plants. The seller, in short, wanted most of the sale proceeds to be reflected in the European assets, and as little as possible in the U.S. plant. This is exactly the issue the IRS had in mind in requiring the *same* allocation to be used by both buyer and seller. Here in this case was a real conflict between the tax interests of the two parties.

The seller then commissioned a *different* appraisal firm to review the first appraiser's report. Not surprisingly, the second appraiser, hired by the seller, found errors in the first appraiser's report. Adjusting for those errors, the true allocation was for the bulk of the sales price to be reflected as related to the foreign plants, and only a small amount as related to the U.S. plant.

This impasse could not be resolved by correspondence or phone, so a face-to-face meeting of all parties—the buyer, the seller, and the two appraisers—was arranged.

After a lot of discussion, the real issue became clear. Both sides were correct! The seller had not been able to turn around the U.S. plant; it was losing money and there was little value in it. By contrast, the two European plants were making money, were growing, and seemingly had a good future. The real value of the total business to the seller was in Europe.

From the buyer's perspective, they knew intimately the domestic business. They were convinced they could turn it around within a year, make a profit, and grow the total volume. They would accomplish this by integrating the plant with other U.S. facilities that had the same customers and technology. From the buyer's perspective, they had been forced to acquire the European plants in order to get the U.S. facility. From the seller's perspective, in order to stop the losses in the United States, they had to give up two profitable plants overseas.

So many tax dollars were involved that compromise appeared difficult. In the final analysis, what the buyer bought was not what the seller sold. The buyer wanted the U.S. plant, which they could make profitable, and did not care about Europe, while the seller was glad to get rid of the U.S. loser, but hated to give up the profitable foreign operation. Common sense might suggest that only the U.S. plant should have been sold, but unfortunately the R&D performed on both sides of the Atlantic was too closely integrated. Also, a substantial amount of components were produced in one country and shipped to the other, so splitting the operations apart really would not have made good business sense.

How did this allocation issue get resolved? At the time this is written, it is not resolved. Each side is filing its own tax return with its own allocation, and in the final analysis the IRS will have to sort out the issue. Not necessarily the recommended solution, but maybe the only answer in this case.

This case demonstrates a couple of truths. What one person thinks he is buying is not necessarily what the other party thinks he is selling. For a deal to work, each party has to think he is gaining.

Thus, getting agreement on what was bought/sold, and what each element is worth, is not only a matter of judgment, but even more so a basis for controversy. While in this situation the controversy was between the two principals, more often than not the real controversy is between a company and its accountants, a company and the SEC, and a company and the IRS.

GOODWILL IMPAIRMENT

We started this discussion about the uncertainties and judgments required in an allocation of purchase price with a discussion of goodwill. Until the Financial Accounting Standards Board (FASB) changed the rules, corporate managers worried about how much goodwill there was going to be, and over what period of time it had to be amortized.

Then, in 2001, the rules changed. Goodwill no longer has to be amortized. Instead, it is treated as having an indefinite life, with no required amortization.

The trade-off for this new accounting treatment is a requirement that companies have to test goodwill that is on their books for impairment at least once a year. Impairment of goodwill is defined as existing when the fair value (appraisers use the term *fair market value*) of the enterprise is *less* than the carrying amount of all the assets, including goodwill, on the balance sheet. In other words, goodwill stays on the books until there is a diminution in the value of the business, and then the goodwill has to be written down, or in some cases completely written off.

This write-down of goodwill is a charge to earnings, and is a reflection of the fact that management either paid too much for the acquired business originally or that what they bought has gone down in value. Corporate management placed a lot of pressure on the FASB to change the rules governing goodwill amortization. They may have traded a headache for an upset stomach.

JUDGMENT REQUIRED IN ALLOCATION

Let us look at some areas where disputes naturally arise in valuing acquisitions for purpose of allocating the purchase price. These include the following tangible assets:

- Inventory
- Land
- Buildings
- Machinery and equipment

The list of intangible assets is virtually endless, but among the most common intangibles that cause valuation problems are the following. These are covered in the next chapter:

- Customer relationships and distribution channels
- Supplier relationships
- Covenants not to compete
- Assembled workforce
- Research and development in progress
- Software
- Brand names and trademarks
- Patents and unpatented technology
- Leasehold interests

Inventory

In most cases, inventories (i.e., raw materials, work in process, and finished goods) do not provide a valuation problem. The acquired firm's regular determination of inventory values, for purposes of closing the books each month, is carried forward. Inventory usually turns over quickly, going from an asset on the balance sheet to cost of goods sold in a matter of months, if not weeks. Any error in inventory valuation is quickly adjusted in the first year's financial statements. Further, public accountants are used to verifying the amount of inventory on hand and auditing the valuation of inventory. In short, appraisers are rarely called upon to determine the true fair market value (FMV) of inventory. However, this does occasionally happen. The following case study not only is true, but led to a bitter court battle.

A distributor of office equipment purchased a manufacturer of office machines. The buyer performed the usual due diligence, and in the purchase contract one of the terms was that the seller's closing financial statements would be prepared consistently with the past and in accordance with generally accepted accounting principles (GAAP).

Two days before the closing, the buyer received notice that, following a physical inventory, the inventory value was some $5 million more than anticipated. Swallowing hard, the buyer agreed to pay the amount, subject to verification.

After purchase and the installation of their own team of financial managers, the buyer discovered that the seller had consistently, for at least 10 years, written off to expense all amounts paid for repair parts. The parts were used both in warranty repair and for chargeable work. This policy was sensible because there were hundreds of models of office machines out in the field, and literally tens of thousands of individual stock-keeping units (SKUs). Setting up and maintaining an accurate perpetual inventory system might well have cost more than the benefits of more accurate internal control of the parts.

From the buyer's perspective, there was no question the parts were there physically. The lack of consistency in accounting was troubling— setting up $5 million as an asset when for 10+ years the items had been expensed—but the deal had progressed seemingly too far to back out. The $5 million was put in escrow for later resolution.

The valuation assignment began when the new management began to be concerned that many of the parts suddenly capitalized turned out to be for very old models, few of which were in use by customers. Having 583 pieces available when there are only 59 machines in the universe that could possibly use the part was the first clue! And this was true in hundreds, if not thousands, of cases.

The appraisal firm was then brought in to determine the FMV of the spare parts inventory. No other assets were to be appraised as part of the assignment inasmuch as the buyer was generally satisfied that the overall purchase price fairly reflected the business acquired.

The physical count made just before the closing date was verified by talking to the managers at several branch locations. There appeared to be no question that the physical quantities of the parts were there (i.e., there had been no cheating on part numbers or quantities).

Next was to verify that the values placed on each part were based on current replacement prices. This required talking to the Japanese trading company that acted as the middleman between the manufacturer and the importer. The prices charged by the manufacturer were the subject of a contractual supply agreement, and there was no evidence that the values assigned to the parts were outside the contractual price.

So, if the parts were there and the prices were accurate, didn't this mean that the seller had delivered what he had promised? The usual definition of *fair market value* is:

The price for which property would exchange between a willing buyer and a willing seller, each having reasonable knowledge of all relevant facts, neither under compulsion to buy or sell, and with equity to both.

The appraiser determined that $5 million was *not* the FMV! How was this determination made? The issue was neither the accuracy of the physical inventory nor the unit price per repair part.

The fundamental issue was the physical quantity on hand. No rational buyer would pay list price for a 100-year supply of a part, much less for a quantity that could *never* be used or sold.

What was the real value of the spare parts inventory, if it could not be used in the business? Did it have *any* value? The next step in the process was to explore the market for used office machine parts. In fact, there is a very active market. After office equipment has reached the end of its useful life in the United States, there is a market in the Third World for technologically obsolete equipment that still works. There is an active U.S. market in acquiring old office equipment and restoring it for export sale. The critical element is the availability of spare parts!

Where there is a demand, there will be a supply. Our client had a supply—a very large supply, in fact—of parts, and there were rebuilders who used parts. Voila!

That was the good news. The bad news was that the economics of rebuilding were such that the going price for parts was essentially 15 cents on the dollar.

The FMV of the spare parts appeared therefore to be about 15 percent of the dollar amount suddenly capitalized at the last minute. One last factor, however, had to be taken into account. After repeated interviews with the repair departments, some of the employees admitted that when a machine came in for repair that was not fixable, the usable parts were stripped from the machine and placed back on the shelf. A customer whose machine was in for repair and got it back in working condition would never know if the required parts were brand new or salvaged from someone else's machine! There was nothing wrong or even unethical with the practice.

When the salvage policy came to light, it did raise a question as to the propriety on the part of the selling company of pricing every part on the shelf as if it were new. Further, in terms of value, much of the inventory was in printed circuit boards. One can look at a bearing and determine its condition. One can not look at a printed circuit board and determine if it is in workable condition or not. The only way is to put the board in the appropriate model and see if the machine works or not.

In discussions with dealers, great skepticism was expressed about the circuit boards, and none of the dealers were willing to bid on that portion of the inventory. In effect, the printed circuit boards had zero FMV, and the boards were a large portion, in dollar value terms, of the total inventory.

The appraisers were able to determine the true fair market value of the $5 million inventory as about $400,000 to $500,000. This was presented as expert testimony in the court suit and was not challenged by attorneys for the other side.

The moral of this case study is that almost every asset has *some* value. With sufficient research, the values can be found. Due diligence sometimes has to be quite diligent, but with enough effort the facts can be determined. Obviously, this example is an extreme one and not representative of most inventory valuations.

Sometimes, *acquiring* companies do want high values for inventory, because the dollar amounts assigned will flow quickly into cost of sales, thus providing an immediate deduction for tax purposes, albeit at the expense of lower earnings in the year of acquisition. A second motivation for wanting high inventory values relates to the fixed total of dollars to be allocated (i.e., the purchase price). The more dollars that go into inventory, the less that must be assigned to goodwill. As we have seen, many managers are allergic to goodwill, perhaps because security analysts tend to penalize companies that have goodwill on the balance sheet. The concept of minimizing goodwill or getting an immediate write-off is discussed in Chapter 13 in the section on R&D. Nevertheless, putting as many dollars as possible in inventory is often a sound business strategy. Companies that have used last in, first out (LIFO) often will have undervalued inventory on the balance sheet, and an FMV study will uncover this hidden asset.

Land

In an allocation there probably is more pressure put on appraisers to value land at its highest possible value than any other asset. The reason is simple: no depreciation. It is an accounting convention that land is not depreciated. Similarly, accounting rules prohibit companies from writing up the value of land, although in some other countries this is permitted and sometimes even required. While nobody claims that land values are forever static, it appears unrealistic to arbitrarily write down land, absent some known economic event. If land were to be periodically revalued upward, pressure would soon mount to revalue other assets; and as we saw in Chapter 2, there would be some very negative consequences were such fair value accounting to come to pass.

The beauty of allocating as much as possible of a purchase price to land becomes immediately visible to every manager interested in higher reported profits. Of course, those who want to maximize tax benefits want as little as possible assigned to land for the same reason (i.e., no depreciation for taxes either).

But for those who want to put as much of the purchase price against land, how much flexibility is there?

Vacant land is basically valued on the basis of comparable sales. In most localities, for most types of land (i.e., zoned as agricultural, industrial, commercial, or residential), there is an active market. Appraisers research what land sales have taken place in the recent past. They then compare the subject parcel to those actual transactions, adjusting for indications of relative value like size of parcel and location. Done properly, a skilled appraiser is able to pinpoint with a high degree of accuracy what land would actually sell for were it to be put on the market. Land may take upward of a year to actually be sold at its estimated FMV, and the time value of money comes into the picture. But at the end of the day, there is actually very little flexibility in valuing vacant land—if the valuation is done properly. Where a degree of optimism can creep in is the assumptions made by the appraiser, for example, agricultural land may be worth more per acre if it were zoned industrial. Will such rezoning be permitted? Reasonable observers may differ, and the appraisal report may state, deep in the report itself, "*If the land were rezoned, then. . .*". But the final land value is no better than the rezoning assumption. So even with vacant land there is some flexibility.

Where there may be more flexibility is in assigning value to land that is presently encumbered with buildings. If you buy a house for $300,000, how much of your purchase price is for the land and how much is for the building? In theory, one looks at the price of vacant and available land that has sold recently. You then compare your lot with the similar lots that sold as buildable for residential housing. The land value so determined, say $60,000, can be subtracted from the total $300,000 purchase price and you could say the house was worth $240,000.

Alternatively, you could determine that a 3,000-square-foot house would cost $75 per square foot to construct. The house would then be worth $225,000, and by subtraction the land is worth $75,000. One method gives the land value at $60,000 and the other at $75,000, a 25 percent difference. Which is correct? Theoretically, the $60,000 land value and $225,000 construction cost are each correct, and this totals $285,000. That is fine, except you paid $300,000 for the total. How do you explain the missing $15,000? It could be based on negotiating skill. It could be based on your need for immediate housing, if you are just moving into the community. The $15,000 could represent the value of housing today, rather than the eight to nine months it would take for you to buy a lot and complete new construction. Or it could be that your lot is a little better located, or the house has some extra feature like a finished basement. The variations are endless.

The point here is that valuation techniques are approximate, not exact. If one wanted the maximum amount assigned to the building (depreciable), the first approach would be preferable. If one wanted the maximum amount assigned to the land (not depreciable), the second approach would be preferable.

Appraisers have some choice in appraisal method and assumptions used. If a client wants one answer over another, there is going to be temptation to utilize the appraisal method, or choose assumptions, that lean toward the desired result. The professionalism of the appraiser is all that stands between a good answer and a poor answer. Nonetheless, even the best appraisers, approaching an assignment in a totally professional manner, do have some leeway, perhaps 10 percent, plus or minus.

In valuing land under an existing building, a 10 percent variation in valuing the total property can lead to a much larger variation in the percentage assigned to nondepreciable land.

Buildings

There is an accounting convention that buildings are depreciated over 40 years. An estimate that 70 percent of all buildings in the country are over

30 years old is probably correct, and few of these structures are going to collapse in the next 10 years. Buildings are far more durable than accountants give them credit for.

The implication of this is that when a company is acquired, the so-called book value, the net amount on the balance sheet, usually understates the FMV of the buildings. More often than not, there is an opportunity to write up the amounts on the seller's books. Since buildings have a very long life for accounting purposes—which means low annual depreciation charges—there is a strong motivation for many purchasers to try and place a major portion of the purchase price on the building account.

Can this be accomplished within the rules of the game? Probably. Appraisers use two major approaches to valuing buildings for a purchase price allocation. The first is the market comparable method (i.e., what other, similar buildings are selling for in the open market). This is the same approach as used in valuing land, described earlier.

The second approach is a cost approach, answering the question "What would it cost today to build the same building, after allowing for depreciation from all causes?" The assumption here is that a rational buyer would not be willing to pay more for the subject property than a new building could be constructed for. The major problem is that construction and design are different today than they were in the past. Warehouses may have higher ceilings to accommodate new material handling equipment. Offices may be directly wired for computers. The layout of a new factory may be more efficient in utilizing new technology. A hotel may have newer and more cost-efficient heating, ventilating, and air conditioning (HVAC). So a new building may even cost more per square foot, but be cheaper to operate.

How do you determine the cost today of a building that would not actually be built? This is where the *judgment* of an appraiser comes into play. Basically, the appraiser determines the cost of replacement, in terms of square feet, and then adjusts the new cost for depreciation from all causes. This depreciation is not accounting depreciation (i.e., just a straight-line amortization of original cost). Instead, an appraiser's depreciation is based on physical deterioration (roof, HVAC, etc.) and functional obsolescence (computer wiring, ceiling height, etc.).

An appraiser must utilize professional judgment in evaluating depreciation from all causes in a building. How much variation would be found in competent appraisals from two different experts in valuation? Again, one would reasonably expect two different appraisals to come within 10 percent of each other. There is, frankly, some room but not much in an allocation to put more or less of the purchase price in buildings.

Just a note on a frequently found situation. Chains of restaurants, retail stores, or service stations may have a standard design. Appraisers, rather than going to 200 separate locations, will price out one or more models, adjust for any regional differences, and utilize this cost of reproduction for all the buildings owned by the acquired firm. This reduces the cost of appraisal and does not materially diminish the accuracy of the final answer.

Machinery and Equipment

The valuation of machinery and equipment (M&E) in an allocation presents one major conceptual problem; otherwise, it is very straightforward. The key question relates to the fundamental assumption as to the premise of value.

Appraisers use the term *premise of value* to relate to the basic assumption used in analyzing the asset in question. Are we going to look to the value in exchange or the value in use? Put in its simplest terms, value in exchange looks at what comparable assets are being bought and sold on the open market. Even this has its choices since we can value the asset on the basis of what a used equipment dealer would pay us to buy the asset from us. Or should we value the asset at what it would cost us to buy the same asset from a used equipment dealer? At a dealer there may be a 30 to 40 percent difference between his bid and ask price for production equipment, particularly specialized machinery as contrasted with general-purpose tools such as lathes and milling machines.

To make the situation even more complicated, perhaps the M&E should be valued on the basis of what it is worth as part of the going concern. After all, nobody assembles a production line just as an exercise in purchasing skill. The assets were bought for a purpose, to be used in making a product for sale to others.

Assuming there is a valid market for the output of the production facility and that the output can be sold profitably, the real value of the equipment is going to be based on the present value of future cash flows from the expected production. The whole is going to be worth more than the sum of the parts. In other words, having assembled a production facility (including the workforce and the distribution channels), the value of the future production should be greater than the cost of the assets in the assemblage.

If the value in use of the M&E is greater than their cost, would it be realistic to capitalize that future income today and allocate it to the assets being acquired? While a theoretical argument might be made that this is the way to accomplish the allocation, in practice neither accountants nor appraisers use this concept.

Rather, the value in use of production M&E is based on the *cost* today to acquire the assets, less depreciation (functional, physical, and economic) from all causes. The reason for using cost rather than capitalized future cash flows rests on the principle of substitution. If an investor could ultimately receive $1.5 million as the present value (utilizing an appropriate discount rate) from sale of the product produced in a factory, then the value of the factory as a going concern is $1.5 million. But what if you could buy from manufacturers today all the equipment in the factory for no more than $1 million? Any rational investor would pay no more than $1 million for the equipment. The difference between the $1 million for the equipment itself and the $1.5 million for the business represents the value of the assembled workforce, the customer base, and the distribution network. While the business is worth $1.5 million, the equipment is worth no more than one could buy equivalent assets from suppliers.

This explanation may be complex and hard to follow. Nonetheless, when examined closely, it exactly reflects the thought process employed by investors. And in a merger or purchase allocation, we are dealing first and foremost with understanding the components of the investment decision, that is, purchase of the seller's business.

Getting back to the value-in-use concept for M&E, as contrasted with the value in exchange, how do appraisers actually do their work? The first step is to take a basic inventory of the assets acquired. This can either be a physical inventory or inspection, which can be time consuming, or reliance on good property records. Chapter 14 discusses property records, and as a generalization here, good property records will more than save the cost of maintaining them. Lack of good property records represents a "penny wise, pound foolish" approach to business. In fact, appraisers sometimes make basic assumptions about a business from the quality of the property records!

After obtaining an understanding of what assets are physically there, appraisers then inspect the assets for condition. Some observers may wonder how any one appraiser can knowledgeably walk through a canning line one day, a foundry the next, and an injection-molding facility the third day and have expert knowledge in all these fields. Realistically, nobody can truly be expert in every facet of production. What a skilled M&E appraiser does have is experience. That experience translates into knowing *what questions to ask* and *who to ask*. Questions about maintenance policy, asset replacement, quality, and operating costs will soon reveal both current condition and hidden costs for deferred maintenance. Virtually everyone likes to talk about his or her job; a good listener (with appropriate questions) will be able to get a very good idea of condition in a short period of time. Skilled appraisers also know when to apply the well-known 80/20 rule and spend their most time on critical assets, typically those with the highest dollar value.

If one knows what assets are in the subject facility and what condition they are in, the next step involves the most time. Appraisers have to determine the cost today of the assets. Cost in this case is defined as cost *new,* typically from the manufacturing supplier. To obtain the actual cost new involves a lot of phone calls to manufacturers. Problems arise when the original supplier is out of business or will not respond to questions. Handling these issues is part of the stock in trade of an experienced appraiser. But assuming a little good luck, the appraiser will determine what it would cost today to buy the assets found in the property being appraised.

From the physical inspection the appraiser will apply a discount for depreciation from all causes. These concepts of depreciation are discussed in Chapter 5. Assume that a new asset would cost $10,000 and that the subject asset is determined to be 30 percent depreciated. Then the cost of the asset being appraised is put down at $7,000. This step is repeated for every asset, although experienced appraisers may take some shortcuts and group like assets together to reduce the time (and cost) of the appraisal.

A second and alternate approach to valuing M&E assets for allocation of purchase price is to apply an appropriate price index to the original cost of the asset(s). A well-constructed price index will measure relative price trends for the category of assets under consideration. If the government has already prepared the index, say by the Census Bureau or Department of Labor, it is neutral and without bias. While some economists have criticized the consumer price index (CPI) for an upward bias, appraisers do not usually use the CPI. Further, the critiques of the CPI center around errors of less than 1 percent a year. Given the inherent uncertainties in utilizing indexes, an error of that magnitude—even compounded for several years— is not going to be serious for most appraisals.

When indexes are used, the appraiser will always test for reasonableness, particularly for the large-dollar items. Blind application of an index, if it provides an obviously erroneous answer, is unlikely. And for the numerous small-dollar-value items, any error in the index is likely to be self-correcting.

There is one caveat about indexing that must be noted. The use of indexes, as compared with direct pricing by an appraiser, is going to save significant time and money. But indexes can be applied only to original costs. Most property records show the date of acquisition and the cost of the item at that time. A computer can then apply a properly constructed index, one covering perhaps a 20-year period. The computer matches up the date of asset acquisition with the corresponding year of the index and multiplies the cost by the index factor; the result is the cost in today's dollars of the asset.

What is often lost sight of is that if the company being appraised was itself the subject of a previous purchase acquisition, the *date of acquisition* on the computer file is unlikely to be the year when the asset was acquired from the manufacturer, nor is it going to be the original cost from the manufacturer.

On the asset file the acquisition date and asset cost, in the case of a previous acquisition, will be the *previously allocated purchase price and the date of the corporate purchase.*

The way price indexes are constructed, based on price trends each year for the same or similar assets, means that they cannot be applied to allocated prices. The reason is obvious. If all the dates on the file are 1995, some of the assets were actually new in 1989, more in 1992, and some in 1994. The actual price change between 1995 and the present, calculated in constructing the index, really bears no relevance to the information available on the assets being appraised. The 1995 allocation took into account not only asset price at that time but also physical and functional depreciation. So a *price index* would be applied to a dollar amount that was not the *price* of the asset in 1995, but the *value* in 1995. There is no known way of indexing values. Prices can be indexed, values cannot.

If indexes are to be used, the solution to this problem can be found only by going back to the original asset records. If they are not available, then indexing really cannot be used.

In setting up a fixed-asset record after a purchase allocation is made, keep the original date and original cost in separate fields. Most good fixed-asset computer programs will handle this approach. A little extra time up front will pay for itself. A further benefit of retaining the original information in the asset record relates to values developed for property taxes and insurance, covered in Chapters 14 and 15.

The basic principle behind the allocation of purchase price is to apportion the total dollars paid over the fair market *value* of the assets acquired. Determining the *cost* of the PP&E, even after allowing for depreciation from physical and functional obsolescence, will provide the *value in use* only if the profitability of the products produced will support the costs.

The typical example used is hula hoops or buggy whips, two products that were widely used and sold at one time and for which there is relatively little demand now. Suppose you had a three-year-old factory explicitly designed to make hula hoops and buggy whips. Three years ago, it was a state-of-the-art facility, and in the interim there has been little technological changes. Determining the *cost* today of the assets, whether on a direct pricing or an indexing methodology, will not tell you the *value* of the facility. The total cash flow reasonably expected from future sales will never support an investment, if the plant assets are valued at today's costs. (Forget for a moment why the plant might have been built in the first place. Mistakes happen!)

If the future cash flows from the plant's output are going to be only $50,000 a year and the cost of the assets is $5 million, would a rational investor be satisfied with a 1 percent return? No. Any reasonable investor would want at least a 10 percent return on investment (ROI). If the cash flows were $50,000, no investor would pay more than $500,000 for the facility. Assume that the liquidation value of the assets, sold piecemeal to a used equipment dealer was only $250,000. (At 5 cents on the dollar, this is about what used equipment actually might sell for.) In this fact situation, the appraiser would not use the $5 million cost of the assets. Rather, he would apply economic depreciation of 90 percent to arrive at the correct answer that the facility is worth only $500,000. The subject of economic depreciation was covered in Chapter 5.

The key point is that using a *cost approach* in allocating purchase price is usually going to provide the right solution, but it always has to be tested for economic reality. If the underlying business does not support the asset values, from the perspective of an investor, then it is up to the appraiser to apply common sense, not just blindly apply indexes to historical cost.

Part of the due diligence effort prior to any purchase of a business should include an analysis as to whether the basic profitability of each product line(s) will support the anticipated asset values. If they do not, and a write-down is going to be necessary, then either the purchase price should be reduced or more dollars will have to be allocated to goodwill. At a minimum, there will be no surprises. Such a preliminary review of asset values and cash flows should be a part of every purchase investigation.

SUMMARY AND CONCLUSION

In allocating the purchase price in a merger or business combination, a large portion of the dollars are usually going to be assigned to working capital (inventory and receivables) and PP&E. The chapter has described how appraisers go about doing this work, the areas where judgment has to be applied, and the range of possible answers.

Recent changes in the FASB's requirements for the handling of goodwill, which no longer has to be amortized, may push companies to desire fewer dollars in tangible assets and more in goodwill and intangible assets. Determining the value of intangible assets is covered in the next chapter.

CHAPTER 13

Allocation of Purchase Price: Intangible Assets

In the previous chapter, we discussed the valuation principles and approaches used in the allocation of purchase price for a business combination. The focus was on tangible assets, that is, inventory and receivables (working capital) and property, plant & equipment (PP&E). In this chapter, we focus on the valuation issues in valuing various types of intangible assets and intellectual property.

COVENANTS NOT TO COMPETE

A covenant not to compete is a good subject to begin the discussion of valuing intangible assets in a purchase allocation. There is a written contract. The life of the asset is known since the contract will have a specific time limit, often three to five years. The contract was freely negotiated between the parties because the tax consequences for the seller differ from that of the buyer. As will be discussed below, other intangible assets often lack one or more of these characteristics.

What is the value of a noncompete agreement? Obviously, the buyer of a company does not want the seller to take his money, move across the street, set up a new business, and then compete directly with his old firm now under new ownership. Many business firms are dependent on the skill of the founder or a key executive, one who is recognized by customers as *the* business. Particularly in service businesses, one or at most very few individuals are in a position to start over again, utilizing their industry knowledge and business contacts.

Without an agreement not to go into competition, the original business actually might not be salable. So it is to the advantage of the seller, as well as the buyer, to agree to the noncompete agreement. The difference of opinion will be the period during which the agreement lasts, with the seller wanting a short time and the buyer a long time.

Assume, however, that this is already negotiated and agreed upon in the purchase transaction. How much is it worth to the buyer for the seller to agree not to compete for a period of time? The approach usually utilized is to ask the question, "How much would it hurt my business if the seller *did* go into competition with me?"

Essentially, the method used to develop this information is to take the firm's own five-year projections, usually made as part of the initial purchase investigation. That becomes the *base case*. Then a second set of projections is made (i.e., sales, gross profit, operating expenses and net income/cash flow) assuming that the seller did start up a new business in direct competition. Obviously, the second set of projections is going to show lower sales and probably higher costs.

The *difference* between the two projections, one with and one without competition, becomes the basis for the calculation. Assuming the covenant not to compete is for five years, the difference in profit/cash flow for each of the five years is discounted back to today's dollars at an appropriate discount rate.

The analysis involved in projecting what sales, costs, and profits would be if the seller did go into competition should utilize reasonable assumptions. For example, it would be unrealistic to assume that the day after the transaction the seller would be back in business at his old sales rate. It would take the seller perhaps six months to actually start up, hire new people, and so on. Further, he would not capture all his old customers. The buyer, meanwhile, would have established some new customers and products and so forth.

The value of a covenant not to compete can be substantial. The value can also be determined in advance of the final closing of the transaction, and it would save a lot of time and effort if both parties would agree on that value and put it into the contract.

ASSEMBLED WORKFORCE

What is the most common saying in the chairman's report to shareholders? "Our employees are our most valuable asset." Actually, if you think about it, the statement, while trite, is probably true. Repeating it so often may have made some employees cynical and shareholders bored. Nonetheless, it is the workforce that separates one company from another.

An assembled workforce has two types of value. One is direct—essentially the *cost* to recruit, hire, train, and place employees in jobs that they understand and can perform effectively. The second is what the workforce can *accomplish* in terms of developing products or services, producing the output, and then distributing it to customers.

No business can operate without people; in the final analysis, *all* of a company's profits—past, present, and future—are attributable to its employees. But employees, at least one at a time, are replaceable. No one is indispensable.

In valuing a workforce, the appraiser looks to the *cost of replacement,* not the future income stream to be derived from the company's overall activities. Otherwise, there would be double counting of income from things like research and development (R&D), customer base, and so forth.

What does it cost to put together a team of employees that understand the business and can produce and sell the product? Nobody ever starts from scratch and simultaneously or concurrently hires all of a firm's employees. Virtually every company today grew, slower or faster, but no firm is born full-size. Employees have been added over time one by one to meet specific growth needs.

Thus, an appraiser does have a database to draw on. What has the subject company spent in the past to hire employees? Presumably, the same costs, per employee, would apply today were *all* the employees to be replaced. That, in essence, is the value of the assembled workforce. The company today has, say, 500 employees. A new firm would have to pay to hire 500 people one at a time.

The cost of hiring an employee can range from a simple want ad in the local newspaper to an executive search firm. But there is far more to these direct costs. Moving expense must be factored in. Training costs, including the time spent by the trainer as well as the trainee, should be included. Wage and salary costs must be paid, starting from day one, even though productivity and output objectives may take three to six months or more to accomplish. Obviously, none of these costs have to be incurred today for an already established workforce, which is why the assembled workforce has significant value.

While a rule of thumb is often suspect, at least it often provides a test of reasonableness. For hourly and clerical workers, a cost equal to three or four months' wages is fully supportable. For executives and managers, a much longer period is correct. An article in *Fortune* estimated that the replacement cost of a departing worker "can be as much as 150% of the departing person's salary."[1] Certainly, the total cost, including loss of profits while a new person learns his or her job, could equal the 150 percent figure.

When appraisers determine the value of an assembled workforce, there is always a second part of the assignment: the length of time over which the dollar amount must be amortized. One argument might be for a long period, say 25 or more years. Support for this position rests on the assumption that even if one person left, the base employees, the long-termers who keep a company going, will remain as employees for more than 25 years. The company life is assumed to be indefinite; the company will always have employees and, therefore, there should either be no diminution of the assembled workforce value or a very slow amortization.

Common practice, however, is to assign a much shorter life, based on the actuarial expectation related to the specific employee base as of the allocation date. The information is developed by looking at actual employee turnover during the recent past, say three years. More often than not, firms want to use the longest possible life for the value of the assembled workforce. To accomplish this may involve a detailed study of the turnover, understanding and adjusting for unusual or nonrecurring items. Realistically, if a firm has consistently experienced 15 percent turnover per year, then a seven-year life for the value of the assembled workforce is going to be the right answer.

Good records about new hires and turnover of existing employees not only would make an appraisal easier. It would also help the company itself develop better policies for employee retention. Almost always, it is less expensive to retain an existing employee than to go out and hire a replacement. Basic data on the costs involved greatly simplifies any management analysis.

It should be noted that the FASB explicitly prevents firms from putting a specific value on an assembled workforce, for purposes of accounting for business combinations. Nonetheless, real economic value exists in an established, cohesive body of employees. Here is a situation where accounting rules should not supersede common sense.

SOFTWARE

As our world becomes more and more controlled by computers and computer programs (think Internet and bank ATMs as examples), software to control the computers becomes a critical success factor for many firms. That software has value is beyond dispute. How to measure that value, contrary to conventional wisdom, is relatively easy.

Software that has been developed for sale to others is like any other productive asset, it generates revenue. Estimating the future net revenue stream and discounting that back to today's dollars essentially controls the valuation. The problem is the estimation of the future stream (i.e., how long into the future should we assume sales revenue?).

Software that is sold to others has very high gross margins since the only cost of sales is an inexpensive disc or CD-ROM, plus documentation. Technical support for existing users also is a cost that must be taken into account. But even so, margins of 90 percent are not uncommon. Two expense elements must also be analyzed. They are the marketing expense, usually categorized in selling, general and administrative (SG&A) expense and research & development (R&D) for new updates of the program(s).

It is relatively easy to project marketing expense, at least in the absence of known changes in the specific market served, e.g., a competitor is coming out with a new and improved product. Once a company has developed a marketing strategy and marketing plan, the expenses tend to be relatively fixed, and fluctuations in sales volume flow directly to the bottom line.

R&D expense in software, as in pharmaceuticals, is a necessary cost of doing business. The cycle of more powerful computers (faster central processing unit, larger storage) generates the ability of software developers to design and implement ever more powerful programs. In turn, those larger programs, in order to run faster, need greater computational power. Users expect something new and improved in software and either your company will provide it or a competitor will. Staying ahead of the competition drives R&D expense.

As a generalization, a particular software program will have a two- to three-year life, before a new version becomes a necessity. The switch from mainframes to personal computers to distributed processing to the Internet shows how technology can drive software. Business history is littered with software companies that were merged out of existence because they had not kept up with industry developments. R&D expenditures are a necessity, but do not guarantee success.

So in valuing software designed for sale to others, one has to investigate SG&A expenses and R&D expense in detail and determine whether the subject firm's product line is likely to be a survivor. Assuming it is, then the standard income approach to valuation, discussed in Chapter 6, applies.

If the appraiser is confident that the software product or product line is being maintained, then a five- to eight-year time horizon is undoubtedly supportable. Much more than that becomes highly speculative, however. Look back eight years and see what were the best-selling software products then and how they are doing today. Other than Windows, few software products, even with good R&D, seem to last longer than about eight years. Even Windows today is a far different product than it was eight years ago. And in the software universe there are few Windows.

To sum up then, valuing software developed for sale to others is a straight-forward exercise in projecting future income and cash flows. The appropriate discount rate is a matter of professional judgment, essentially relying on an understanding of the competitive position of the subject product or product line. A dominant product has lower risk and therefore a lower discount rate. A marginal product in a mature area has much higher risk and demands a higher discount rate—which, of course, leads to a lower valuation.

Software developed for internal use also has value. Sophisticated Enterprise Resource systems, or administrative and accounting systems, are very expensive to develop, and the cost to replace them would be substantial. One measure of the cost of software was the effort spent to correct the so-called Y2K problem. Many business firms literally found it cheaper to install new software than try to fix old 'legacy' programs. Estimates for the economy as a whole of fixing Y2K ranged upward from $100 billion.

How do you value software used internally (i.e., not developed for sale to others but rather used to run the business)? A superb internal system may provide significant competitive advantage (i.e., reduced operating costs and/or increased sales). But trying to separate the role of a software system from all the other elements of management becomes quickly an exercise in futility.

It is almost impossible to determine the fair market value (FMV) of internal-use software by trying to develop an income stream. The income approach to value is not ordinarily used to value internal software.

Rather, one has to look at the cost approach. How much would it cost to-day to replace or replicate the software? Basically, the answer can be found by analyzing the time it would take today to replicate the software. Programmers are paid perhaps $45.00 per hour. The systems manager or other qualified individual is asked to estimate the time it would take to develop equivalent software. This time estimate should be *less* than the actual time originally spent in the development inasmuch as the second time should require less effort (e.g., time will not be wasted on "blind alleys"). Multiplying the new time estimate by the rate per hour gives a fully supportable answer as to the value of the internal use software.

Again, one of the key questions asked of an appraiser is the length of time over which the value of software should be amortized or written off. Software for internal use does not have to be rewritten to keep up with competition, as does software that is sold to third parties. A longer life, perhaps 6 to 10 years, can be supported in most instances. Companies simply do not reengineer their distribution systems, their procurement systems, or their accounting systems that often. When they do, the software is only a small portion of the total cost. Put another way, the life of the software should best be measured by inquiry as to the elapsed time before the next expected process redesign.

Basic accounts payable software, even from five years ago, is going to work perfectly well for several more years, in terms of calculating discounts, printing checks, and preparing expense ledgers. The only reason to throw out accounts payable software might be if one were planning to go completely to electronic data interchange or business-to-business internet (EDI). In this case, we would be talking about a major redesign of how the company operates, and new software would be but one small piece of the redesign cost. As companies found out when confronted with the Y2K problem, there was a lot of 20-year-old software still in use! Companies do not lightly change internal operating methods, and this implies a relatively long life for software that comfortably processes today's operations.

SUPPLIER RELATIONSHIPS

Most observers would agree that customer relationships (discussed in the next section) are more valuable than supplier relationships. Nonetheless, a good base of high-quality, low-cost vendors can provide a very strong competitive advantage. This advantage, in turn, has value and can be quantified as an asset in a purchase allocation.

A large chain of retail stores specializes in manufacturer and distributor closeouts. They buy upscale goods that are overstocked, last year's design, or simply errors on the part of the supplier. In turn, the stores

are able to sell to the public at seemingly low discount prices; yet the chain has an above average gross profit margin.

In analyzing this business strategy, the key element separating the company from other retail chains is its ability to locate such merchandise, negotiate good prices, and then deliver it on time to its many retail outlets. The chain's buyers, over the years, have developed many sources that are able to provide good merchandise year in and year out. In this case, good equals brand names that can be sold at very low retail prices while maintaining margins.

The company decided to split its buying and warehousing operation from its retail store operation, in part for operational control and in part for potential savings on state taxes. It was necessary to value separately the two parts of the business—the buying/warehousing function as separated from the retail operation.

Basically, the supplier relationships built up over time represented the essence of the buying division's value. By looking at the incremental gross profit (as compared to other comparable retail chains) one was able to capitalize this amount on a present-value basis. The resulting value for the buying division value was substantial.

One could ask, why couldn't anyone else do what they had done? Someone else could have done it in the past. Now most of the good suppliers had well-established relationships with our client firm and it would have cost a lot of money and time for a competitor to come in and try to replicate the operation.

Another example of the value of supplier relationships can be found in the automobile industry. Historically, the Big Three had put all of their parts purchases out to bid each year. The feeling was that competition among suppliers would keep prices down, thus accruing to the auto company the lion's share of the profits. The parts suppliers, in turn, did compete furiously for each contract, and the result was in many cases profitless prosperity.

Then the Japanese auto companies came in with a different business model: cooperation with suppliers instead of competition. One or two suppliers of each part were chosen, and the Japanese company worked closely with them in terms of design, quality, and cost. At the end of the day, the Japanese companies had lower supplier costs, higher quality, and a healthy spirit of cooperation in advanced design. In practice, the chosen supplier became an extension of the car company's own design team, thus further reducing costs to both parties.

After 10 to 12 years of losing market share, the Big Three finally saw the light. Instead of trying to beat up their suppliers, in a dog-eat-dog attempt to get the lowest price today, the Big Three essentially adopted the Japanese model. They started to develop long-term relationships with a few key suppliers. While late in terms of competitive position, the Big Three started to realize the economies inherent in good supplier relationships.

A way to value supplier relationships, in total, is to look at the cost of the procurement function, capitalized over, say, a 3- to 5-year period. It takes time to identify the best suppliers, who may in practice not have the lowest unit prices but make up for it in terms of on-time delivery, high quality, and good design. Any reader who has moved to a new town and has to spend time finding a good plumber, a good restaurant, and a good dry cleaner will accept the fact that customer/supplier relationships both take time to develop and have real value.

CUSTOMER RELATIONSHIPS AND DISTRIBUTION CHANNELS

Many definitions of goodwill deal with the phenomenon of satisfied customers coming back to trade with someone because of successful previous relationships. This tendency to continue to do business with those you have dealt with in the past has value. In fact, it is the *primary reason* a buyer is willing to purchase an established business rather than starting anew.

In the past, buyers were not always necessarily interested in separating out the specific value of customer relationships and the related distribution channel from the more generalized goodwill. Now that the FASB has explicitly mandated this separation, increasing emphasis will be placed on quantifying this asset. Techniques are available for quantifying specifically the value of customer relationships. Why might this be desirable?

If a portion of the business is later sold, then having quantified that portion makes it easier to determine the gain or loss on the subsequent disposition. This is particularly true for tax purposes. Two examples follow on putting a value on customer relationships. In the first, rather than have a 20-year life for goodwill, the appraiser was able to quantify the asset on customer relationship and establish a supportable 35-year life. In the second, the relationship was actually a negative in terms of valuing the business.

A studio photographer bought a competitor who had a long-established relationship with a major chain retailer. Several hundred studios were scattered around the country in the lessor's stores. Customers made reservations to have their children's pictures taken, the photos were shot, and a week or two later the finished prints were delivered back to the store where the customer picked them up. From the photographer's perspective, the relationship was excellent because customers really thought they were doing business with the store, not a separately owned and run firm with no name recognition. From the chain store's perspective, the studios brought in traffic to each store at least twice, and the rental income (based on volume) was very attractive on a per-square-foot basis. In fact, the individual photo studios were among the most profitable parts of each store.

The contractual arrangement was a one-year lease, renewable each year unless either party decided not to renew. In the industry, relationships comparable to this had been established for at least 30 to 35 years. As long as the photo studio did good work and brought in traffic, the retail chain was happy. As long as the retail chain had a good reputation and brought in customers, the photography company was happy. Certainly, this symbiosis explained the long-term relationships that were established in the industry.

Had the value of this relationship, essentially the purchase price of the company, been allocated to goodwill, the Securities and Exchange Commission (SEC) might have insisted on no more than a 20-year life. But by showing that the industry norm was for the photo studio/chain store relationship to continually be renewed (even though the contract was only for one year), a 35-year life was established and supported.

By lengthening the life of the asset, the annual charge for amortization was significantly reduced, in turn increasing reported earnings in the forthcoming years.

Here was a perfect example of a customer relationship that was expected to continue, could be quantified in terms of future net cash flows, and for which a specific life was determined, in this case based on the industry history.

This next case, however, had a slightly different outcome.

A small plastics manufacturer had developed a line of craft items that were very well received. Low selling prices per unit were offset by wide distribution. There were, however, several competitors because the manufacturing process was actually fairly simple. Brand name recognition was minimal. The key to success in the industry was distribution.

The subject company was being valued for estate tax planning purposes. More often than not, the owner (or his attorney) is looking for as low values as possible, minimizing gift and estate taxes.

In this case, the company had one major customer, a giant discount retail chain with distribution throughout North America. The basic business was profitable, manufacturing facilities were being expanded, and the outlook was positive. However, in valuing the business, the fact that the one chain store customer accounted for 70 percent of total volume had to be considered a key factor. That customer's business was profitable and growing.

In valuing the business, we had to look at it from the perspective of a prospective buyer. How would a buyer like to acquire a company virtually all of whose profits came from one customer? The original owner had established a strong relationship with the chain's buyer over several years. The chain store was very satisfied with the level of service (order fill rate, timely deliveries, etc.) and with the pricing.

What would have entered the mind of a prospective buyer of the firm was whether the retail chain couldn't suddenly switch suppliers. As noted, the manufacturing process was simple, and there were several competitors. Essentially, the firm's owner had established a strong personal relationship with the purchasing managers at the retail chain.

Could this relationship be extended to a new owner? What were the risks? The business being appraised had very positive cash flows and good growth potential—both positives. But the appraiser also had to take into account the big negative—dependence on one customer.

The conclusion of the valuation was that in determining the appropriate discount rate to apply to the projected income stream, a higher rate was necessary, thus lowering the business enterprise value (BEV). Ad-

justing the discount rate was more appropriate than trying to estimate the probabilities that the single large customer would or would not continue to buy in the future.

In this case, the dependence on one customer affected the answer in a way that gave the owner of the business the answer he was looking for. But, in practice, things do not always work themselves out so neatly. Sometimes, the appraisal client wants a larger value and the appraiser cannot comply. But that is a different story, not applicable in a chapter on allocation of purchase price.

There really are two ways of valuing customer relationships and the associated distribution channels. As noted above, appraisers can utilize the income approach to value, essentially capturing the future cash flows and discounting them to today's dollars.

The second method is to look at the *cost* of developing a customer base. In practice, this is not as difficult as it sounds. The fact is that in most lines of business a successful marketing program, with good advertising, sales promotion, and direct selling effort, can capture a share of that market.

It is necessary for the appraiser to estimate how long it would take to capture the market share of the company being appraised. Say that with determined effort it would be possible through lower selling prices, better delivery, and higher product quality to capture a 15 percent market share. This could be done perhaps in five years.

The cost approach would then quantify the costs over that five-year period of providing higher quality (higher manufacturing cost), lower prices (lower gross profit), and direct selling and advertising (out-of-pocket costs) to accomplish the goal.

Putting the exercise in those terms, it is possible to demonstrate that for a subject company that already has a 15 percent market share, the cost of replicating it would be $8 million, to pick a number. In other words, a newcomer to the industry would have to spend $8 million to capture a 15 percent market share, so someone already there has an asset, intangible though it may be, that is worth $8 million.

Generally speaking, it is the professional opinion of many appraisers that customer relationships have a relatively long life. There is always a basic assumption that management is focused on the business and devotes its energies to developing satisfied customers, through continuing high quality, low prices, and so on.

In establishing a life, the real issue deals with changes in products. A visit to a large grocery store or general merchandise chain would show that the products being sold today are not necessarily the same as those sold 20 years ago. In the food area, prepared foods are taking a much larger share of the customer's dollars. In the chain store area, electronics in the broad sense has also captured purchasing dollars.

Thus, any projection for much more than 20 years out, in terms of customer relationship, has to deal with the question of whether the subject company will continue to sell the same product(s). One of two possible outcomes would be that the customer/supplier relationship will continue (and thus has value) but the actual specific products may change. Alternatively, one can put a 20- to 25-year time limit on the customer relationship. This acknowledges that over a 25-year period customer tastes will change, distribution channels (i.e., Internet sales) will change, and today's relationships will be so altered that trying to value them for more than 25 years is an exercise in futility.

The one thing that is true about valuation is that each case is different. Approaches to valuation may be the same, but application of the techniques always has to be focused on the unique attributes of each business. Therefore, determining the amount of value in customer relationships, or the length of time for which the valuation is appropriate, is always fact specific. So-called rules of thumb have little place in an allocation of purchase price.

BRAND NAMES AND TRADEMARKS

That brand names and trademarks have substantial value is beyond question. Think Coca-Cola or Oreo cookies. In fact, for most consumer goods companies, the investment in developing customer loyalty through branding may well exceed any other investment on the balance sheet. But a buyer will look in vain on the seller's balance sheet for any sign of brand name values.

Accountants, including the FASB and SEC, have consistently and persistently precluded firms from capitalizing advertising and marketing expenditures. These expenditures are designed to enhance the long-run sales of the branded products, just as an investment in plant machinery and equipment is designed to produce those same branded products that will be sold over the long-term. Machinery and equipment is capitalized on the balance sheet as an asset. The trade name Coca-Cola is reported by accountants as having zero value since it is not listed any place as an asset at all.

However, investors are much smarter than accountants. People who buy companies know what they are getting. For a well-known consumer name, the buyer is acquiring not only the brand name, production facilities, and know-how. Shelf space and distribution channels are equally important. Does a popular brand sell well because it gets shelf space, or does it get shelf space because it sells well? Obviously, they go hand in hand.

Separating out the value of the brand name from the value of the distribution channel is possible, and probably worthwhile. Typically, a good brand name will have a much longer life than today's distribution network. Several studies by independent researchers rate the world's top 10 brand names, and most of them go back 50 years or more. In contrast, distribution channels today are far different than they were even 20 years ago, and the rise of Wal-Mart and the demise of Montgomery Ward & Company are evidence. Valuation of customer relationships and distribution channels is covered in the next section.

If we want to place a separate value on brand names how is this done? Brand names, *per se,* are rarely sold, although it does happen. Occasionally, one will read about a liquor brand that is sold. But 99 times out of 100, not only is the brand name sold but the buyer also acquires production and distribution facilities. The brand name may be the motivating factor, but at the end of the day it is a total business that is transferred.

Thus, we cannot use the so-called *market comparable* approach. There simply are too few transactions. Worse, the value of a brand name is really a function of prospective sales volume and profitability. What good does it do to know that Brand name "T" of a frozen foods manufacturer was sold for $20 million if we are trying to determine the value of a soft-drink brand?

If we cannot use the market comparable method, how about the *cost method?* Recall that the cost method looks at what it would cost today to replace or reproduce the asset in question. How would you ever replicate the name Colgate for toothpaste or Campbell for soup? Yes, someone else could duplicate the products, but in the consumer's mind, the brand names of Colgate and Campbell on the package stand for something more than the physical toothpaste or soup.

Someone once visited a production facility at which very well-known cosmetic products were produced. The visitor was asked, "Would your wife like some face powder?" Upon receiving an affirmative answer, his host promptly scooped up some powder from the end of the production

line, put it in a bag, and handed it to the guest. In terms of quantity, it was a lifetime supply.

Unfortunately, when he got home that night his wife was less than thrilled with her gift. Without the brand name and packaging, the product *appeared* extremely pedestrian and she really did not want to use it. There was nothing wrong with the product and it was the genuine brand, but without the brand name on the package it appeared to be what it could have been—generic powder.

The cost approach to value will work when we are dealing with machinery and equipment, with real estate, even with the cost of assembling a workforce. But for a unique asset, the cost approach fails. No matter how much you spend today, you cannot create a new Rembrandt painting. You can buy an already existing painting from someone else, but you cannot get a brand new one. In real estate you can buy an existing building or you can have a general contractor erect a new building to your specifications. The market approach will work for antiques and fine art, but not for brand names. The cost approach will work for real estate and production equipment but not for brand names.

This leaves the *income approach,* which determines the net present value of future income and cash flows and discounts that back to today's net present value. The value of a brand name has to be in the income it produces for its owner.

Some observers have approached the brand name valuation problem from the perspective of the total profits produced by the brand. As a hypothetical exercise, if Procter & Gamble's (P&G's) Tide brand generates $100 million a year in profit, then allowing for a 10 percent return on investment, one could estimate the value of the brand at $1 billion, 10 times the annual profit.

That approach might be a start for valuing the brand itself, but certainly not the brand name. The reason is that the detergent is produced in factories that were designed to make that and other similar products. P&G has a very well established marketing and distribution chain, excellent relations with retailers, and a strong advertising and brand management system. The P&G system is geared up to managing literally dozens of brands, and each of the separate brands, Tide included, benefits from the system.

The value of the brand name Tide can be calculated only on the incremental profits related to packaging the detergent in a box with the brand

Tide on the box. The investment has already been made in P&G's infrastructure and they could, and do, sell detergent under several different brand names. All the operating profits of Tide cannot and should not be attributed to the brand name. The prior investment in all the *other* P&G assets requires a return, and this return on investment (ROI) is not properly part of the Tide profits, no matter how P&G keeps its books.

To value a brand name properly requires the appraiser to (1) estimate the *incremental* quantity of the product sold; and (2) determine how much higher a *price* the seller is able to realize. What we try to do is estimate what the brand name itself does from the perspective of the customer. Assume there are two cans of soup on the grocery store shelf, one labeled Campbell's and the other with the store's own generic brand name. At the *same price* more shoppers will pick up the Campbell's can. At a penny or two higher per can, the store will sell its own brand about 50 percent of the time. But that incremental 1 or 2 cents per can will translate into significantly higher gross profit for both the store and for Campbell. The Campbell's brand name on the can affects both volume and price. Depending on the product line and the strength of the brand name, either price or volume may be more affected. It is the analyst's job to estimate this impact. It should be recognized that the estimate of the price effect or the volume effect is still just that—an estimate. Thus, brand valuation is not an exact science. The margin for error is relatively high. The one thing that is certain, however, is that the accountants are wrong when they say that the value of a brand to a company, for financial statement purposes, is zero.

One way to *estimate* the value of a brand is to look at expenditures for marketing, sales promotion, and advertising. If one kept a record each year of such expenditures, then perhaps the sum of the most recent five years' outlays would be a close approximation of value. As discussed, the cash expenditures made do not necessarily equal the value of a brand name, but a good estimate is better than zero.

A second way of looking at the value of a tradename is related to *royalties* paid on it or on comparable products. Licensing of a brand name has become ever more prevalent, and a perfect example is the use of an athlete's name on basketball shoes or a team name on a cap. There are literally thousands of examples.

What each has in common is the use by one party of an asset, the name, owned by someone else. While the specific transactions are each individually negotiated, the common thread is a royalty payment by the licensee to the licensor almost always based on sales volume. There often is an additional up-front one-time fee required by the licensor, an amount that can act as a minimum royalty or is simply the price of admission.

Royalty rates are usually quoted in percentages, say 3 percent of sales or 8 percent of sales. Within an industry or product line, royalty rates usually fall within a range. High-margin products, say perfume, can usually afford much higher royalties than lower-margin products such as clothing.

Valuing a trade name thus can mean examining actual royalty rates, if the name has been licensed to others, or estimating the royalty rate that the name could command *if it were licensed.* An appraiser will then take the actual or theoretical royalty rate and conduct a discounted cash flow analysis. The royalty rate is applied to projected sales, discounted at a reasonable interest rate, and the resulting amount is one indication of value.

When a company has a good brand name, one that has *not* been licensed to others, this method of capitalization of what a royalty rate might be (even though in the real world no royalty is actually being paid) is referred to as a "relief from royalty." The appraiser values the brand name *as if* a royalty were being paid, a royalty equivalent to what a different party might charge on an arm's-length basis. The use of a relief from royalty methodology provides a perception of precision. In practice, it is no more accurate than the choice of theoretical royalty rate. To the extent there are good comparable rates available, the resulting answer can have a good degree of reliability. Unfortunately, there is not a good database of publicly available royalty rates.

PATENTS AND UNPATENTED TECHNOLOGY

Of all forms of intellectual property, patents may be the best known. Given a legal monopoly by the government, albeit for a finite number of years, the owner of the patent can produce the product—or utilize the process—on an exclusive basis. Some patents have no value, because they have been superseded, or because there is no consumer demand for the product. But many patents have great value, such as those owned by pharmaceutical firms for one-of-a-kind drugs.

Again, as with other intangible assets, the cost of a patent is irrelevant. Accounting conventions allow only the out-of-pocket cost of applying for the cost to be capitalized on the balance sheet as the value of the patent. Thus, a drug that cost $100 million to develop might be on the balance sheet for $15,000, representing the legal expenses associated with filing the patent. How cost is defined by accountants (i.e., the $15,000) bears no relationship to value as we use the term in a purchase allocation.

The real value of a patent is the income that the owner can derive from his exclusive legal monopoly. It may be a lot, or it may be little, or it may be nothing. We determine the value, based on future income, by asking what benefits the patent actually provides. Does it allow exclusive sale of the product, as in a pharmaceutical? Does it add an exclusive feature to an otherwise standardized product? Does it reduce production costs because of an exclusive process? A patent can provide all of these exclusive attributes.

An appraiser, in valuing a single patent or a portfolio of patents, asks about the exclusive features and tries to understand the impact of the patent on sales volume (i.e., cash inflows) or reduced expenses (i.e., lower cash outflows). From an understanding of the cash flows that the patent(s) provides, it is relatively easy to project these cash flows out for the remaining life of the patent and discount the future cash flows back to a present value.

Sometimes, it is hard to estimate directly the cash flows. Again, appraisers will utilize the relief from royalty approach discussed earlier. For the relief from royalty technique to be applicable the appraiser must find other, more or less comparable license agreements dealing with comparable technology. Often, it will be easier to project the cash flows directly than to use the indirect relief method.

The royalty method is applicable in valuing patents when the owner has, in fact, licensed use of the patent to some other party. The licensing agreement will spell out the royalty rate to be paid by the licensee. This then represents a direct and known cash flow *rate*. Valuing the patent directly then involves only a projection of future royalty amounts, essentially the sales volume forecasted for the licensee against which the royalties are payable.

Unlike some intangible assets, the *life* of the patent is always known exactly because of the fixed period for which the patent is valid. Every patent expires at some point, and the cash flow projections should be carried out only to the expiration date. But what if there are numerous patents, one overlapping the other?

Multiple patents, sometimes involved in cross-licensing agreements, really have to be treated as a group. Look at a specific electric toothbrush, for example, a product covered by three different patents, expiring at three different dates. Further, the manufacturer is continuously working on improvements, some of which may be themselves patentable. In this type of situation it may be more appropriate to look at the underlying business, and value the product line, rather than to try and separate out the impact of the patents from the other assets involved in the line of business.

In this situation the controlling factor is not necessarily the expiration date of the earliest patent nor even the latest patent. A reasonable assumption may be that the life of the product is longer than the patents and all the patents together at the point of valuation can be valued as a business, with a more realistic time horizon than the arbitrary expiration of one of the many patents involved.

The concept of *unpatented technology* is obvious when it is pointed out. Sometimes referred to as *know-how*, many firms explicitly do not wish to disclose publicly a secret manufacturing technique. Keep in mind that the essence of a patent is disclosure, telling the world what you have discovered, how it works, and what it does. In exchange for public disclosure the government provides the owner with the exclusive right to exploit the knowledge.

But often, simply knowing that something is possible is extremely valuable to competitors. Many observers thought that the secret of the hydrogen bomb would never be able to be kept secret. As soon as the Soviet Union found out that a hydrogen bomb *could* be made, they were able quickly to replicate the feat. The key piece of information was that a hydrogen bomb could be developed using an atomic bomb as the trigger. Everything else after that was engineering effort. Simply disclosing that a hydrogen bomb had been successfully exploded gave the Soviet Union all the information they needed to proceed expeditiously.

Many manufacturers in competitive industries feel the same way. If they have discovered a better way of producing a product, then by patenting it, they alert their competitors. Further, if the intellectual property deals with a *process,* how will the original owner ever find out if competitors are in fact using that process. The first company will never have access to the second firm's factory to find out if the patented technique is being infringed!

Rather than patent a new process and risk unknown infringement, many firms choose quite consciously *not* to patent new techniques even though they would be patentable under current law. When evaluating an acquisition, a competent appraiser will determine the unique manufacturing and processing techniques that provide a cost and competitive advantage. These unpatented techniques and processes, what we refer to as *unpatented technology,* have real value. A dollar amount and economic life can be established for this asset.

Once the unpatented technology has been identified and analyzed, the actual valuation requires application of the income approach. How much is saved in production costs, and for how long will the savings continue to be realized? Again, once these questions are answered, the valuation is straightforward. The real skill comes in properly identifying the un-patented technology, in effect being sensitive to the potential and then looking for it.

LEASEHOLD INTERESTS

Many prospective target companies have an asset that is often overlooked in a due diligence analysis. A lease is a signed contractual agreement for use of property. The terms of the agreement control the economics of the situation. A company has a real estate lease with eight years left. How can this be an asset? Appraisers often find that the lease-mandated rent, per square foot, is substantially *less* than current space is being rented for. If a retailer is paying $9.00 per square foot when comparable space is currently being rented for $11.00, the $2.00 savings is an asset!

After all, relative to competitors the subject firm has a cost advantage. The total value of this cost advantage is measured by taking the $2.00 per square foot times the total number of square feet. That equals the savings per year. Then on a present value, discounted cash flow basis, the savings are added up for the total period between the date of the appraisal and the end of the lease. The assumption of course is that at the end of the lease any renewal would be at full current market prices. There is no reason to expect a landlord to continue to favor a particular tenant. The only reason for the below-market rate today is that at the time of signing the original lease, the tenant got a better deal.

Can this go the other way? Can a company be paying too much under terms of a lease? The answer is obviously in the affirmative. Just as a below-market rent is an asset, so an above-market rent is a liability. But as a practical matter, most buyers, in a purchase analysis, do not pay too much attention to this phenomenon. The assumption is that the rent ex-pense on the most current profit and loss statement reflects the total cost being incurred, and most purchase decisions are based on earnings, not analysis of specific assets and liabilities.

The purchase price allocation we have been discussing is almost always an after-the-fact study. The search is always for *assets,* in order to minimize goodwill. Reflecting the liability for the above-market rent would simply increase the goodwill, which is not the objective. Technically, the purchase price analysis should be objective and reflect economic conditions as they are, favorable or unfavorable. But since above-market rents are often immaterial in terms of a total purchase price for a business, more often than not this aspect is overlooked and nobody is really hurt. The SEC doesn't care, so the independent auditors do not scrutinize this aspect.

The only time above-market rents do become material is in a bankruptcy situation. The debtor has to get out from under onerous cash flows. Without going into the legal technicalities of abrogating leases, the valuation of leasehold interests, favorable and unfavorable, can become a critical element in any reorganization plan.

RESEARCH AND DEVELOPMENT IN PROGRESS

In 1974, the then new FASB made a fundamental decision that corporate expenditures on R&D must all be expensed immediately. Many firms had been capitalizing R&D on the grounds that the amounts spent had future benefit. The amounts capitalized would then be written off as the new product or service went into production and generated revenue. Thus, the argument went, there was a proper matching of revenue and expense.

The FASB took a look at this and said it was true that R&D expenditures were designed to provide future benefits, but capitalizing all such expenses on the balance sheet did not reflect the real value. In other words, some firms were capitalizing the R&D, but then not writing off the costs of unsuccessful projects, perhaps arguing that *maybe* things would work out in the future.

In any event, by edict the FASB simply ruled that all R&D must be expensed and was not an asset. It could not be capitalized, irrespective of how successful or profitable the investment might ultimately be. It was less important to match revenue and expense than to avoid overstating values on the balance sheet.

Jump ahead 20 years. Software and biotech firms, among others, live and die by the success of their R&D efforts. When IBM bought Lotus, management determined that a significant portion of the purchase price was really for the work Lotus then had in progress to update existing software and develop new applications, activities that fit the classic definition of R&D. But, guess what? The billions of dollars IBM paid for the R&D in process under the original FASB ruling could not be considered an asset. It would have to be written off immediately to expense. This immediate write-off of purchased R&D in process was actually to the benefit of IBM. Rather than showing the billions of dollars as an asset that would have to be written off over five to ten years, it was immediately written off with no future impact on the income statement. In one fell swoop companies had found a way to get rid of a substantial portion of goodwill—just call it R&D in process.

As with anything that is too good to be true, writing off purchased R&D in process was abused, and the SEC reacted by putting increasingly severe limits on what could be called R&D in process. Further, they promised scrutiny of the financial statements of any company that charged off a high percentage of purchase price to R&D. Companies were forced to scale back the somewhat aggressive posture they had been taking. It will be interesting to see what approach companies take, after issuance of SFAS141 and SFAS142. Now goodwill is not going to be amortized and R&D has to be changed to expense. One can imagine a role-reversal with the SEC now looking for companies to charge *more* to R&D.

Nonetheless, until the FASB says that R&D expenditures can be—or even must be—capitalized, firms do have to write off purchased R&D in process. The only issue then is how to calculate the amount of R&D in process at the date a target company is acquired.

The methodology involves application of straightforward valuation principles. Keep in mind that in the allocation process, the goal is to determine the *value* of acquired assets, not what they originally *cost* the company in the first place. Consequently, one does not really have to look at past expenditures previously identified as R&D on the target firm's books.

Rather, the emphasis is to look at the products or services under development and determine the future income-generating potential. The future sales of the products or services under development are estimated and the relevant costs of providing those services subtracted to arrive at an operating profit. The costs to complete the R&D in process at the acquisition date also must be accounted for.

It is necessary not only to develop the *value* of the R&D in process but to estimate the useful life that the product or service will have once it is commercial. The useful life affects the value itself. After all, if the product has a three-year life, the cash flows and present value will be materially less than if the product can reasonably be expected to have a five-year life. Because all of the R&D in process at the date of purchase will be written off immediately to expense, minimizing the dreaded goodwill, acquirers at times get fairly optimistic about the chances for success. R&D in process, by definition, is not yet a successful product so even assuming there will be future profits is itself a leap of faith, albeit one based on experience and sound business judgment.

The valuation of R&D in process therefore involves significant estimations. Just how long will the new product be viable before *it* is itself superseded? Some purchasers of software firms made the assumption that the next version of the software, the one currently in process, will last forever. Of course, this is not literally true, but assumptions have been made assigning all future profits of all future versions to the current R&D in process. This may give a desirable answer but is extremely hard to defend logically.

The nature of software, and most other products and services for that matter, is that new versions are a way of life. If at some point you do not update your own products, you can be sure your competitors will, thus forcing you to develop new versions. Nobody seriously expects that when today's R&D efforts are successfully completed all R&D will cease. The very nature of R&D is that it is a continuing *process.*

The importance of recognizing a realistic life for in-process R&D cannot be overstated. Shareholders, security analysts, auditors, and even the SEC scrutinize the amounts written off. Inasmuch as the assigned life effectively controls the amount of the write-off, choosing a supportable life and then justifying it becomes a critical part of the valuation.

SUBSCRIPTION LISTS AND DATABASES

There are a number of intangible assets that actually increase in value over time, not decrease. A good example is a database that is assembled item by item. A dictionary with 500 words in it is less valuable than one with 5,000 words, while a 50,000-word dictionary is at least an order of magnitude still more valuable. But putting together a 50,000-word dictionary file is going to cost more than 10x the cost of the 5,000-word file. Each definition has to be researched individually, so there are no possible shortcuts. Once assembled, however, the file has significant value over time.

Assume that a buyer acquired the dictionary database from its assembler at the point that there were 6,000 items in it. Valuing it could be done by looking at the *cost* spent to date. Alternatively, one would estimate the future sales and profit potential, less the cost to complete the project (i.e., develop the remaining 44,000 entries). These two approaches might well provide somewhat different answers, but in either case the database does have value. It would be hard to argue that this was R&D in process. In fact, what was bought was a database that has potential for expansion. The database has present value and potential for even greater value in the future.

Assuming the dictionary project is to be continued, assigning any arbitrary life to the asset will give a wrong answer. If the database at the 6,000-word level is worth $30,000 ($5.00 per entry), then assigning it even a 30-year life means that the buyer will have to write off $1,000 a year for the next 30 years.

But think through what was really acquired. One year later the database may have 8,000 entries and be worth at least $40,000. In that year, the *value went up.* Writing off $1,000 tells shareholders the value went down, which in fact did not happen. Accounting rules mandating amortization of intangibles are simply out of touch with economic reality when dealing with assets that increase in value over time. Some, if not most, intangible assets do diminish in value as time passes, but others do not depreciate.

SUMMARY AND CONCLUSIONS

Intangible assets, sometimes referred to as intellectual property (IP), are becoming an increasingly significant part of corporate assets. Appraisers have developed techniques for valuing virtually every type of IP. Many of them have been covered in this chapter.

As technology develops and new fields of endeavor are exploited, undoubtedly the variety of IP will expand over the years. Yet the methodology for valuing intangible assets can be applied.

In the past, and still today, many companies wanted allocations of the purchase price of their acquired companies to accomplish certain financial, tax, and accounting goals. Appraisers have tried to be responsive to client wishes, but are still constrained by the fact that their work is going to be scrutinized by the client's independent accountants and the SEC.

Changes in accounting for goodwill undoubtedly affect the way companies are treating allocations for purchase accounting. Whereas in the past pressure was on to minimize goodwill, now that has been reversed. Nevertheless, most purchased companies still have an assembled workforce, customer and supplier relationships, technology, and R&D. Good valuation techniques are still available, and prudent management should at least endeavor to find out just what was bought and what it is worth. Whether the information so developed is actually reported in the financial statements is actually a different issue.

ENDNOTE

1. "You Hired 'Em. But Can You Keep 'Em?" *Fortune,* November 15, 1998, p. 247.

CHAPTER 14

Good Property Records Increase Value and Save Money

Most companies have poor property records. There are a number of reasons for this. First, in most accounting departments, the job of property accountant is near the bottom of the list of desirable jobs. Second, the property record function does not *appear* to contribute directly to profits, although as will be discussed in this chapter, this is not true. Third, with the advent of computerized property record systems, the job appears both clerical and mechanical. Finally, neither outside auditors nor Internal Revenue Service (IRS) agents typically spend a lot of time going over accounting records for property. In the final analysis, there is an assumption that any errors will correct themselves in terms of future depreciation charges.

In short, the best and brightest management accountants coming out of school want jobs in cost accounting, budgeting, general accounting, and operational analysis. To most observers, property record accounting is a dead end, so many controllers put either the newest accountant on the job or the individual near retirement who is being phased out of a career. Consequently, in many firms, turnover among accountants in the property record job function will have been very high, and there will be numerous different approaches to keeping the property records.

Why are good property records so important? Good property records can help increase profits through:

- Increased return on investment (ROI)
- Secured lending
- Reduced insurance expense
- Reduced property tax

- Better product pricing
- Reduced capital expenditures
- Control over maintenance expense
- Component depreciation

INCREASED RETURN ON INVESTMENT

Many companies measure performance of division managers in terms of ROI, with the investment base being working capital and property, plant and equipment (PP&E). For many firms, PP&E is larger in absolute amount than receivables and inventory combined. Exhibit 14.1 shows this.

The chances are very high that at most of these firms far more manpower and resources are devoted to keeping track of and controlling the receivables and inventory than of the PP&E. Yet in terms of assets employed, the opposite is true.

One of the big problems with fixed assets is that they are not truly fixed; that is, fixed assets move within a company. To verify this, try two small experiments. First, take a sample of 10 items physically located in a specific location and try to find them in the fixed-asset record. Most computerized records have one or more fields showing the location of the asset. So, theoretically, the 10 items geographically together should appear in the same section of the record. The chances are that they will not. The second test is just the reverse. Take 10 items from the fixed-asset listing that all

Exhibit 14.1   PP&E as a Percentage of Receivables and Inventory

Company	Receivables and Inventory	Property, Plant and Equipment	PP&E as a Percentage of Receivables and Inventory
IBM	$32,486	$39,616	122%
PepsiCo	$ 2,704	$ 5,438	201%
Merck	$ 6,936	$14,347	207%
Sara Lee	$ 4,715	$ 5,362	114%
P&G	$ 6,400	$23,221	363%
Newell			
Rubbermaid	$ 2,213	$ 2,955	134%
Supervalu	$ 1,478	$ 2,920	198%

In millions of dollars.
Source: Company annual reports.

show in the same location, and try to find them. The chances are that they will not be contiguous to each other, if you can even find them.

Now if you were a division manager, being measured on your ROI, how would you like to have several hundred thousand or even millions of dollars of assets on your books that really belonged elsewhere? The formula for ROI is earnings divided by the asset base. The bigger the asset base, the lower the ROI for a given level of earnings. Therefore, if the denominator of the equation is overstated, the worse the manager will look.

The answer is to have good records that are updated periodically through a fixed-assets inventory. That subject will be covered below. At this point, the reader should be aware how ROI calculations will be in error if the asset base is incorrect.

The bottom line here is that physical assets are constantly being transferred, moved from one department to another, one plant to another. Keeping track of machinery and equipment is not a trivial task, and stringent controls have to be in place and enforced if the system is to maintain its integrity.

ASSETS PRESENT BUT NOT ON THE BOOKS

Just as there are usually numerous assets on the books that cannot be found, and presumably no longer are functional or even in existence, the opposite is also true. There are many assets present and still in active use that have been written off to zero value. When an appraisal company takes a complete physical inventory of all PP&E, discussed below, invariably both types of errors are present. Assets exist that are not on the books, and assets are on the books that cannot be found.

Sometimes, people wonder just how assets could be present that are not on the fixed-asset accounting record. That can come about for a variety of reasons:

- Many companies at times have had overly strict controls on capital expenditures. A local plant manager is not allowed to spend $10,000 for a machine, but he needs the machine to cut costs and meet his operating budget target for the year. How to get the machine? One way is to split up the purchase into two projects for $4,900 since the local plant can spend up to $5,000 without permission. The two expenditure projects have to be treated as expense rather than capital, so they never are on the books.

- Cannibalization of obsolete machines, discussed earlier, can be a useful source of parts for a newly built piece of equipment. Many plant engineers in a factory like to tinker and solve problems, and occasionally they will create a new piece of equipment custom-designed for a specific manufacturing problem. The unit works and is on the shop floor, and the costs were never run through the books.
- A vendor of new production equipment will accept a trade-in as a disguised form of price reduction. In point of fact, the vendor has no use for the old asset itself, and lets the company keep it on the floor. The factory superintendent, assuming the space is available, likes keeping the unit just in case there is a need for it. In every factory, unexpected production requirements come up. The more complete the complement of equipment, the better able management is to respond to short-term challenges. Retaining an asset that theoretically was traded in provides an insurance policy.
- Finally, some companies take assets out of their accounting system once they are fully depreciated.

FULLY DEPRECIATED ASSETS

Depreciation for accounting purposes, computed in accordance with generally accepted accounting procedures (GAAP), bears little relationship either to the real value of the asset(s) being depreciated or to the useful life of those assets. For most companies, depreciation expense is charged on an annual basis (split into 12-month increments) based on some estimate of useful life determined at the date of acquisition.

Some companies will have accounting manuals or policies for setting useful lives. Others rely on tax accounting requirements. Relatively few companies make a concerted effort to understand actual expected useful lives and develop accounting policies appropriate for their unique circumstances.

A brief history of depreciation accounting is in order. During World War II, companies were trying to minimize their reported profits, in order to reduce taxes due at the very high rates in effect. One way of doing this was to charge as a current expense all maintenance performed on PP&E, and to use the shortest possible lives for setting the amount of annual depreciation. The shorter the life, the higher the current year's depreciation charge, the lower the reported income and the less taxes payable. Companies at that time essentially chose to use the *same* life for books and for taxes.

The IRS, trying to maximize tax revenue, was in constant fights with taxpayers about capitalizing large maintenance expenditures (on the ground they extended the lives of assets) and on the choice of lives themselves. The IRS issued regulations that effectively set the minimum lives for most categories of PP&E. These lives were generally recognized as being too long, at least in the period after World War II when technology was rapidly changing. The steel industry, for example, took the lead in arguing that the long IRS lives were prohibiting them financially from investing in new equipment. By 1960, these arguments appeared to have some validity. In order to stimulate investment, the government shortened the lives for PP&E and instituted the Investment Tax Credit, a way of utilizing the Tax Code to impact the economy.

From this point on, depreciation policies at the IRS were essentially set on the basis of politics and economic policy, not on actual experience. There have been numerous twists and turns in the intervening years. The net effect is that IRS guidelines, with the possible exception of personal computers, now provide for lives for tax purposes that are *shorter* than actual experience would dictate. This, of course, helps companies reduce their tax bill. But it has had a perverse impact on financial reporting.

Companies, by and large, still tend to set lives for financial reporting that are consistent with tax lives. While there is no requirement for this, and software programs can handle different lives, nonetheless the old tradition hangs on and many companies use tax lives for financial reporting. Therefore, if the IRS allows seven-year or 10-year lives on production equipment, it is easier for the company to use the same lives for financial statements.

However, most production equipment in manufacturing, as well as office furniture and fixtures lasts well beyond 20 years. In fact, go to any long-term manufacturing facility and you will find many assets still in use that are more than 20 years old. Under current approaches to tax and book accounting, these have been fully depreciated, but obviously still have value.

One more complexity must be mentioned. Under GAAP, as pronounced by the Financial Accounting Standard Board (FASB), companies must write down their assets if they are impaired (i.e., worth less than book value). But this is a one-way street because if assets are worth *more* than they are carried on the books, they cannot be written up. They can be written down, but *never* written up, unless the total company has been sold, and this allocation is discussed in Chapter 12.

Appraisers, if performing an allocation of purchase price on a merger and acquisition transaction invariably find lots of fully depreciated assets in use, with values that can and now must be written up. We are not advocating changing to some sort of fair value accounting and reporting system, whereby companies automatically write up assets, although this is done in a number of foreign countries. What we are advocating is twofold.

First, companies should disconnect the choice of lives for financial reporting from tax requirements. The lives for tax purposes are now set by statute and regulation, and an IRS agent cannot come in and say, "Lengthen your tax lives to correspond with your financial reporting." There is no conformity requirement for asset lives that is comparable to LIFO reporting for inventories. Under tax law, if companies use LIFO for taxes, they *must* keep their books the same way. For lives and depreciation methods this is not true, although many companies act as though it were.

Second, companies should really try to estimate the effective economic life of assets they acquire. Perhaps personal computers are replaced every three years, so use a three-year life. However, if milling machines last 30 years, then use a 30-year life. This will have no impact on cash flow because taxes and tax payments will not be affected. Reported earnings will be higher, which may or may not be considered desirable. What will happen are those book values for PP&E will now more closely match economic value. There will still be no provision for writing up values, but there will also be less need.

ARE BOOK VALUES TOO HIGH OR TOO LOW?

There are two forces pushing in opposite directions concerning the accuracy of property records. On the one side there are assets that can disappear—be on the books but not there. In the opposite direction are assets that are not on the books but are definitely in use.

Any generalization in this area is dangerous, but by and large one will find that these two may offset each other. Perhaps 15 percent of the assets on the asset listing cannot be found. Offsetting this could be 10 to 15 percent assets that are there, but do not appear in the records.

It is fundamental in accounting that offsets are not desirable, essentially because two wrongs cannot counter each other. There really are two separate problems that should be addressed. Because one is plus and the other minus makes the sum of the two perhaps immaterial. But in terms of property taxes and insurance, to be discussed below, they do matter. The fact is that every company is different. The fact that on balance for the U.S. economy the two may offset does not mean this is true in any specific situation.

There is a second factor to be considered in looking at book values relative to property records. As has been mentioned several times, book values on the accounting records represent original cost less accumulated depreciation. What book value does not represent is the current fair market value (FMV). As discussed in Chapters 2 and 3, there are several definitions of FMV, primarily value in use and value in exchange. Book value in the accounting records bears no direct relationship to either.

Nonetheless, when our firm performs an appraisal of a total business for purposes of allocating the purchase price, it is often the case that the real FMV, on a value-in-use basis, is roughly equivalent to book value. We have given this some thought trying to explain it. There is no direct connection between the original purchase price of an asset 10 years ago and today's book value. Take a $100,000 machine tool purchased in 1991 and being depreciated over a 15-year life. In 2001, the book value would be $33,000, disregarding any salvage value.

In the intervening 10 years, technology has improved through electronics. The price of electronics has come down steadily. Offsetting this are inflationary factors for all remaining costs of machine tools. So a new and improved machine tool would sell in 2001 for $125,000. The 15-year life understates the period of time over which the old unit will still function. But the new machine, with better electronics, is faster and uses less labor and material. This causes an appraiser to ascribe a cost penalty to the old unit.

Take all these factors together, and it is possible to see how the FMV, on a value-in-use basis might approximate book value. Any example like this can be made to come out to a predetermined answer. But our experience suggests that looking at book value provides, at a minimum, a rough approximation of value-in-use.

What book value does not do is even come close to the FMV on the premise of sale (i.e., value in exchange). When a lender looks to assets to support a loan on a collateralized basis the lender is not interested in value in use. If the loan cannot be repaid, the bank does not want to try to run the business, utilizing the assets that are there. After all, if the borrower cannot make a go of it, how can the bank's officers do a better job? When a loan cannot be repaid, the bank wants to sell the collateral and recoup its money.

Sale of assets at a time of loan distress involves what appraisers refer to as liquidation value, either orderly or forced. This is value in exchange. The prospective buyers for collateral are usually dealers, auctioneers, or competitors. None of them have an incentive to pay top dollar. Experience suggests that in this situation, essentially forced sale, sellers are going to be lucky to obtain 50 cents on the dollar of book value. While book value may approximate value in use, it almost always exceeds value in exchange.

SECURED LENDING

Many companies borrow from banks and other lenders, using their fixed assets as collateral. Here we show how important property records are.

A major chemical company wanted to undertake a sale and leaseback transaction. The lender would buy the specific assets and lease them back to the borrower. At the end of the lease term, the borrower would have the right to repurchase the assets at the then fair market value.

The purpose of the transaction was twofold. First, to borrow money at relatively low cost because the lender had good collateral. Second, if the transaction were structured properly, the borrower would treat the financing as an operating lease. The PP&E would come off the balance sheet, and no debt would show, inasmuch as the monthly lease payments were an operating expense, not a capital lease.

To accomplish these objectives, the specific assets subject to the lease had to be identified, and values determined twice. First, the parties needed current values at the time of the lease, and second, they needed an estimate of the FMV in five years (i.e., at the conclusion of the lease).

The appraisal company was called in to develop the values, and the dollar amounts were satisfactory to the lender. However, there was a new accounting rule dealing with sale and leaseback transactions. It stated that the costs to take down or deinstall the asset(s), ship them elsewhere, and reinstall them elsewhere could not exceed 10 percent of the lease.

Therefore, the appraisers had to estimate not only the FMV of the assets themselves, but also the deinstallation, shipping, and reinstallation costs of those same assets. In many companies, inbound shipping costs and installation costs are captured separately and entered as a separate line in the computer record.

In this case, the assets had been transferred from another plant, and there was one giant entry on the computer record that essentially said "transferred assets" and carried forward the depreciated cost of $8 million. So the original cost was missing, the original date of acquisition was missing. The original inbound freight and installation costs were also missing. In short, the appraisers could not go to the borrower's own accounting records to obtain the requisite information to comply with the new accounting requirement.

The problem was ultimately solved by working with the plant engineers and purchasing department and in effect recreating what the costs would be today. The borrower lost a lot of time, and incurred significant additional expense, as a result of the poor condition of the property records.

When PP&E is used as collateral, the lenders want to know not only the current values, which are never available from the property record, they also need to know exactly which assets are and are not included in the deal. Good property records provide this information.

REDUCED INSURANCE EXPENSE

How do good property records reduce property insurance expense? Years of experience with many companies have shown that invariably there are numerous assets on the books that no longer are physically present. How can this happen? In most cases, the explanation revolves around poor record keeping. Old assets are traded in on new equipment. The company records the net cost of the new asset (list price less allowance for old equipment) in the property record system. The property accountant, however, does not ask the appropriate plant engineering personnel to initiate documentation to remove the old asset from the accounting system. Even as soon as the next day, the accountant goes on to some other task and quickly forgets that the old asset is still on the books.

The outside auditors, when they come in for the annual audit, do not typically review internal workpapers to see if documentation for the old asset was issued. The thought process they go through is essentially as follows: "If there is a mistake in the records, the annual charge for depreciation expense, this year and in future years, will sooner or later write off the old asset to zero. Further, in comparing this year's operations with last year's, there is no significant difference inasmuch as both years showed the same (straight-line) depreciation. Both balance sheets also were comparable. So, what is the problem?"

Consequently, it is easy for the old asset to leave the factory, and not be recorded as such; there is nobody to worry about it. Time, in short, will ultimately solve the problem. It is not like inventory shrinkage, in which there is a real loss due to employee or customer theft. Not processing paperwork for traded-in assets is simply an accounting problem.

A second way that assets are no longer in the plant, although still on the books, deals with cannibalization of units to obtain currently needed spare parts. One reads about airplane mechanics in the Air Force, taking parts off one plane to fix another, expecting to repair the second unit when the spares arrive. It is fairly easy to see that a plane on a runway missing perhaps a landing gear is going to be repaired as quickly as possible.

In real factory situations, however, current production emergencies are solved however possible. Many pieces of production equipment have been taken out of service. This is either because they have been replaced with newer and better equipment or they are simply in a stand-by situation in case a particular part or assembly is needed sometime in the future. Meanwhile, to a desperate maintenance man, the availability of his needed part from equipment that not only is currently unused, but also may never be used in the future, is a "no-brainer". Once a machine has started to be stripped down for spare parts, it can very quickly lose its identity. Soon there will a discontinuity between the fixed-asset record and physical reality. The accounting records will show a machine that no longer can be found.

There are other ways besides trade-ins and cannibalization that assets are not physically located where the records say they should be, or worth what the books show as the cost. One would imagine that if a milling machine were moved from Plant A to Plant B in another state, the net effect would be zero, from the corporate perspective. True, assets of one plant are overstated and in the other are understated, but the shareholders are not affected in total. They have bought and paid for one unit and the company still has it.

However, what accounting entries have been made? On day one, when the asset went into Plant A, incoming freight and installation were undoubtedly capitalized as part of the acquisition cost. This is in accordance with GAAP. When the item was moved from Plant A in one state to Plant B in another state, the remaining freight and installation cost in Plant A should be written off, as well as the new freight cost to move it to Plant B, plus the Plant B installation cost now capitalized on Plant B's cost. That is the theory. In practice, anything can happen. Often, the original freight and installation will be left on the books and the company will now capitalize the new freight and installation. This will have the effect of doubling up the costs, overstating the value of the unit.

To get back to the insurance question, the poor property records will result in paying insurance on assets no longer physically present or owned by the company. If the trade-in is not removed, the cannibalized unit not written off, and the freight and installation cost on the transferred item doubled up, the net impact is to overstate the cost of PP&E.

Basically, insurable values are based on the books of account. If the books are wrong, the insurance coverage will be wrong, and the insurance premium will be too high. The one thing a reader of this book can be sure of is that the insurance company is not going to send in its auditors or adjusters before a loss to make sure the insured is not claiming too many assets. After a loss, the records may be scrutinized closely, but even then, any overpayment of premiums because the assets were not there will not be refunded.

REDUCED PROPERTY TAX

Good property records are essential if real estate taxes, on land, buildings, and personal property are to be kept to a minimum. In this section, we will touch briefly on the records themselves. First, as a generalization, property taxes are a local government concern, usually at the county level. Thus, there are as many different requirements as there are jurisdictions.

Local assessors have the right to come and inspect the property, and homeowners occasionally see them or their representatives during periodic reassessments. For major commercial and industrial properties, local assessors have neither the time nor the expertise to determine what assets are present and what is the current fair market value. Keep in mind that so-called *ad valorem* taxes are supposed to be based on value (valorem).

The starting point then is for the taxpayer to provide the assessor a listing of taxable assets in the jurisdiction. Ordinarily, the taxpayer will also supply the original cost of the assets. Each year a form is filed showing new additions, at current cost, and deletions due to retirement, sale, trade-in, and so forth.

The local assessor typically then adjusts the previously reported assets by index numbers representing price changes, offset by an allowance for the increasing age of the assets, which of course reduces their computed value. The asset base, as computed, then becomes the tax base against which the local tax *rate* is applied, thus determining the total taxes due.

It can be seen that if the property listing supplied to the assessor is incorrect, then the tax base and the taxes due will be incorrect. This makes it critically important, in order to keep taxes at a minimum, that all sales, transfers out of the jurisdiction, trade-ins, and cannibalizations be recorded accurately. With a good property record, correct and minimum assets will be reported to the county, minimizing taxes due.

Local assessors will typically not come in and perform an audit or physical inventory of the assets. If it is hard for a company to do this itself, discussed below, it is totally unrealistic to expect a third party, the assessor, to look very hard for assets on which taxes are being paid but which may not be present.

Just as good property records are necessary for proper insurance coverage, and minimization of premiums, so the same good record will keep property taxes at a minimum. The emphasis for property taxes has to be on assets in the records, and no longer there or in use. Ordinarily, assets that are present physically but not on the books will not be reported to the tax authorities because the input forms require that new additions be reported. Ordinarily, corrections of the record itself would probably not be reported. Explicitly, we are not recommending anything other than full compliance with specific local tax reporting requirements. There is little doubt that too much tax will be paid unless assets are promptly removed from the record.

BETTER PRODUCT PRICING

A number of companies have adopted activity-based costing (ABC) as a means of better identifying costs and product profitability. One of the concepts of ABC is specific identification of costs with cost drivers. So, as an example, instead of spreading selling expense over all sales as a straight percentage, the company identifies which customers require more help from sales representatives. Those customers then get charged in the ABC analysis with the correct allocation of selling expense.

Companies that adopt ABC often find out that high-volume product and product lines are more profitable than expected, even if gross profit margins are lower. This is because fewer resources have to be committed as compared to the special handling of small custom-type orders. Based on the ABC analysis, some companies have raised selling prices of low-volume products and even cut selling prices of high-volume lines. Total profits can increase significantly.

How do good property records aid in an ABC analysis? Before ABC was established, most product-line profitability studies tended to spread depreciation expense ratably over all production. High-volume pieces received the same charge as low volume items, even though the latter had more setups, more material handling, and more labor.

In a properly conducted ABC study,[1] depreciation expense will be specifically allocated to piece parts, assemblies, and final products based on the PP&E actually utilized in the production of the specific items. Thus, it is critical that only active equipment be in the fixed-asset listing, assets on which depreciation is properly computed. The alternative, of having missing assets charged to current production, obviously provides erroneous information for decision purposes.

CONTROL OVER MAINTENANCE EXPENSE

Many companies are able to integrate their fixed-asset record with their plant maintenance system. As assets age, they require more maintenance, in order to maintain tolerances and correct inevitable problems associated with wear and usage. Individuals experience this phenomenon with their own homes as well as their automobile. Older assets cost more in upkeep.

Most companies have capital expenditure control, whereby proposed expenditures, whether for new products or replacement, must meet some minimum return on investment, based on the firm's cost of capital. Fairly elaborate procedures are in place to ensure that the required minimum ROI is met. Formal review procedures are in effect, as well as postcompletion audits.

One of the most difficult tasks in capital budgeting is knowing the optimum time to replace existing equipment. New productive assets usually are technologically advanced over what they are replacing. In fact, experience shows that for most firms one-for-one replacements are extremely rare.

Calculating the proper ROI for a newer asset, as contrasted with the older existing asset, has to take into account the dollar savings on *not* having to maintain the old asset. There are further savings due to the higher productivity of the new equipment. Offsetting these savings is the actual out-of-pocket cost of the new asset, less any trade-in.

Companies usually have more projects they wish to undertake than they have funds or staff available. There are even a lot of resources consumed in the capital budgeting process itself. If a company has a good database of maintenance expenditures for each piece of equipment, a process can be set up to flag those assets for which the expenditures exceed a certain percentage of the assets' cost.

This approach will simplify the capital expenditure budgeting process. Further, it will assure a firm that limited resources are devoted to those projects promising the highest ROI. Without an accurate database of maintenance expenditures by asset, the firm cannot be sure that replacements will be properly selected.

REDUCED CAPITAL EXPENDITURES

Tied in with using a fixed-asset listing to control maintenance expenditures is the benefit of a company-wide asset inventory. Many times, a company will buy new assets, when similar assets are elsewhere in the organization. These can be either idle or underutilized. This problem is particularly prevalent in multiplant and multidivision companies.

In most one-site companies, personnel are personally familiar with all assets, what is being used and what is idle. By the same token, however, Plant A's staff is probably not familiar with what is available in Plant B.

If a business has a consolidated fixed-asset listing, classified by type of asset, then before major new acquisitions are made a quick review can be made to see if the same or a similar item is available elsewhere. Even if it is in use part of the time, it may be better to transfer the asset to the new location, and let the minimal requirements at the old plant be met in spare time capacity at the new location. True, there will possibly be transfer pricing issues between plants, with arguments as to who should pay how much; nonetheless, from the corporate perspective the objective is the greatest possible utilization of existing asset. Avoiding duplicate purchases, even once a year, of a major asset will pay for a pretty good fixed-asset system with proper coding of type of asset.

PHYSICAL INVENTORY OF PP&E

Every year, when the external audit is finished, the auditors write a management letter to the client in which the auditors present their recommendations for better controls. In virtually every such letter there will be a recommendation for better controls over fixed assets, including a suggestion that the client periodically take an inventory of its PP&E and reconcile this to the books.

This is a terrific suggestion. Then, why does the recommendation continue to appear year after year? Because companies do not follow the recommendation. They do not take such an inventory.

For raw materials, work in process, and finished goods, GAAP effectively mandates either a perpetual inventory system or an annual inventory. If the firm has a perpetual inventory system, portions must be tested regularly. In short, physical inventories are routinely taken on inventories in current assets, but hardly ever taken for PP&E.

Despite the strong recommendations of the auditors, and a knowledge by corporate controllers that they should take such an inventory, it simply is postponed from year to year. Why is this so? It is simple to explain, and hard to solve.

There are two ways to take a physical count of PP&E. The first is to go out on the shop floor, warehouse, and office and count and list the items. That provides a 100 percent sample of what is there. Now the fun begins, in trying to reconcile what is there to what the records show. Having tried this once, few people ever want to do it again, for reasons described later.

The second approach is to take the fixed-asset listing, sorted by department and floor, and try to find the items. This provides a 100 percent test of the record, but it is a certainty that many of the items on the asset listing cannot and will not be found where they are purported to be located. Further, there will be many assets present that are not on the record. It is relatively easy to write off the missing items, except that this may turn out to be a rather large number, and the company does not want to report a big write-off, charged to current year's expense. This is understandable. Even worse, in reality the missing items have simply been moved or transferred elsewhere.

To take a simple example, the property record listing may show that in Department 201, on floor 3, there should be three desks and five chairs. Physical inspection reveals only two desks and four chairs. Common sense suggests that the missing desk and chair have been moved somewhere else. Where they may be is indeterminate, short of physically locating every desk and chair and tying it back to the record.

The truth is that going from the record to the assets does not work. Neither does going from the assets to the record. This is why so few companies actually take a physical inventory of their PP&E and reconcile it periodically to the books. It would be nice to do. The benefits of having it done are great. But the resources involved in doing it correctly, and reconciling the differences, always appears overwhelming.

Since doing nothing means that this year's depreciation expense ends up being similar to last year's, and any overstated assets will be written off sooner or later, it is easy to rationalize, "Let's wait until next year."

MINIMUM CAPITALIZATION POLICY

There is a solution to this problem, which we discuss in this section. But first it is necessary to minimize the number of items which we are trying to account for and keep track of.

We strongly recommend that companies adopt a policy that requires a minimum dollar amount for capitalization. Below that amount all items are charged to expense, irrespective of how long they are expected to last. In other words, the definition of an asset to be capitalized is related to the dollar size, not its economic life.

Many companies use a $1,000 or $2,500 cutoff, but we recommend going even higher, to $10,000. At first glance this may seem like a large amount, because it effectively means that an asset costing $8,500 will be charged to current year's expense, when acquired. If capitalized and depreciated over 10 years, this year's P&L would be hit with only $850.

Why do we recommend such a high dollar limit? Our previous discussion indicated how hard it was to control fixed assets, particularly when one is attempting to reconcile what is on the floor with what is on the records. Minimizing the number of items one is trying to control reduces the management issues going forward. Further, there are studies that suggest it costs $5.00 or more per item per year just to maintain the records in the accounting system.

Even more fundamental to a high minimum capitalization is the premise that management has to focus its efforts. If you try to control everything, you end up controlling nothing. The truth is that for most firms, the property record system or process accomplishes virtually nothing other than to compute depreciation expense for books and taxes. Actual control over assets is impossible if you cannot find every asset when you want to. Having literally thousands of individual small dollar amounts in the records makes it much harder to locate the important records.

If a reader is skeptical, take the existing record and sort it in descending dollar amount. See what percentage of the total item count and what percentage of the total dollar amount is accounted for by assets below $5,000 or $10,000. The "80/20 rule" undoubtedly applies.

It is probably impractical to write off in the current year the undepreciated balance of all items under $10,000. But going forward from this point, a lot of money will be saved by adopting this capitalization policy.

An argument will be made that going this route will cause a company to lose control over assets like personal computers. If they are not controlled, people will steal them or lose them or whatever. Two answers make sense.

First, with PCs now costing less than $2,000, how much time and resources should be devoted to this kind of control? If virtually every employee has one PC, then each individual is responsible for control of his own unit.

The second answer is that a company can set up controls over assets without having them as part of the fixed asset accounting system. Vendors have programs that will keep track of every computer, how it is configured, what version of software is on it, and so on. Maintenance of this software record of all PCs can be, and should be, independent of the accounting records.

The final argument against a high capitalization policy is that individuals will spend money unwisely. Most companies have quite strict capital expenditure policies and procedures. These are usually tied in with the fixed-asset accounting system, on the assumption that all approved capital expenditures will be capitalized. This, however, is just an assumption. One could set up a process requiring approvals at several levels for PCs, or for items over $1,000, and still not have to treat the items when acquired as capital assets.

Finally, the argument is heard that if we have a high (say $10,000) capitalization level then lower level managers may try to "beat the system" by splitting a $25,000 purchase into three separate $8,500 items. Yes, this can be done. It is also why firms have internal audit departments. Further, sometimes a really urgent need arises and a plant manager, for example, does not want to wait 60 days for the approval process to take its time. He needs the $25,000 item now. Unfortunately, accountants and controllers sometimes place greater emphasis on the system than on results. It is possible that beating the system really is in the best interest of the shareholders.

The alternative to a high capitalization limit was seen several years ago.

A large appraisal company acquired a much smaller firm in the same line of business. The corporate controller went out to visit the newly acquired firm's offices and met with the accountant to go over the transfer of the accounting function back to the corporate headquarters.

At one point, the discussion turned to the property record system. Before the days of computerized records, the bookkeeper had maintained the records on individual 5″ × 8″ index cards. She pulled out a sample record and it was for "wastebasket—$4.75." This elicited a question and the next card, literally, was "ashtray—$2.70."

Asked why the company kept track of such small items, the accountant explained that almost all the employees were small stockholders in the appraisal company. The owner paid out dividends based on reported earnings.

By capitalizing literally everything she could, she managed to boost reported earnings, albeit by a very small amount. After 10 years or so, the system was self-defeating, because the annual depreciation then hurt earnings, whereas if the small items had been written off the year acquired there would be no further charges. Nevertheless, the accountant was very proud of her system. The corporate controller switched them over to the existing parent's system, and immediately wrote off all the small-dollar amounts. The cost of transferring the information to the new system would have been greater than the value of the items.

ASSET DESCRIPTIONS AND ORIGINAL COST

Before going on to describe the best way to set up a property control system, we need a brief mention of asset descriptions. A complete list of incomprehensible asset descriptions we have seen would fill a chapter in this book. Many accountants, who at one time were responsible for the fixed-asset records, have not taken their successors into consideration. Descriptions such as "Remodeling—$295,306" or "Asset Installation—$32,477" may make sense on day one, because there is a vendor invoice for each of those amounts. However, the descriptions, while perhaps passing the test of an auditor checking for numerical accuracy, do not pass the test of subsequent utility. How do you find remodeling or installation three years later, if you do not know to what the amounts originally referred?

The basic problem, of course, is that computer records, until recently, were severely constrained in the length of each field. If a complete fixed-asset record had to fit on a single 80-column punch card, maybe no more than 14 letters of description would be allowed. Abbreviations and contractions were understandable, if not desirable.

In today's environment there is no excuse for poor descriptions, because storage space in the computer is no longer a constraint. It is hard to set up a standardized policy as to asset descriptions in a property record. The individual responsible for the asset listing should ask herself, "Will someone else be able to find or identify this item in the future?" All a controller can do, to ensure compliance, is to have someone spot-check new listings for comprehension and future utility. Space limitations in the record no longer should control what is put down. In terms of description, too much information is always preferable.

CARRYING FORWARD ORIGINAL COST

One additional desirable aspect of a good property record system deals with original cost. There is a difference between the cost the first buyer paid to the vendor, one that includes incoming freight and installation, and the type of cost that arises during a business combination when the purchase price is allocated over all the assets acquired, as discussed in Chapter 12. From the perspective of the new owner, whatever dollar amount was allocated to that particular asset represents its cost, its dollar outlay to acquire that asset as part of the total transaction.

What is important here is that subsequent valuation of the asset cannot be based on that allocated cost. Only the original vendor sales price represents a base from which subsequent current values can be derived through application of index numbers.

For both property taxes and insurance, the most common basis of determining current value is for the company, the tax assessor, or the insurance company to apply standard cost indexes to the original cost. Cost indexes are developed by linking together the current cost each year for a specific type of asset. The index represents a factor that converts the original cost in the year of acquisition to the current year.

Inasmuch as the index is always developed from actual selling prices of the asset(s) on a new basis by the vendor or manufacturer, it is inappropriate to apply such an index to the value derived from an allocation. In other words, indexes can be applied to cost, but they cannot be applied to values. We know of no reliable indexes of value as determined through business combinations.

In order to simplify the process of determining current costs, it is highly desirable if a company's fixed-asset accounting system retains the original cost, as well as the allocated value derived from allocation of the total business enterprise to the individual assets. In a business combination treated as a purchase, the buyer *must* set up as an asset what he paid for each of the assets acquired. This is done based on a value-in-use concept, taking into account technological obsolescence, physical condition and economic conditions for that asset at that point in time.

Assume there were two simultaneous business combinations, involving two different purchasers and two different acquired firms. In each purchase, there was an identical model Cincinnati milling machine with identical features. As part of the appraisal of each of the acquired companies, the appraisers would have looked at the condition and utility of the milling machines, and quite likely would assign *different* values for what might appear to a layman to be identical assets. For this reason, it would be inappropriate to apply the same cost index to the two different values.

The solution is easy. Any time there is a business combination, and allocated values are determined as the new starting point, just make sure to keep the original cost and date of acquisition as an additional part of the new record. Given the flexibility of today's PC-based property accounting systems, this is very easy to do. Then, if and when it is necessary to determine current cost(s), the appropriate indexes can be applied to the original cost field in the record.

SETTING UP A PROPERTY CONTROL SYSTEM

Two fairly recent developments have made possible implementation of a useful and easy-to-maintain property control system. The first is design of computerized accounting programs to run on PCs. The second is application of low-cost bar-coding technology.

Manual systems on index cards worked reasonably well through the 1960s, but the larger the file the more difficult it was to control. Essentially, the records in that day were used solely to compute annual depreciation, which was one reason that tax and book accounting were so closely joined together. Manually computing two sets of depreciation expense would literally have doubled the workload.

Then came the era of mainframe computerized property record accounting systems. These automated the calculation of depreciation and could easily handle separate tax and book accounting issues. With first punch cards, and then magnetic storage, the files could be large. Sorting of the files, for example by location, permitted inventories to be taken, or analyses made for property tax appeals. In short, the mainframe property record systems were a great advance over manual methods, but they suffered from two big faults. They were expensive to buy and costly to install and maintain. The property accountant had to schedule with the management information system (MIS) department if she wished the files updated or a special analysis made. The mainframe systems lacked flexibility.

The advent of the personal computer was soon followed by several PC-based fixed-asset accounting systems. At first, the small memory capability of the early PCs was a hindrance. That is, the large files stored on a mainframe could not be processed and manipulated on a PC. Over time, of course, PCs grew in power and storage capability to the point that virtually any fixed-asset record can be handled today on a desktop. (Don't forget to back up those PC-based files!)

The second development that has aided fixed-asset control is the application of bar code technology. Low-cost readers, combined with preprinted and numbered tags, means that physical identification is now mechanical. Rather than hunting through a computer listing, hoping to match up the asset in front of you with one of the lines on the printout, you wave the bar code wand over the preattached tag, and instantly find the asset listing.

This technology now provides a relatively low cost means of setting up a good property record and control system. Step one is to order the bar code tags and apply them to the assets that will be treated as capital assets. A decision will already have had to be made as to what to do with the dollars representing the numerous small assets that should not be maintained on the new record. One approach would be to determine the dollar amount and decide simply to write off the total ratably over the next three years or next five years. That charge to expense would have happened anyhow, as part of the old system. Not including the small assets in the new system does *not* require instant write-off.

The next step is the hard one. With the bar code tags on the assets to be controlled, it is then necessary to enter the new bar code tag number into the existing computerized record. For perhaps 70 percent of the items, this will be easy. That still leaves a large number of tagged items without a home on the listing, offset by many items on the listing that cannot readily be located.

What will really have happened is that there is a pool of dollars on the listing representing assets that do not exist, cannot be found, or cannot be identified. On the other side are assets with tags that cannot be identified to any specific entry on the existing asset listing.

The next step is to develop a description for the tagged items not found on the existing list, an estimate of when they were acquired, and a best guess as to their current value. Professional appraisers do this kind of valuation all the time, so some firms may wish to obtain guidance and support from an appraisal firm. In other cases, the internal staff can reasonably estimate the current value.

However derived, the total value of the assets not on the listing should be compared to the total dollar amount on the listing that cannot be found. It is unlikely that the two dollar amounts will be the same, but they should be reasonably close. The difference, whatever the amount, has to be disposed of.

If the value of the assets, either through appraisal or judgment, is greater than what is on the books today, the company can either record a net gain in other income and expense or can take it into income ratably, thus offsetting the higher future depreciation expense.

If the value of the tagged assets not on the record is less than the missing items on the existing asset listing, then again the dollar amount can be written off to expense at once, or charged ratably in the future, thus offsetting the future lower depreciation expense.

Either way, the accounting records will now match the assets, the assets will have been tagged and are readily identifiable in the future through the bar code system.

MAINTAINING THE SYSTEM

There are four steps that have to be implemented for this system to continue to work, assuming the company wants to maintain good control. Step one has been accomplished, and that was to develop a PC-based accounting system with all assets identified and bar coded. This provides the tools necessary to do the job, and the flexibility to provide whatever kind of information is needed about PP&E.

The next step is to put one person in charge of maintaining the system, making her responsible for the accuracy of *all* information. The problems in maintaining the system do not lie in capturing new asset acquisitions. All approved capital expenditure requests are followed by purchase orders, vendor invoices, and coding to capital assets. The detailed property record can be reconciled each month to the trial balance, which will have picked up all expenditures charged to PP&E.

The problems in maintaining the system revolve around the issues discussed earlier in this chapter. These are:

- Transfers
- Trade-ins
- Cannibalization for spare parts

Transfers within a plant or building are, frankly, hard to keep track of. "Emergencies" will arise and assets will have to be moved quickly. Whoever approves the move will say to himself, "Let's get the job done today and we will worry about the paperwork later." Of course, later never comes, the paperwork is not filled out, and the poor property accountant never finds out about the transfer until the next physical inventory reveals the move.

The only real solution is for printouts of PP&E charged to a given department to be provided to each manager as part of the annual budget process. The current year's depreciation expense is compared to the projected expense to be charged next year, *if the individual manager still has the assets.* Some, not all, managers are going to look at the list and in an effort to reduce projected expense monitor it for assets no longer under his jurisdiction. This is not a perfect solution, but is better than none.

For trade-ins, the best approach is to make sure that the capital expenditure request form (every company has a different name for this) has a blank space to be filled out. It would indicate any trade-in proposed. This will alert the property accountant, and when the project is closed out, she can check the vendor invoice to see if credit was given for the trade-in. Further, she can go directly to the plant engineer or person in charge of the project and ask explicitly about any trade-ins.

Finally, with regard to cannibalization of idle equipment for spare parts, the company should try and maintain a separate listing of idle equipment. Only rarely will active equipment be the source of needed spare parts. What really happens is that unused equipment appears to be a fine source. So the issue is how a company controls idle equipment.

One way would be to set up a separate department to hold idle equipment. Depreciation on these assets would not be charged to individual departments; rather, it would be a corporate overhead expense. The motivation would be to have individual managers identify as early as possible those assets they are not using. Getting them off the department's books will reduce their expense as well as their asset base, important if the company measures performance on an ROI basis. If this idle equipment is separately identified, it is relatively easy to monitor it periodically for condition.

This is not to say that maintenance foreman should be discouraged from using spare parts from idle equipment. This may well be the low-cost solution to a pressing problem. What is wanted is to make sure that if an asset is no longer functional that it be retired, so property taxes and insurance are not paid, and incorrect depreciation expense not be charged.

Inasmuch as few systems are foolproof, and fixed-asset accounting systems have a low priority in most accounting departments, what has been suggested above will produce good results, not perfect results. However, it will be so much better than 95 percent of all companies in the country that the accounting staff can take pride in their performance.

The final control, certainly, is the actual matching of the records to what is on hand (e.g., the physical inventory of PP&E). Just as most auditors recommend the company do this, even though it hardly ever is done, with the system described here the inventory will no longer be perceived as a hopeless undertaking.

The asset listing is printed out by location, the bar codes are swiped, and the subsequent reconciliation should be pretty straightforward. Having assets only over some high dollar limit captured in the system means that hundreds or even thousands of items will no longer be tracked, thus freeing up time for resolving any real issues that have a significant dollar implication.

COMPONENT DEPRECIATION

One final topic can be discussed briefly, and that is component depreciation. Some accountants, particularly for tax purposes, have had the idea of setting up separate asset classifications for components of a larger item. For example, if a giant 1,000-ton press has been installed in a 15-foot base, it is highly unlikely to be moved. So the dollars associated with the installation would be identified separately, and given a long life. The press will not be moved, and a long depreciation period for that aspect can be justified.

The electronic control system for the press, perhaps computerized, would be given a very much shorter life. Justifiably, one can expect development in electronic controls and computers to move rapidly. In fact, a five-year life for that portion of the total cost might be justified. So just for this one asset the total cost could be broken down into three components, each with a separate life.

While this component depreciation is possible for machinery and equipment, it most often is used with buildings. Most observers would expect that the elevator system would have a different useful life than the heating, ventilation, and air conditioning (HVAC) system, and both would differ from the roof. Just discussing this will stimulate the imagination into the almost infinite detail with which a large office building, warehouse, or factory can be split.

This approach to component depreciation got started when the Investment Tax Credit (ITC) was part of the Tax Code. ITC was not allowed on buildings, but was allowed on productive equipment. What was and what was not productive equipment became a matter of dispute between the IRS and taxpayers, and ultimately the courts. Inasmuch as ITC is now relegated to the history books, we do not need to discuss it further, other than to say that it was the genesis of component depreciation.

For a large and complex building, the savings in property and real estate taxes can be substantial. The savings will usually pay for a professional engagement that develops and supports the cost segregation.

For other assets it is probably a matter of dollars and cents whether to undertake component depreciation. Offsetting the tax benefits is the fact that the property record system will not easily be reconcilable to the assets that have property tags. On the 1,000-ton press, for example, one would need three bar code tags representing respectively the electrical system, the installation and the press itself. All three tags can be grouped together. But every time you make a system more complex, and component depreciation is more complex, the harder it is to maintain the system. This is a trade-off only company management can make.

SUMMARY AND CONCLUSIONS

The material in this chapter should aid financial managers to develop and maintain a first-class property record system. This is not a short-term project, nor will it be inexpensive. There will be a positive ROI for the investment made in the new system. Property taxes and insurance premiums will go down. Financial reporting will be more accurate. Maintenance expenses will be analyzed, and subsequent replacements of capital equipment can be forestalled if the equivalent asset is available elsewhere in the company.

ENDNOTE

1. Recommended is *Implementing Activity-Based Management in Daily Operations* by John A. Miller, John Wiley & Sons, New York, 1996.

CHAPTER 15

Don't Overpay Property Taxes!*

Property taxes are considered by many simply a nuisance—in terms of monitoring and controlling the payments, getting check requests processed on time, and properly filling out the forms. Others focus on the dollars involved, feel put upon in terms of cash outflows to some distant governmental unit, and shrug their shoulders, saying ultimately, "These property and real estate taxes are a fixed cost and simply a cost of doing business in this jurisdiction." In short, like the weather, many feel that property taxes are something to complain about but that cannot be influenced.

Most firms fill out the local assessors' forms each year, showing new additions for the year, any deletions due to retirements, sale, or trade-in. The municipality typically will have its own price index and own depreciation schedule, the net effect of which arrives at a value for the assets in that jurisdiction. Some communities have one additional complication, and that is they may assess personal and real property at some discount to current value. So, as an example, land and buildings may be carried on the tax roll of that tax jurisdiction at 60 percent of fair market value (FMV). Private residences are often carried at significantly less than true FMV.

It should always be remembered that there are two elements to every property tax. First is the assessment, in absolute dollars. Second is the total amount of property taxes to be collected. The assessor divides the total taxes by the total value of all assessed property, thus arriving at a *tax rate,* usually stated in terms of dollars per hundred dollars of valuation.

It can be seen that if *every property* is assessed at 70 percent of FMV, or every property is assessed at 90 percent of FMV, the actual tax bill will be

---

*The author is indebted to, and would like to recognize, Mr. Jack Chernobyl for information in this chapter.

the same. Inequities arise only when *some* properties are assessed at 90 percent of FMV while *others* in the same jurisdiction are assessed at 70 percent.

As a generalization, tax assessors rarely assess at 100 percent of true FMV. They prefer to have a uniform 95 percent assessment level for one reason. If a homeowner comes in and complains about the assessment, the official asks one question, "Would you be willing to sell your house for the amount we have it assessed at?"

If the uniform assessment is really at 95 percent, but taxpayers are told that all values are supposed to be at 100 percent, then the taxpayer is likely to say, "Well, my house is assessed at $285,000 but I would not sell it for less than $300,000, so I guess I cannot complain." The real point is *not* whether the assessment is at $285,000 or at $300,000. The only important fact to be determined is whether your house is assessed at the same relationship to its true FMV as all other houses in the community.

It is useless to complain to the assessor that your tax bill is too high unless you can demonstrate that there is a disproportion between the real value of your house and its assessment relative to other houses with the same true FMV. If there were two identical houses, each worth $300,000, and one was assessed at $285,000 and the other at $250,000, then there is inequity. If they are both assessed at $285,000, there is little one can do.

For example, tax revenues for a particular jurisdiction are collected by spreading the desired revenue over the total assessed value of all property in the community. It is easy to see that it makes very little difference if property is valued at 40 cents on the dollar, with a tax rate of $1.50 per $100 of assessed value, or a tax rate of 60 cents per $100 of assessed value if the assessment is at 100 percent of FMV (see Exhibit 15.1).

This example deals with residential property, but the identical concepts apply to *ad valorem* taxes on businesses.

There are two separate issues that financial executives should keep in mind in reviewing property taxes for possible savings. First, many tax bills do not show the equalization rate on the face of the bill. Thus, the bill might show your property is assessed at only $100,000 when you know it is worth a lot more. But you may not question the assessment because of the seem-

Exhibit 15.1   Tax Rates versus Assessed Value

Assessed Value	Fair Market Value	Tax Rate	Tax Collected
$100,000	$250,000	$1.50	$1,500
$250,000	$250,000	$ .60	$1,500

ing bargain. What is needed is to understand the relationship between assessed value and true FMV.

The second problem is that companies have themselves reported each year their new additions, and many companies historically have *overstated the cost and value of new construction and newly acquired PP&E.*

EQUALIZED VALUE VERSUS ASSESSED VALUE

As shown above, the dollar amount on the property tax statement, against which tax amounts are computed, need not be the assessor's real estimate of the true FMV. Assessors may not raise the assessed value each year, as real estate values increase, for one of two reasons. For example, in dealing with private residences, by having a low assessed value, relatively few people are going to complain about their relative share of the tax load. Of course, everyone complains about too much real estate taxes, but that is a political issue. How much of the total tax is paid by each homeowner is a function of your assessed value as a percentage of the total assessed value in the community. By undervaluing your home, you are less likely to complain.

The second reason for underassessing is that the tax assessor then does not have to update all the thousands of records in his or her jurisdiction. By keeping old values on the books, the clerical work in the assessors' offices may appear to be reduced.

Nonetheless, most states require property taxes to be based *ad valorem,* or to value. This is usually defined as fair market value. If the assessors' records are old and really out of touch with current values, the overall values are often adjusted by an equalization factor. Thus, if school district A in the state has its property assessments recorded at an average of 40 percent of FMV, while next-door district B has its property assessments at an average of 75 percent, there is no good way to compare the tax burden in A to that in B.

The state will then come in and apply an equalization factor, effectively multiplying the values in A by $2.5\times$, and those in B by $1.33\times$. In this way, the dollar amount of tax on a two-story, three-bedroom house in each community can be compared on an "apples-to-apples" basis.

In every community it is possible to obtain the equalization factor, the ratio by which property is undervalued, or occasionally overvalued. Keep in mind that the tax base and equalization factor affects only the relative tax contribution of each property owner, one with another. As long as *all* the assessments are truly at 40 percent, or at 75 percent, it does not affect the total taxes paid on any specific property.

The basic fairness problem related to property taxes is that most property cannot be assessed each year at fair market value by a tax assessor hired by the tax jurisdiction. Actual assessments for business and commercial property are ordinarily based initially on what the taxpayer himself has reported, whether it was right or wrong. The assessor's subsequent computation for depreciation, plus the impact of any inflation index, will probably not accurately reflect true changes in current fair market value (i.e., what the property could be sold for). Further compounding the problem, no system of historical cost, combined with depreciation and inflation indexes can possibly take account of changes in technology and external economic factors.

COST VERSUS VALUE

Should taxpayers report the *cost* of assets acquired, as they appear on the books, to the assessor? In a word, probably not. Most companies fill out an annual tax reporting form for that year's additions utilizing the dollar amounts capitalized as fixed assets (PP&E) on the company's financial statements. In other words, if an amount is treated as PP&E for the balance sheet, it is usually reported as a capital expenditure addition, for the same dollar amount, to the local tax authorities.

There is no inherent reason why the dictates of financial reporting should govern or control tax reporting. In terms of taxes on income, accountants are thoroughly familiar with differences between book and tax income. The fact that these differences have to be reported on Schedule M does not dissuade tax-knowledgeable accountants from trying to minimize reported taxable income and hence taxes on income.

The same principle holds true for property tax assessments versus capitalized amounts on the balance sheet. Here are just a few examples of where the two should differ.

- The company makes a 10,000-square-foot addition to an existing 40,000-square-foot building and spends $1.2 million ($120/sq. ft.) to build the addition. The company now owns a 50,000-square-foot building. Assume the original structure was reported originally as costing $3.6 million ($90/square foot). Now, according to the tax assessor's records, the taxpayer has a single 50,000-square-foot building with total original costs (phase 1 + phase 2) of $4.8 million, which works out to $96/square foot.

Included in the costs of phase 2 was the demolition of the end wall, a second HVAC system, and replacement of the landscaping. Do any of these costs add value to the structure? The answer is that they do not. Assume that a new 50,000-square-foot building could be constructed for $90/square foot or a total of $4.5 million. Yet the tax assessor would be charging tax on a $4.8 million asset. Worse, by applying inflation indexes each year, this $300,000 extra cost would incur taxes for the next 30 years.

The solution is clear. The taxpayer should report as the cost only $900,000 for the new phase 2 addition. When added to the cost of phase 1, the assessor's records will now reflect the true Fair Market Value of a 50,000-square-foot building.

- A second example would be replacement of an old analog telephone switch with a new digital switch, along with the attendant wiring and instruments. It is likely that a single contractor was engaged to manage the project, and the contractor's total invoice would be capitalized. A couple of questions come to mind. While the actual cost of the old switch and instruments was probably removed from the books, what about the wiring that might have been performed by the original electrical contractor. This would represent duplicate costs. Second, if the new telephone switch were programmed for the current building occupant, those costs would be of no value for the next occupant. Finally, costs associated with previous moves of extensions of the old system may have been improperly capitalized; if so, they probably cannot even be located in the records. A significant discount from the cash price paid to the contractor for the new telephone system would be appropriately reported to the assessor.
- In assembling a large acreage of land, perhaps to put up a distribution center, a real estate agent acting on behalf of the buyer will probably be forced to pay a significant premium for the last two or three parcels, as sellers get wind of the new development. While it may be expensive to pull together a large parcel, if that same acreage were put on the market as a single offering, the price per acre might well be reduced. The fact is that the demand for large parcels is substantially less than for smaller parcels. They take longer to sell, and the price per acre upon sale may be less.

Thus, in determining the amount to report to a tax assessor, adding up the price actually paid will probably overstate the current FMV of the assembled parcel. The solution here is to obtain a current appraisal of the land, either before starting construction or prior to filing the first property tax return. It is perfectly proper to report only the current FMV of the land, not what was paid.

- Finally, in putting a large machine tool into service there will be a lot of costs associated with its design, acquisition, transportation, installation, debugging, and initial quality acceptance. Many companies, for purposes of increasing currently reported earnings, will tend to capitalize a lot of management time associated with the transaction.

However, if the property tax requirements call for the true FMV of the asset, it would appear prudent to review the construction-in-progress detail, and eliminate all the recorded costs not directly associated with the machine tool itself. For example, the management time in engineering, purchasing, and production is of no value to any subsequent purchaser of the equipment who will undoubtedly use it for some other purpose, probably even moving it to a different location.

It is hard to generalize as to what specific costs should be excluded in filing property tax returns, but the first step is to recognize that what was done for financial reporting need not control what is filed for property taxes.

This is not to say that the decisions controllers may make in a given year as to what should be capitalized and what should be expensed are necessarily consistent from year to year. Different accountants make different decisions. In a year with higher-than-expected income, the emphasis may be on charging as much as possible to expense. The next year, possibly below budget, will find the same accountant leaning the other way, trying to capitalize as much as possible, thus increasing reported income.

We are not judging the propriety of such changes in accounting philosophy. The fact remains that at different times the same company will choose opposite approaches to capitalization policy. Combine changes in capitalization approach with changes in personnel applying those philosophies, and it is easy to see that there is, in many circumstances, a total lack of consistency in reporting of costs to tax assessors.

This lack of consistency is *not* going to be discovered by the tax assessor, much less reported back to the taxpayer. At least in theory, if an IRS agent finds, following an audit of your return, that you have overpaid your taxes, he is supposed to bring this to your attention. This approach does not hold true with respect to property taxes.

What taxpayers submit to local assessors is rarely reviewed or audited, barring some tremendous disconnect between reporting and the assessor's visual inspection. If you reported a building addition of $100,000 for the year to the assessor, but your firm had bragged in the local newspaper about your new 100,000-square-foot addition, with employment going up by 200, this would trigger an audit. Buildings simply cost more than $1.00 per square foot. But if you reported a $4 million addition in your return, then $40 a square foot *might* be reasonable and probably would not trigger a specific review.

There are a number of reasons why the dollar amount capitalized on the books for PP&E should *not* be the amount reported on the property tax return. This assumes, of course, absolute good faith and high ethical standards by the taxpayer. Obviously, we are not condoning anything illegal or immoral. Nonetheless, the rules for property tax reporting are not the same as generally accepted accounting principles (GAAP).

Wiley GAAP 2001,[1] dealing with the recorded costs of PP&E, states:

Recorded Cost. Any reasonable cost involved in bringing the asset to the buyer and incurred prior to using the asset in actual production is capitalized. Examples include sales taxes, finders' fees, freight costs, installation costs, breaking-in costs, and set-up costs. These costs are **not** to be expensed in the period in which they are incurred.

The *Miller GAAP Guide*[2] puts it slightly differently, albeit with no change in basic concept:

Asset Cost. The basis of accounting for depreciable fixed assets is cost, and all *normal* [emphasis added] expenditures of readying an asset for use are capitalized. However, unnecessary expenditures that do not add utility of the asset are charged to expense. For example, an expenditure for repairing a piece of equipment that was damaged during shipment should be charged to expense.

For property tax assessments the basic principle has to be fair market value, what the proverbial willing buyer would be willing to pay for the asset. Further, there is, as we saw earlier in the book, a difference between value in use (VIU) and value in exchange (VIE). On a VIU basis, a new buyer would properly expect to pay for cost involved in breaking in and setting up the machine, as well as freight in and installation. On a VIE basis, assuming a third-party outside buyer wanted to acquire the asset(s) for use elsewhere, all of these costs would be truly non-value added.

EQUALIZED VALUE VERSUS FAIR MARKET VALUE

As we have seen, the assessed value developed by an assessor is usually derived from the original cost information supplied by the taxpayer, subsequently adjusted by indexes for inflation and depreciation. But, as indicated, different assessors utilize different approaches in updating the information to what is supposed to be the standard of fair market value.

One approach, not necessarily utilized frequently, is to attempt to determine the true FMV of all property in the jurisdiction each year. Given the mix of residential, commercial, and industrial property in most communities, and the limited staff and resources available to the assessor, this gold standard of valuation is hard to achieve.

At the other end of the spectrum, also fortunately not too common, is essentially a frozen approach to value. Whatever is on the assessor's tax roll stays there. Then the required revenue is spread over the dollars on the tax roll, a rate determined and applied to those dollars. The impact of this approach is that new properties pay more than their fair share, and older properties, not adjusted for inflation, pay less than their share. In a residential neighborhood this approach to property taxation is somewhat facetiously referred to as a "Welcome to the Neighborhood," since new neighbors pay disproportionately high taxes based on the recent purchase price of the home. The very same house next door, but one that had never changed hands since it was built in 1955, might literally pay only one third the taxes.

This approach is certainly not in the spirit of fairness to all taxpayers, but may be politically attractive inasmuch as older residents probably have more political clout.

It is to avoid situations such as this that states often mandate periodical revaluations. When professionally performed, an independent team of appraisers simultaneously determines the current FMV of all property within the jurisdiction. Frankly, this is the only fair way for *ad valorem* taxes to be assessed. But, as can be imagined, it would be prohibitively expensive to do this every year. Anyhow, there probably are not enough appraisers in the world even to attempt this.

So in lieu of reappraising all property, local assessors adopt two shortcuts. We have referred earlier to the use of indexes for this purpose. Typically, an assessor will utilize one of several standard published indexes to adjust for price changes. These work well for buildings, reasonably well for common equipment (machinery and office furniture and fixtures) and vehicles. Indexes do not work at all for land, and are usually ineffective for technology-based assets.

So, step 1 in the assessors' valuation process is to take the original cost reported by the taxpayer and apply a price index. That arrives at an estimate of what the asset might cost if acquired new today. But, as assets age, they lose value due to depreciation and physical wear and tear. Thus, assessors will then adjust the new cost by an index that attempts to measure depreciation. For example, if a machine tool is estimated to have a 15-year life and a salvage value at that time of 20 percent of original cost, the assessor's computer will make the computation each year.

What this means is that at the end of 15 years, assuming 3.5 percent inflation, the 20 percent residual at the end of 15 years will show a then current value of 67 percent more than the original estimate, or some 33 percent of the original cost of the asset. Is a 15-year old machine tool worth one third of its original cost today? Whether it is or not, that is what the taxpayer will be paying taxes on.

How accurate are the price indexes used by assessors? How reliable are the depreciation estimates? It is hard to generalize, but our firm's professional experience suggests that the real FMV of many assets is often substantially less than that estimated by the assessor in the absence of a full-scale reappraisal by the assessor.

Applying the local equalization ratio to the assessment will tell the taxpayer what the assessor thinks the FMV of the asset(s) is. What the assessor believes, or at least shows on his records, and what the true FMV is, are often likely to be far apart.

Remember that the basis of property taxes remains fair market value, *not* what the assessor's records show. So if the taxpayer believes the assessor is wrong, that the assessment is too high, the state provides a mechanism for appealing the assessor's valuation. However, the burden of proof is likely to reside with the taxpayer.

APPEALING PROPERTY TAX ASSESSMENTS

Every tax jurisdiction has a legal procedure for challenging the assessor's valuation. Typically, this will require the services of a local attorney who specializes in real estate, plus an independent third-party appraisal.

The basic approach taken by appraisers is to review the assessor's records to see just what is being taxed. Often, the assessor will be showing buildings that were long since demolished, personal property (PP&E) that is no longer present physically, and in some cases even an incorrect record of total acreage.

Step 1, therefore, is to communicate with the assessor as to the assets presently located at the property, in essence correcting the assessor's records for content. This is prior to looking at values.

When it comes to the valuation issues, the following are the steps that most appraisers would take in performing an appraisal for *ad valorem* purposes.

- The appraiser will carefully review the assets that are physically there to determine current cost. One of the disadvantages of indexing, as used by assessors, is that any errors in the base record are compounded year after year. So after many years, the indexed values may bear very little relationship to what the assets could be acquired for today.
- Next, the appraiser determines the real depreciation from physical wear and tear. This puts the assets on an as-is basis.
- The next step is to look at functional obsolescence. In most manufacturing environments, there have been significant advances in technology. Indexes cannot effectively capture such changes. So, while the old assets physically work, there may be a significant cost penalty associated with using the older assets. Put a different way, if the assets were acquired new, current production costs would be substantially lower. This cost penalty per unit is capitalized and on a present value basis represents a *subtraction* in value. This approach is premised on the assumption that any prospective purchaser would offer only an amount to buy the assets that encompassed the cost penalty.
- The appraiser would inquire about environmental problems and the cost of remediation. The subject of environmental damage and remediation is beyond the scope of this book. Suffice it to say that if the company knows the dollar amount of current and future remediation expenses that would be incurred before the asset(s) could be sold, such remediation costs are a legitimate subtraction in determining value.
- The final step would be to assess the economics of the business. As noted before, no rational buyer would pay an amount for assets that was so high he could not earn a reasonable return on that investment. Assume the total cost of a facility, using all the previous steps above, was $25 million. If, because of competition or raw material costs, the output could only be sold for an amount that provided $1 million of after-tax profit, no investor would pay $25 million. It is far more likely, if the assets were put on the market, that they could be sold for no more than $10 million. Legally, the $10 million value should be the basis on which property taxes are assessed and paid.

Having said this, some companies are reluctant to go all the way in reducing the valuation of their property in a particular taxing jurisdiction. We have seen several instances in which our client was the largest taxpayer in a community. The employees of that company represented a significant portion of the total populace.

In such situations it may be difficult to cut the company's property tax without adversely affecting the level and quality of public services (e.g., education or placing the burden back on the employees themselves through higher taxes on their individual residences). What is "fair" to the company will be perceived as "unfair" to the employees.

In such situations, a politically satisfactory compromise is usually arrived at. At the end of the day, a lot of valuation issues in property taxes are settled through negotiation. However, even then, the starting point has to be a supportable appraisal that the assessor can use in his discussions with elected officials as to why he lowered Company A's assessment and hence property taxes.

We are not in a position to discuss assessments in highly political jurisdictions, with perhaps Chicago as a prime example. It is a common belief that to obtain tax relief in such locations it is advisable to hire one of a very few politically connected attorneys. Where the legal fees ultimately go is not considered to be a concern of the taxpayer.

SOFTWARE

There are several vendors of software who provide turnkey systems that automate all aspects of record keeping related to property taxes. If a company has more than a dozen locations, whether offices, distribution centers, terminals, factories, or any other geographically decentralized assets on which taxes are collected locally, we recommend acquisition and use of such software. No two tax jurisdictions do things the same way, and simply keeping track of filing due dates and payment due dates will pay for the software. Then there are benefits in terms of handling all the various types of assets, and the cost and depreciation indexes used in each state or locality.

As stated earlier, it is all to easy to think of property taxes as a fixed cost of doing business. It really need not be that way. Property taxes can be *managed.* Good software is available, and it would not pay for a company to try and develop its own.

SUMMARY AND CONCLUSIONS

The starting point for property tax review has to be an independent appraisal. There are some firms that offer to perform the appraisal, and carry on the negotiations and appeal on the basis of a contingency fee. Most larger appraisal firms charge only on the basis of time spent, and the fee is not contingent on the outcome.

In terms of credibility, a contingent fee raises more questions than can be answered about the independence and supportability of the answers provided in the appraisal report.

Larger companies have specialists in their tax departments who do nothing but property tax work. After a while, they get to know the appraisers and understand the process in each major locality. Smaller companies do not have such specialists, and either pay little attention to property taxes or hire outside specialists.

It is very feasible to ask an appraisal firm to look at the assessed levels in major corporate locations. You can ask them to provide a professional judgment as to whether or not it is worthwhile committing the resources to appeal assessments in a given area. The appraiser will review the property records, the assessment records, perhaps make a one-day site visit, and can then state authoritatively whether the cost/benefit tradeoff looks favorable.

ENDNOTES

1. *Wiley GAAP 2001,* John Wiley and Sons, p. 339.
2. *Miller GAAP Guide,* Dryden, 1996, p. 11.04.

CHAPTER 16

Adopting SFAS 141 and SFAS 142

July 1, 2001 represented a red-letter day in the history of valuation. For the first time *all* business mergers had to be treated as purchases, inasmuch as pooling of interest accounting was abolished. Goodwill no longer had to be amortized. For appraisers these two accounting pronouncements were outweighed by the equally new requirement that companies had to test, every year, all goodwill for impairment. This impairment test, in turn, mandated determining the value of all business units that had goodwill.

For the first time companies now had to determine the Fair Value (FV) of segments of their own business. And, if there was an apparent impairment, the company had to evaluate the FV of all the assets, both tangible and intangible, in the business unit that had the goodwill impairment.

While accounting rules had all along required companies to develop FV estimates of *financial* assets, as well as derivative *hedges,* now companies had to look to Property, Plant and Equipment (PP&E) values, and determine also the FV of all other intangible assets. Some observers started referring to SFAS 141 and SFAS 142 as the "Full Employment Act for Appraisers."

INITIAL IMPLEMENTATION

In this Chapter, readers will be lead through the steps required to implement the new accounting standards. Note that the standards are applicable initially only to companies that have goodwill on their books. The standards do apply, in the future, to all *new* merger and acquisition (M&A) activities.

For those businesses with goodwill the very first step, after reading the two documents, is to decide on the firm's objectives. There are two schools of thought and each has merit.

1. Companies can plan and apply the new standards to *maximize* the amount of immediate goodwill write-off.
2. Companies can plan and apply the new standards to *minimize* the amount of immediate goodwill write-off.

This determination can only be made by the company, in light of its financial reporting objectives and its approach to investor relations. The latter is discussed in Chapter 11. There is no consensus among publicly traded companies as to which approach is preferable; this suggests that either course of action will work.

MAXIMIZING THE INITIAL WRITE-OFF

Many companies want to get as much goodwill off their balance sheets as possible. The way the FASB drafted the new standards certainly encouraged this. Any initial goodwill impairment loss incurred as a result of adopting the standards can, must, be written off as a *change of accounting.* This, in effect, tells the world at large that the write-off would not have taken place absent the new accounting rules. Thus analysts examining the company will tend to overlook the impairment writedown as unrelated to the company's main business.

Putting emphasis on this interpretation, any *subsequent* impairment losses, after the initial adoption of the standards, *must* be charged in the Profit and Loss statement as a part of operating results. Even if the company is able to highlight and explain a subsequent impairment writedown, the very fact that it is to be charged to operations is likely to reflect adversely on management. Put a different way, management is not responsible for the FASB's determination to change accounting rules, but will be responsible for subsequent losses.

This motivation to get rid immediately of as much goodwill as possible is enhanced by the desire to avoid future impairment losses. After all if you write-off all goodwill, then by definition you can not have any future losses. For companies in cyclical industries, or where the future is not crystal-clear, taking minimum pain now (impairment as a change in accounting) appears far superior to the possibility of major pain in the future (a reduction of operating profits).

In the subsequent section the steps that can be taken to maximize the initial write-off of goodwill are described.

MINIMIZING THE INITIAL WRITE-OFF

Many companies prefer to leave existing goodwill on the balance sheet. Since goodwill no longer has to be amortized to earnings every quarter, many financial managers see no reason to take an immediate charge. Further, if the business outlook is favorable, under the new rules it can be highly unlikely that an impairment loss will ever have to be taken.

Companies that have expanded primarily through internal growth usually have very substantial intangible assets that are *not* on the balance sheet. As discussed in Chapter 11, it might have been desirable to have disclosed the value of these assets in supplementary reports to shareholders. But whether disclosed or not, the fact is that the formal financial statements did not, and still do not, reflect such things as an assembled workforce, customer and supplier relationships, brand names, technology and favorable contracts.

The only time such assets appear on a balance sheet is when they were acquired in the purchase of another company. Self-developed intangible assets are just as real as are those that were purchased. But, as noted in Chapter 11, while one set of intangible assets is on the balance sheet, the other, the self-developed group, are not.

As discussed below, the basic test for impairment is to compare the Fair Value of the business unit to the book value (amount on the balance sheet). As long as the FV is in *excess* of book value, by definition there is no impairment.

This means that if a unit has essentially grown internally, with but one or two small acquisitions that generated goodwill, then the FV of the unit is likely to be well in excess of a book value that totally omits all the self-generated intangible assets. For example if a profitable retail chain has bought a small competitor, and converted it to the buyer's name, then there will be a small amount of goodwill, and a large value for the buyer's existing trade name. But the value of the existing trade name will appear nowhere on the buyer's financial statements.

In effect there is often going to be a 'cushion' of intangible values, not formally recognized in the financial statements. This cushion will tend to offset any decline in the value of the goodwill from the prior acquisition(s).

Thus for firms with little goodwill on the book, and valuable intangible assets, the financial manager's assumption that future impairment is highly unlikely is a pretty safe bet.

In the next section we discuss the steps that must be taken to formally implement the new standards.

INITIAL IMPLEMENTATION

Reporting Units

The first step is to determine the "reporting units" that the company has. The FASB starts out with the presumption that each segment separately reported in the footnotes in accordance with SFAS 131 is a "reporting unit." However, companies are permitted, but not required, to go down one level from the SFAS 131 segments and establish additional reporting units. The very first choice a company must make in implementing SFAS 141 and SFAS 142 is in the reporting units.

The basic guidelines set forth by the FASB are that the economic characteristics within a segment are consistent. If diverse types of business are encompassed within an existing reporting segment, then the firm should treat each as a separate reporting unit.

The reason that the choice of reporting units is critical is that, as discussed in the next section, existing goodwill has to be assigned to the reporting units that have been chosen. While the FASB provides guidelines as to how the goodwill is to be allocated among the reporting units, there is still room for discretion in the initial assignment.

Assuming a decision has been made to *maximize* the immediate impairment writedown, a company would choose reporting units in such a way that the FV of certain units is likely to be *less* than the book value; the book value against which the comparison is made, *includes* the goodwill. So if you want a big loss, the goal is to put as much goodwill in reporting units that have the lowest Fair Value.

By the same token, if you want to *minimize* any initial goodwill impairment loss, then one tries to assign existing goodwill to profitable units that have low book values and high intangible assets not already on the balance sheet.

Readers should understand that the FASB does not provide companies with a "free choice." The standards do, however, provide some flexibility and companies should make their decisions regarding reporting unit based on their overall financial reporting objectives.

Assigning Goodwill

If the choice of reporting units has been made based on corporate objectives, the next step is to take existing goodwill on the balance sheet and assign it to the reporting units. Note that *all* goodwill must be assigned. It is not acceptable to leave out a chunk and call it a 'corporate' asset.

If goodwill can readily be traced back to the acquisition that generated it, and that acquisition is still identifiable in one of the new reporting units, then that is where it must be placed. Companies with good accounting records and few acquisitions may be at a disadvantage relative to those with many acquisitions and poor records.

In many instances companies have integrated newly acquired firms into existing business units. In turn, following one or more corporate reorganizations, say from functional to geographic management, the original identity of the goodwill may have been lost.

If a company can not readily allocate existing goodwill based on historical records, then it must be allocated to the reporting units based on reasonable application of management judgment. This could be as simple as sales volume, or operating profit or assets. Some rational basis must be used, and the company has to be able to defend its methodology.

The standards provide one out. Suppose, as an example, a company buys a manufacturing business; the benefits of the purchase are going to accrue from selling the new product to the buyer's existing customers, thus reducing selling expense. The company is going to combine the new firm's manufacturing assets with its existing plants. If the company has a manufacturing reporting unit, and a selling reporting unit, it would make sense to apply part or all of the goodwill, which is due to the synergies, to the selling unit. In short, the standards permit goodwill to be separated from where the assets are placed, if real synergies can be identified.

While the standard discusses assigning newly acquired goodwill based on these synergies, the same analysis can be, and should be, applied in allocating existing goodwill to reporting units.

Assigning Assets and Liabilities

The next step in the process is to assign all corporate assets to the reporting units. By definition the operating assets of each business will already have been assigned to the respective reporting units.

But for existing segment reporting purposes, under SFAS 131 many companies have chosen, and been fully correct, in retaining certain assets in a 'corporate' segment. This might include pension assets and liabilities, deferred tax assets or liabilities, cash, and money market investments and notes payable.

The standards require that all such assets be assigned to one or more reporting units, using some systematic basis for the allocation. Thus cash could be allocated based on sales volume, or receivable balances, and so forth.

The stated purpose of doing things this way is so that when measuring possible impairment, the book value of each reporting unit will be as high as necessary, thus increasing the possibility of an impairment of goodwill. If the 'corporate' assets had not been included, it is less likely that the Fair Value of the reporting unit would be in excess of the book value. Recall that if the book value is higher than FV, then it is likely that an impairment loss exists.

TESTING FOR IMPAIRMENT

Both at the time of the initial implementation and subsequently at least once a year, companies have to test each reporting unit that has goodwill for possible impairment. Impairment testing is mandatory under the standards and hence is an integral part of GAAP.

The FASB set up a two-step approach to testing for impairment. In step one the Fair Value of the reporting unit is determined. This can be done on the basis of the Income Approach (Chapter 6) or the Market Approach (Chapter 7). Ideally, in practice, both approaches would be utilized and the results correlated. Many companies are going to obtain outside professional assistance in the determination of the Fair Values.

The SEC has indicated that in case of an impairment writedown at some point in the future, they will ask the registrant to go back and show why the loss was not taken earlier. If it is the company's own self valuation that prevented a prior writedown, this will be a cause for concern by the SEC. However, if the company has in its file an independent third-party valuation report, this should be good-faith evidence that the impairment took place this year, not in a prior period.

If the FV of the reporting unit is well in excess of the book value of all the assets, including goodwill and allocated 'corporate' assets, the company can stop there. Thus for profitable and growing business units only a simple FV calculation is necessary each year.

If the FV is close to book value, or if it is actually below book value, then the company *must* go to Step 2. Step 2 is essentially the equivalent of a *new* allocation of all the assets as though the unit had been bought this year from a third party.

In Chapters 12 and 13 we discuss what such an allocation entails. Essentially the same work must now be done on all the unit's assets. In other words we ask, "What is the *current* Fair Value of the assets in this unit in today's business environment?" This is equivalent to asking what someone else would pay to buy the business from you if you were planning to sell it.

After you have the FV of the overall unit itself, and the FV of all the tangible assets, and identifiable assets (discussed below), you subtract the assets from the FV of the business. The difference is now a new 'implied goodwill'. This calculated implied goodwill is compared to the goodwill that is on the books. If the goodwill on the books is greater than the calculated implied goodwill an impairment loss must be recognized.

In effect, the new calculation of 'implied goodwill' for the reporting unit now becomes the new book value; the difference between the two has to be written off through the income statement. After the initial implementation, all such impairment losses have to be treated as expenses of the current year's operations. Management of most firms will be unhappy with this result. Again, this is the reason that some far-sighted firms are striving to reduce or even eliminate existing goodwill as part of the initial implementation process.

It should be noted that if this impairment review results in a new and lower goodwill, no other assets need be revalued. You will have determined the current FV of the assets but what is on the books stays. There is no write-up or write-down of the assets to reflect their current Fair Value.

PURCHASE ACCOUNTING FOR NEW MERGERS

With the issuance of the new standards the FASB effectively killed pooling of interests accounting. Many companies, particularly high-tech firms, initially argued that precluding pooling accounting would have strongly adverse consequences. Forcing companies only to use purchase accounting, and then making mandatory the amortization of goodwill, would cause fewer business acquisitions, they claimed. The reason was that for such high-tech firms, there often was very little in the way of tangible assets, and most of the (high) purchase price typical of the industry would be denominated as goodwill.

The SEC was taking a hard line on goodwill amortization and in many cases mandating that it be written off in no more than 20 years. Given the economics of the business, and the purchase prices relative to sales volume, mandatory purchase accounting combined with mandatory goodwill amortization would effectively wipe out reported earnings.

Now every observer agreed that goodwill amortization did not affect cash flows. Most observers agreed that values of businesses were dependent on cash flows, not reported earnings. Nonetheless, few managers were comfortable running a company that not only had current losses, but was likely to have reported losses as far into the future as could reasonably be anticipated.

The big breakthrough came in the dispute about accounting for M&A activity when the members of the FASB had an epiphany. Maybe goodwill did not have to be amortized! After all, accounting rules are a man-made construct. Amortization of goodwill was the rule for 30 years, but that did not mean it always had to be.

The day the FASB decided that goodwill did not have to be amortized was the day the opponents of abolishing pooling accounting stopped fighting. To show how serious the fight had been, however, many of the high tech firms literally had gone to the U. S. Senate and asked for legislation prohibiting the FASB from doing away with pooling.

The thought of Congress writing accounting rules scared a lot of observers because, after all, it was those same Congressional representatives who had brought us a 20,000 page IRS Code and Regulations. Nobody really wanted that for financial reporting, but at least some people argued that Congressional involvement in accounting was preferable to doing away with pooling of interests accounting.

But as soon as the FASB gave up on amortization of goodwill, all serious obstacles were removed. However, it was obvious that goodwill could not be allowed to remain on a company's balance sheet forever. Hence the mandatory testing for impairment, discussed above.

So, on all new M&A activity, a company must use purchase accounting, develop the goodwill, and not amortize it. Instead, once a year, all existing goodwill has to be tested for possible impairment. If it is not impaired, the balance sheet stays the same. If it is impaired, it gets written down to its new value, and the charge flows through the P&L.

The basic rules in Chapters 12 and 13 on how to perform an allocation are carried forward unchanged from previous practice, with one major exception. PP&E is handled identically as in the past. Accounting for working capital is also unchanged. What is different is the identification, valuation and life of intangible assets *other than* goodwill.

IDENTIFIABLE INTANGIBLE ASSETS

In theory companies were supposed to allocate the purchase price of every acquisition to all the tangible and intangible assets that were acquired. The same explicit requirement has been carried forward, with but one or two modifications. What has changed is that whereas before not too much care was taken in identifying specific intangible assets, now it is mandatory.

Why was so little attention paid to separating goodwill from other intangible assets like a customer list or technology or a brand name? Essentially, up to SFAS 141 and SFAS 142, there was no material difference in the accounting treatment. What difference did it make if $100 million was put into goodwill, or $20 million into technology and $80 million in goodwill? If both were amortized over identical 20-year periods, neither the P&L nor the balance sheet were affected. Since many companies lumped goodwill and intangible assets in a catchall category of 'other assets,' readers of the financial statements were none the wiser, nor did they care.

But with non-amortization of goodwill, and mandatory amortization of other intangibles, it now makes a big difference in terms of reported earnings. Again, cash flow is not affected, but the primary purpose of financial statements is to determine income, earnings per share, not cash flow or cash flow per share.

Companies, for the first time, have a tremendous incentive to maximize goodwill and minimize dollars allocated to other intangibles. The members of the FASB are sophisticated, and in drafting the new standards they were fully aware of this potential bias on the part of companies.

What the Board did was to make explicit the separation of identifiable intangibles from goodwill. Further, the Board provided users with a full-page checklist of these identifiable intangibles. No longer can statement preparers say, "it makes no difference what we do" since now it does make a difference.

The SEC has made it clear that they too will be scrutinizing closely how companies allocate the purchase price. The SEC is particularly concerned that companies do not overstate income, and every dollar put into goodwill is a dollar less that has to be charged as an expense over its useful life. The SEC staff accounting staff that had been dealing with pooling issues (SEC sources claimed 50% of their time was spent on pooling) now had nothing to do on pooling so they were switched over to monitoring application of SFAS 141 and SFAS 142.

The FASB in Appendix A to SFAS 141 lists five major categories of intangible assets that must be identified and valued, if the target company has them:

1. Marketing-related intangible assets
2. Customer-related intangible assets
3. Artistic-related intangible assets

4. Contract-based intangible assets

5. Technology-based intangible assets

The key point about this FASB list is that in order to be recognized and valued:

"it shall be recognized as an asset apart from goodwill if it arises from contractual or other legal rights (regardless of whether those rights are transferable or separable from the acquired entity or from other rights and obligations). If an intangible asset does not arise from contractual or other legal rights, it shall be recognized as an asset apart from goodwill only if it is separable, that is, it is capable of being separated or divided from the acquired entity and sold, transferred, licensed rented, or exchange (regardless of whether there is an intent to do so)."[1]

In case this seems difficult to comprehend we think that what the FASB means is that the intangible asset has to arise out of a legally enforceable right, *and/or* be separable without affecting the rest of the business.

For example if a company like Land's End can rent its customer list and generate income, that would be an identifiable intangible asset. But a professional service firm can not sell its relationship with its clients to another firm since the clients have no contract for anything beyond the immediate service currently being performed.

MARKETING-RELATED INTANGIBLE ASSETS

Included in this category are:

- Trademarks, tradenames
- Service marks
- Trade dress
- Internet domain names
- Non-compete agreements

It is obvious that these assets, if present, are protected by legal grants from the government or by contract. Further, they can be licensed to others. The number of licensing agreements is huge, with a cap company licensing the Harley-Davidson name, or an ice cream manufacturer licensing the Starbucks name. Thus both Harley-Davidson and Starbucks are generating income from their name, while totally retaining the rights for their own motorcycles and coffee.

If either of these firms were acquired, the buyer would have to quantify the value of the name and show it as a separate intangible asset, apart from goodwill.

Now, we indicated earlier that it is necessary not only to value such intangible assets, it also is necessary to set a life on them. What is the effective economic life of well-known tradenames such as Oreo™ or Coca-Cola™? Under the previous accounting rules the maximum life allowed for such assets was 40 years. Almost everyone agreed that over time well-known tradenames *increase* in value, they don't diminish. Thus amortizing tradenames was one of the basic complaints prior to adoption of SFAS 141 and SFAS 142.

The FASB responded by saying that *if* the life of an intangible asset was "indefinite," that is, could not be determined definitively, then such an identifiable asset did not have to be amortized but instead would be tested for impairment. The impairment test for intangible assets other than goodwill is discussed below.

The bottom line therefore is that the new rules require valuation of tradenames and similar assets, but do not require that they be written off. Only non-complete agreements with a stated life in the contract would have to be amortized, and that does reflect any change from prior practice.

CUSTOMER-RELATED INTANGIBLE ASSETS

Realistically, most M&A transactions are undertaken in order for the buyer to acquire the seller's sales volume and customers. But the way the FASB wrote the rules, that the asset has to be severable or based on a legal contract, means that in practice this particular category of intangible assets is not likely to attract significant value.

For example if a retail chain is acquired, say a chain of shoe stores in malls all over the country, or a chain of grocery stores, the customer base is very valuable. Buyers shop every week at the grocery store and every couple of months (if the family has kids) at the shoe store. But by the same token how could the buyer transfer the customers to another chain without exiting the business? Therefore, as the definition is written, a buyer of a chain of retail stores would probably not ascribe value to the customer-related assets and the economic benefit would instead show up in the non-amortizable goodwill category.

ARTISTIC-RELATED INTANGIBLE ASSETS

Since this category, according to the FASB includes ballets, literary works, musical works, photographs and television programs, it is quite specialized and in this book we will omit a full discussion. Suffice it to say that appraisal firms are experienced in valuing such assets and in determining a supportable life.

CONTRACT-BASED INTANGIBLE ASSETS

These are defined by the FASB to include:

- Licensing agreements
- Advertising, construction management, service or supply contracts
- Lease agreements
- Construction permits
- Franchise agreements
- Operating and broadcast rights
- Use rights such as drilling, water, air, mineral timber cutting
- Servicing contracts such as mortgage servicing contracts
- Employment contracts

The issue in valuing such contracts is the benefit itself. For example, a landlord has a lease agreement with a tenant at a rental that is at market prices. If this tenant did not rent the space at $20 a square foot someone else would. The real value in the contract is the avoidance of selling expense, which is likely to be relatively low.

Similarly, an employment contract—from the perspective of the employer—may not have much value. A 5-year contract with a sales manager for $200,000 a year plus bonus provides the company with a competent executive. But if the employee quits, how much would have to be paid a replacement? Probably $200,000 a year plus bonus! Salaries are generally quite competitive and a company will not keep a key employee if she is underpaid. Similarly if she is overpaid this represents a liability, not an asset.

In our experience these intangible assets do have some value, and often relatively short lives. So, to comply with GAAP it is highly likely that buyers will attach some modest amounts to each category, with relatively short lives. Keep in mind that if the life is short, the dollar amount of the asset's value is going to be less.

TECHNOLOGY-BASED INTANGIBLE ASSETS

The FASB defines this category to include:

- Patented technology
- Computer software
- Unpatented technology
- Databases
- Trade secrets, such as secret formulas, processes, recipes

This is going to be the surprise for many companies. Patents are well-known and have been valued for years. But putting the proper valuation on computer software, unpatented technology and trade secrets is going to cause some acquisitions to show lower reported profits in the first few years.

Proper valuation of technology and software, in the broad sense, is going to lead to large amounts in many cases. As an example, one of the critical success factors for Amazon is its one-click software. Valuing the software is relatively easy, but setting the appropriate life on it involves certain assumptions.

For example, software is constantly being upgraded and improved. When new computer hardware becomes available, with greater speeds and more capacity, software is rewritten to take advantage of the hardware. Now the question is, is the software a year from now, which will differ in some way from today's code, the 'same' software or is it 'different' software. In one case you would assign a long life, perhaps 5 to 8 years, with a substantial value. However, if you value the software only until it is modified slightly the value is going to be low because of the short life.

This issue, as to the life of software, first came up when the SEC was evaluating In-Process Research & Development (IPR&D). Companies tried to assign as much as possible to the value of an acquired company for the software under development; this was because R&D must be written off immediately and therefore the amount of amortizable goodwill was reduced. The SEC argued that you could not include the value of the next generation of software after development of this version was complete. In other words, at some point the new software differed enough from the old that a discontinuity had taken place.

Ironically, companies used to try and maximize IPR&D to minimize goodwill. Now companies will want to minimize IPR&D, to maximize goodwill. Total role reversal inasmuch as the SEC will now argue for *greater* allocation to IPR&D!

The unresolved issue in all of these technology-based assets, other than patents which have a definitive life, is going to be to define carefully the specific asset being valued and the life of *that* asset. Companies are going to looking for low values and short lives, and SEC examiners will want the opposite.

TESTING INTANGIBLE ASSETS FOR IMPAIRMENT

Intangible assets other than goodwill have to be tested for impairment and for changes in useful life. Thus, if the life of a tradename is going to be short, say because the product will cease to be manufactured and distributed, an impairment loss must be recorded or the asset written off over its now shorter life.

The interesting thing is that impairment testing for intangible assets other than goodwill is *not* based on Fair Value. Instead, SFAS 121 has to be applied, and this calls for an analysis of future cash flows related to the asset. If the sum of future cash flows, on an *undiscounted* basis, is less than the carrying amount, then an impairment loss must be recognized.

SFAS 121 is the only place in business where undiscounted future cash flows are captured and analyzed. All other uses of future cash flows are converted to *present value* by discounting at an appropriate rate. Most people believe that a dollar five years from now is worth less than a dollar today. Only for purposes of this impairment test does a company add up cash flows without discounting.

This anomaly was deliberately put into SFAS 121 in order to minimize the number and amount of impairment losses on PP&E. The FASB has now carried forward that approach to identifiable intangibles other than goodwill. "Two wrongs don't make one right" as the saying goes. In this case the FASB has made the same mistake twice. Undiscounted cash flows are a meaningless concept. Nonetheless they are captured in GAAP and represent the law of the land as far as financial reporting is concerned.

ENDNOTE

1. SFAS 141, paragraph 39.

CHAPTER 17

Valuing a Start-up Firm: Cheap Stock Options

Valuing a newly formed business, sometimes referred to as a Start-up, presents a lot of problems to an appraiser. The entrepreneurs want *high values* demonstrated for the business as a whole, in order to bring in new equity investors. They want *high values* for the company's assets, usually intangible in nature; such assets are often referred to as Intellectual Property (IP). These values are provided to lenders, so that the larger the valuation the greater the potential loan. Finally, the owner/entrepreneur wants *low values* to support issuance of options to key employees. To comply with tax and financial reporting requirements options must be granted at their then current Fair Market Value, and for a start-up a low value may be realistic.

Now it is very difficult for one appraisal report to show high values in order to attract outside investors and lenders, and low values to comply with IRS and SEC requirements. What usually happens is that appraisers are called upon to submit a formal valuation that supports the low option price. Then the owners approach Venture Capital and other equity investors totally independently, with just their own Business Plan, and in effect provide those outsiders with their own opinion of value, i.e., a high price.

Hopefully, six months later the company has an Initial Public Offering (IPO) at a price in excess of that derived from the most recent round of financing. The impact of this is that the low-price options, given to management and employees are suddenly very valuable.

However, before the IPO can become effective, the company's financial statements must pass SEC scrutiny. Assuming the options were granted six months ago at $5, and the IPO is at $20, the SEC argues that 'cheap stock' was granted and this is a disguised form of compensation. They can then make the company go back and restate its P&L statement, adding to compensation expense and decreasing earnings. Worse, this may trigger the IRS to disallow the favorable benefits of stock option treatment to the employees lucky enough to own the options.

CONFLICTING VIEWS AS TO VALUE

The Securities and Exchange Commission ("SEC") has recently viewed the valuation of options granted to employees prior to an Initial Public Offering as a matter of concern. If the strike price of the option is low relative to the IPO price to the public, and the options were just recently granted, say within six months, the SEC argues that management is taking advantage of the new shareholders. The SEC, in order to level the playing field, argues that the favorable options really represent compensation. Consequently, if this is correct then the registrant's reported income was overstated as a result of the understatement of salary expense. In short, the SEC often questions the valuation of a company and its options in the period prior to the IPO.

What must be kept in mind is that valuation issues almost always reflect a conflict between two parties, one of whom wishes a high value and the other a low value. In this case the registrant argues for the propriety of the recent low option value and the now current high valuation of the company. The SEC argues that the company could not possibly have gone up in value, say four-fold, in perhaps six months.

When this writer first joined an appraisal company, his implicit assumption then was that most clients, in most situations, were likely to want the *highest* possible value that could be supported by the appraisal report.

- A building owner planning to sell would want to receive the maximum price for the property; what was the highest amount the appraiser could support?
- A manufacturer would want the highest value on its equipment in order to support the largest possible loan.
- In a purchase price allocation the buyer, a publicly held company, would want maximum value ascribed to the land, in order to minimize depreciation expense.
- If options were being offered to employees the company would want the highest possible value ascribed to the company; management could justify a higher strike price, thus bringing in more funds upon exercise, and reducing potential dilution.

Whether or not in each case the appraiser could justify the high value, the client's pressure almost invariably was going to be in the direction of maximizing the answer. That was the initial assumption. Reality soon presented a contrary picture.

In practice, it soon became apparent that many clients, if not a majority, look to the appraiser, and the appraisal report, to *minimize* the value. How could this be?

- In contrast to the seller, the buyer wants the lowest possible value ascribed for the building.
- The bank wants the most conservative value ascribed to the collateral just to be on the safe side, thus minimizing the loan amount for the borrower.
- In a purchase price allocation, many privately-held firms want to maximize depreciation for tax purposes, and want the least amount ascribed to the land.
- The employees, in contrast to the company, have the most to gain if the company valuation was low so that the options would likely be granted at a lower strike price.

What the author had failed to take into consideration in his initial implicit assumption about high values, was that in every transaction there are always two parties, with opposite goals. Buyers want low prices, sellers want high prices. In estate tax cases involving closely held companies, taxpayers want low values, the IRS wants high values. Borrowers want to maximize the loan while lenders want to minimize risk. Privately held companies want to minimize taxes and publicly held companies want to maximize reported income.

It is this conflict between the parties, usually with diametrically opposite interests, that causes one side or the other to hire an independent appraiser. From the client's perspective the appraiser's goal, whether achievable or not, is to support the client's position against some third party. This is not the place to discuss what happens when each party hires its own appraiser and the two so-called independent experts come out with diametrically opposite answers. Put bluntly, this is what keeps lawyers and the court system in business.

Suppose, however, that the client just wants the 'right' answer, is not looking to prove a point. The appraiser is treated as a true expert, an independent professional whose sole goal is to find the 'truth'. For the purposes of this Chapter, which deals with the valuation of stock in privately held start-up companies, assume the only criterion is the true Fair Value. Even with no pre-conceived answer, how an appraiser approaches the real-life problem of valuing options in a start-up environment is, at times, subject to differences of opinion.

BUSINESS ENTERPRISE VALUATION APPROACHES

Is determining the market value of a new business really any different than valuing an existing well-established company? After all, appraisers have derived techniques for valuing business enterprises; these approaches have withstood the test of time, as well as many court challenges. In fact, the bread and butter of the appraisal business, day in and day out, is valuing business entities. Should start-up companies be any different? Unfortunately, the answer is both Yes and No.

We must digress a moment to look at just how appraisers do value business enterprises. There are three, and only three, approaches to valuing any asset. As discussed in earlier chapters these are referred to in the appraisal profession as:

- Cost Approach
- Income Approach
- Market Approach

The *Cost Approach* asks what it would cost today to acquire the same or similar assets. If you are valuing a building, the upper limit on value is going to be the price you would have to pay a contractor today to build the same building. A rational buyer would not acquire an existing building at a price of $120/square foot if a comparable new building could be constructed at $100/square foot. Similarly, in valuing machinery and equipment appraisers look to the prices of new assets from the manufacturer. Where necessary, adjustments are made for technology and productivity improvements. The cost approach is highly reliable in dealing with tangible personal property and real estate. It is not generally used by appraisers in valuing financial assets, including business enterprise values. For practical reasons, it would be difficult to identify today just what it would cost to replicate an existing, on-going business enterprise.

The *Income Approach* involves the capitalization of anticipated future income streams. This method is predicated on developing net income or cash flow projections, which are then discounted for risk and the time value of money, to indicate a present value. The residual value of the business at the end of the projection period is also considered. This method also takes into consideration capital expenditures, working capital requirements, and depreciation estimates.

The discount rate used to calculate the present worth of the cash flow is based upon an analysis of the risks associated with their realization. This discount factor accounts for the time value of money and its selection must consider the yields available to investors on alternative investment opportunities.

The *Market Approach* is a technique whereby the operating performance of the subject company is compared to that of other companies in similar or related lines of business which might provide an alternative investment opportunity. Relative risk is measured by rates of return or earnings multiples required by investors in the comparative companies. These multiples are derived from companies engaged in similar lines of business whose stocks are publicly traded. Although there are typically differences between the comparative companies and the company being appraised, all are subject to similar economic risks and would be considered alternative investment opportunities by a prudent investor. These multiples are then applied to various indications of earning power for the subject enterprise, in order to arrive at an indication of value.

Because there are virtually no publicly traded start-up businesses, appraisers can not realistically utilize the market comparable approach. Measuring a start-up's projections against historical performance of established companies in most cases would be an 'apples to oranges' comparison.

Neither can an appraiser really utilize effectively the cost approach in a start-up company. What has been spent to date is clear. How much will have to be spent in the future, in order to make the firm truly viable, is really part of the forecasting or projection used in the income approach.

Thus valuing a start-up firm, and the associated stock options, falls back on the income approach.

APPLYING THE INCOME APPROACH

As noted in Chapter 6, the income approach assumes that investors have numerous alternative investment possibilities, ranging from risk-free U.S. government securities to venture capital startups. Assuming the investment market is reasonably efficient, and that investors demand greater potential return in exchange for assuming additional risk, the question then becomes, "What kind of return can an investor reasonably expect in exchange for making the investment in this privately held, non-marketable start-up?"

Today's value is based on investor expectations of the investment's future returns; in turn this is directly related to the future income and hence cash flow that the business will earn. So, application of the income approach simply involves projecting the future. How does one project the future for a start-up? Usually, for established firms, this is accomplished by studying the past performance, as a guide to the future. But there is always a degree of uncertainty in any forecast, and particularly so for a new business venture.

- Where will the sun rise tomorrow morning? Based on millennia of experience an answer that the sun will rise in the East is an excellent bet.
- Where will the Chicago Cubs finish in the National League? Based on the last 50+ years, it is a very good bet they won't win.
- What gasoline mileage will I get on my next 1000-mile trip? Based on my car's performance to date 24 to 25 mpg seems a pretty good estimate.

These three projections of the future can reasonably be made by most observers, and there would probably be little disagreement. When it comes to corporate performance for established businesses, however, there is a much higher degree of uncertainty.

- What are Ford's earnings going to be next year?
- What will OPEC do regarding oil production and what will ExxonMobil's earnings be?
- The patent expires on Prozac. How much will Eli Lilly's earnings go down and how much will generic maker Barr Labs go up?

Obtaining answers to these three questions is far from trivial, yet today's stock prices for these well-established firms depend in large measure how investors collectively evaluate the individual situations. In fact one can probably more easily answer the questions of what do other investors expect (and investors collectively can be wrong) than of what will actually happen to Ford, Exxon or Lilly.

The truth is that ever since the Greek oracle at Delphi, man has tried to foretell the future, with notable lack of success. Projecting earnings for established companies keeps Wall Street security analysts in business. These experts often disagree. A small cottage industry has grown up trying to correlate and report on security analysts' earning projections for individual companies. *The Wall Street Journal* then dutifully reports after the fact how close companies came to meeting the analysts' forecasts. Miss by one penny a share and a company's stock price can go down by 15% or more.

Now look at an even more difficult situation. For a start-up business there is no past to use as a guide.

If Wall Street's best and brightest have difficulty for *established* businesses in forecasting earnings one year out, or even one quarter out, how is an appraiser supposed to forecast earnings for an individual start-up company? Which is more difficult, to forecast GM's earnings next year or a five-year outlook for a new biotech company? Most observers would, overall, anticipate greater accuracy with the former.

Projecting earnings for a start-up company involves making a definitive judgment on the probabilities of success of a new business. Compounding the difficulty, while the product and business model may be good, how well will the specific company *management* be able to translate the anticipated sales into profits?

The point is that if it is hard to forecast earnings for companies with a 50-year history, how much harder it is to forecast for a company with no history. Yet, at the end of the day, somebody has to set a value on a start-up company in order to determine an option striking price that is supported by an objective assessment of Fair Value.

VALUING A START-UP COMPANY

We have pointed out some of the very real difficulties in valuing any company, much less a start-up company. Nonetheless, this has to be done, and appraisers are hired every day to do it. What procedures are used in practice? In this article we can only describe our own approaches; undoubtedly others are available and in use.

Most start-up companies have developed a business plan. This is utilized by the entrepreneur(s) to go out and raise capital, assuming the founders can not rely solely on their own resources. Every business plan we have ever seen starts out with initial losses, and then very quickly swings over into profits. Assuming the projections are accurate (discussed below), the business plan thus makes a strong case for investors to put in their money and very rapidly achieve a satisfactory ROI.

In order not to scare off prospective investors, who are assumed to be leery of losses, these business plans invariably have rapidly growing sales volume, with expenses never going up as quickly as revenues. Many expenses thus are assumed to be 'fixed', and will be incurred irrespective of volume changes. The most significant difference among initial business plans is whether the switch from initial losses to profits takes place within the first six months, or will require all of twelve months!

Business experience, however, suggests that almost invariably it takes much longer than a year, much less six months, to develop a new business and start to have a positive cash flow. It is the rare start-up company, indeed, that starts to have positive cash flow, never mind reported earnings, in less than two years.

The typical Discounted Cash Flow model utilized in the income approach to valuation weights near term results heavily. Results ten years out, no matter how high the projected profit, have little impact on value, at least using the high discount rates (25%–40%) that Venture Capital (VC) investors typically look for. This is why, in attempting to present an attractive investment, business plans shy away from projecting near-term losses.

The only way a business venture will have a positive Net Present Value, if one discounts the future at 40%, is to assume low losses in the beginning and high cash flows quite quickly. Knowing that VC investors are going to apply high discount rates leads the entrepreneur to overly optimistic assumptions. But those same VC investors also know the realities of business and that is why perhaps only one out of a hundred business plans even merits a second look by experienced VC investors.

It is very easy for a VC to 'pass' on any specific proposal, and therefore not have to do any more work on that venture. Appraisers who accept a valuation assignment must come up with an answer, and one that is supportable.

Where do we start? The same place as every one else, and that is the sales projection. How reasonable are the assumptions? Competition is almost always present, and we look at what competitors are doing, and even more important, likely to do. Many business plans overlook this aspect. For a truly new product, a new dot-com application or a new biotech venture, it is even harder to get a handle on the realism of the overall sales projection, i.e., acceptance by paying customers. In practice the real issue often is whether or not the business enterprise will still be in existence in three or four years.

In the final analysis the appraiser either has to accept the entrepreneur's sales projections or modify them to a more 'realistic' level. Once the appraiser substitutes his or her judgment for that of the client the appraiser is put in the difficult position of then justifying and supporting his or her own view on the sales outlook. Does the appraiser know more than the client about the client's work?

The answer is that the appraiser knows less about the client's product or service than does the client, but may well know more about growth trends for new businesses in general. The appraiser can always challenge the client by saying: "Give me an example of another product/service that has had an equally rapid growth curve." For every Microsoft or Genentech there are 10,000 failures, so when the client points to one of those super-successful companies, the response has to be, "What are the real-life chances of that happening again?"

At some point the appraiser has to develop a cash-flow projection, including *realistic* assumptions for capital expenditures and working capital requirements. Then comes the fun part, choosing an appropriate discount rate. Depending on the risk characteristics of the product/service being successful, we have seen discount rates range upwards from 35% to above 50% being applied. At a 50% or above discount rate, the appraiser is essentially saying "I don't really believe this is going to succeed, but there is always a chance that lightning can strike."

However, not all start-up ventures require such a high discount rate. A well established company, with a much lower cost of capital, and with a track record of successfully initiating new products, may justify a much lower discount rate, say between 20% and 30% for a new venture. As a generalization, the more optimistic the sale projection, the higher the discount rate that an appraiser applies. One tends to offset the other.

TESTING ANSWERS USING THE MARKET COMPARABLE APPROACH

A look back at the dot-com fiasco shows clearly that short-term market psychology can (for a period) draw away from economic reality. Think tulip bulbs. How many dot-com companies were recommended by well known sell-side security analysts on the grounds that "If Company A is selling at 50x revenues, then Company B should at least sell at 35x revenues."

Whether most readers of such optimistic selling recommendations knew it or not, the writer of such a report was using what appraisers call the market comparable approach. If the last 3-bedroom homes in the neighborhood sold for $275,000 to $290,000, it is reasonable that another 3-bedroom home coming on the market today could list at $289,900. Whether the seller will get this price or have to settle for something $10,000–$15,000 lower depends on a lot of factors. But the $289,900 asking price is at least grounded in economic reality.

But how many companies in history have consistently sold at 10x revenues, much less 30x or 40x? Justifying price B by looking at transaction A works only if the actual market transaction being used as a comparable makes sense itself, and the two companies are in fact truly similar.

The truth is that for most start-up companies there are few good comparables. Yes, there may be large publicly traded companies in more or less the same industry. And appraisers often look to such companies to set a starting point. But one has to *adjust* the price per share, or market capitalization, of the publicly traded companies for the following factors.

Our subject company undoubtedly:

- Is smaller
- Is not as well capitalized
- Has a much shorter, if any, history
- Is not publicly traded

Now, appraisers have techniques for adjusting downward from publicly traded companies, by applying 'discounts' for each of the above factors. However, it should be noted that there is a degree of subjectivity in the choice of discount for each of these factors. Again, an outsider reading an appraisal report may well challenge the reasonableness of the specific discounts applied. Lower the discounts and the value goes up, and vice versa.

Appraisers try, whenever possible, to use two or even all three of the standard approaches to value. In reality, sometimes the income approach appears to provide the better answer, at least to the extent of the reasonableness of the cash flow projections. In practice, it is often hard to find publicly traded firms that are comparable with any particular new venture. Using well-established large firms as the basis for comparison requires a whole series of assumptions. Keep in mind that a chain is no stronger than its weakest link, and an appraisal is no better than its weakest assumption.

LESSONS LEARNED

The two most appropriate methods of valuing a start-up company are the income approach and the market comparable approach. Unfortunately the income approach, as noted, is sometimes limited because of the uncertainty of the future success of the company, much less its revenues, expenses, and cash flow. The market comparable approach, however, is also often limited because there are usually few truly comparable publicly trade companies for a new or very young company.

Notwithstanding these problems, if such a start-up company does wish to grant options to its employees, then a valuation is required in order to comply with both tax and financial reporting requirements. And, despite these difficulties, independent appraisers are usually called upon for this task.

Based on the author's experience here are some guidelines:

- Appraisers will probably develop lower, rather than higher, values and their answer may be less than the principals of the valued company like. The value of the company, and hence the option price, may well be less than the overall enterprise valuation placed upon the business by one or more outside investors in a recent round of financing.

- "Many are called, but few are chosen." The Bible had it right. Many companies are started, but few end up with a successful IPO.

- Most appraisers tend to be conservative. Therefore the valuations they present to their clients tend not to assume that the best conceivable outcome will occur. Put a different way, values are likely to be lower than higher.

- Assume that ten start-up companies have valuations prepared at some early stage in their operation. Later, perhaps in 6 or 12 months, only one out of these ten goes public in an IPO. The 6-month prior option price for the single IPO company, based on the earlier business enterprise valuation, will likely be significantly less than the current public IPO price. The remaining 9 companies out of the starting 10 will never be looked at by the SEC. One cannot judge the accuracy of a single appraisal with hindsight, unless at the same time one looks at the accuracy of the other comparable appraisals by the same appraiser.

- This apparent 'jump' in value does not mean that the original appraisal (option price) was wrong. It was probably correct *at the time*. Compounding the problem is that appraisal reports almost universally provide a single point answer, rather than a range. The apparent precision of a single point answer masks the economic reality that value usually lies within a range. For start-up companies that range may in practice be quite wide.

- The question is often asked, then, "How can the value of Company X increase so much, in such a short period of time?" The answer is that at the date of the IPO we are dealing with a different company from the one at the earlier time period. Whatever tests the underwriter performs in deciding to take a particular company public, those tests have now been met. Twelve months ago, even six months ago, Company X did not pass those tests.

- Finally, at the date of the IPO one can evaluate the then current projections of the company by looking at the previous projections and seeing how accurate and reasonable they were. In all likelihood the company will have beaten the earlier projections, whereas many of the other start-up companies from a year ago are either out of business or still struggling.
- In short, hindsight is a wonderful thing. We all should have bought IBM in the 1930s and Microsoft in the 1980s. But at the time each of those companies had many competitors, often with greater financial strength. It is easy to say now that it was 'obvious' then that IBM and Microsoft were 'screaming buys'. Somehow, however, not everyone saw it the same way at the time.
- Evaluating the fairness of an IPO pricing today, based on a contemporaneous valuation twelve or even six months ago, is truly comparing apples and oranges. If the registration statement prepared for the IPO properly relates the company's history, and expansion difficulties, along with the current risk factors, the earlier low valuation usually was appropriate. The current higher IPO price, in fact, may be the problem, in that it is too high. Recent issues where the subsequent trading range was *below* the initial offering support this thesis. Certainly the IPO experience in 1999 through early 2000 (opening day trading at 2x or 3x the IPO price) has not been replicated in recent times.

CONCLUSION AND RECOMMENDATIONS

The so-called cheap stock problem may not be a real problem after all. If options were granted six or more months prior to an IPO, and if a contemporaneous appraisal was prepared by a reputable firm, then indeed the IPO price *can* be significantly higher than the option price.

What is important is that every appraisal be grounded in economic reality. If the income approach is utilized by the appraiser, then the projections should be carefully reviewed and tested for reasonableness. How likely is it that sales will grow at the rate shown? What, if anything, will competitors do? Are all expenses accounted for? Have reasonable time frames been allowed for the product/service to be accepted by customers? These and many similar questions should, in a good appraisal report, be answered.

We have found that if a company is planning an IPO at some point in the future that it makes sense to have a new appraisal report prepared every quarter or at a minimum every six months. This way progress against previous projections can be monitored, and a higher degree of confidence felt in the earlier forecasts as well as the most recent valuation. Further, assuming the company remains on track, the progressively higher valuations will give credibility to the earlier values, values that may have been the basis of option grants.

Finally, it should be recognized that in terms of Fair Value, or as appraisers use the term, Fair Market Value, there is often a substantial difference between the enterprise value of a privately held company and one that is now publicly traded.

It is a fact of life that investors are willing to pay a significant premium for shares in a publicly traded company, in comparison with one that is still privately held. The very fact of an IPO can increase value by 25% to 33% or more. The obverse of this is often referred to as a 'marketability discount' that is applied to privately held companies. This marketability discount is recognized by the IRS and accepted by the courts. While not the sole factor or perhaps even the most important factor, it does go a long way to explaining the difference between a low option price and a current high IPO price.

Index